Nocturne

Nocturne

A Journey in Search of Moonlight

JAMES ATTLEE

HAMISH HAMILTON
an imprint of
PENGUIN BOOKS

The author gratefully acknowledges the financial assistance provided
by the Authors' Foundation towards the travel undertaken in this book.

HAMISH HAMILTON

Published by the Penguin Group
Penguin Books Ltd, 80 Strand, London WC2R ORL, England
Penguin Group (USA) Inc., 375 Hudson Street, New York, New York 10014, USA
Penguin Group (Canada), 90 Eglinton Avenue East, Suite 700, Toronto, Ontario, Canada M4P 2Y3
(a division of Pearson Penguin Canada Inc.)
Penguin Ireland, 25 St Stephen's Green, Dublin 2, Ireland (a division of Penguin Books Ltd)
Penguin Group (Australia), 250 Camberwell Road, Camberwell, Victoria 3124, Australia
(a division of Pearson Australia Group Pty Ltd)
Penguin Books India Pvt Ltd, 11 Community Centre, Panchsheel Park, New Delhi – 110 017, India
Penguin Group (NZ), 67 Apollo Drive, Rosedale, Auckland 0632, New Zealand
(a division of Pearson New Zealand Ltd)
Penguin Books (South Africa) (Pty) Ltd, 24 Sturdee Avenue, Rosebank, Johannesburg 2196, South Africa

Penguin Books Ltd, Registered Offices: 80 Strand, London WC2R ORL, England

www.penguin.com

First published 2011
1

Copyright © James Attlee, 2011

The moral right of the author has been asserted

Set in Bembo Book MT Std 12/14.75pt
Typeset by Jouve (UK), Milton Keynes
Printed in Great Britain by Clays Ltd, St Ives plc

A CIP catalogue record for this book is available from the British Library

ISBN: 978-0-241-14432-9

www.greenpenguin.co.uk

For Rosemary and David

Contents

Moonrise

Sky Maps and Ghost Ships

Strange indeed are the places that give birth to the ideas that later, for better or worse, find physical form as books. I first encountered my subject lying on my back in a dentist's chair. In an effort to distract the minds of those undergoing treatment, the dentist in question had attached a large photographic poster to the ceiling depicting the earth at night, seen from space. It is to this distant yet familiar world that his patients cast their eyes, sometimes blurred by tears, sometimes pre-naturally sharpened by the effort of ignoring their discomfort. What they learn is that much of the planet we inhabit no longer experiences 'night' as it was once understood. Ever-increasing swathes of it are bathed in artificial light twenty-four hours a day and glitter like amber jewels when observed from the air; only the great deserts and oceans offer large areas of darkness. Those of us who inhabit these regions of eternal day (most of us, in other words) are increasingly cut off from the movements of the silent satellite that controls the tides, linked in the human mind for centuries with love, melancholy and madness. So if you asked what it was that inspired me to write about moonlight I would tell you that it was not the moon at all but *an absence of moon*, as well as of stars, meteorites and the rest of the celestial light show rendered spectrally pale today by the intensity of our self-regard.

This was one defining moment; the next was as unlike it as the range of an ordinary life allows. I was walking with a friend one hot August night along the coastal path that borders that rugged and isolated promontory in Cornwall that is named, for reasons rendered obscure by the passage of time, the Lizard. The air was rich with the smell of gorse and the scent of the springy turf that bordered the path; to our right the ground fell away in a steep slope, punctuated by rocky outcrops, which ended abruptly in a sheer cliff down to the sea. As we rounded a corner we were both halted mid-stride by what lay before us. Looking out across the ocean we saw what appeared to be the lights of a great ship approaching, glowing orange across the water. We had been idly tracking the movement of vessels all day, as visitors to the coast will do, pleasure craft and small fishing boats mostly; we had seen nothing of this size. As we watched, we realized our eyes had been playing tricks on us. What we were seeing was the rim of the harvest moon emerging from the sea, a monstrous, swollen apparition, its shape distorted by the atmospheric conditions; glowing and pulsing like an ember, craters and canyons were clearly visible on its surface like purple veins. We stood for a few minutes before hurrying back along the path to the house where we were staying and calling our friends outside to toast the moon as it wobbled up into the sky. Later that night I was woken by the mournful bellow of a foghorn. Going to the window I saw that the moon had changed colour from tangerine to silver and was casting a blade of light over the perfectly still sea, across which a solid wall of fog was advancing towards the shore. On this night at least, in this distant corner of our crowded, congested archipelago, the moon still reigned supreme.

Despite all the technological advances and new forms of entertainment our world offers, the majority of humankind still retreat into the cocoons of their dwellings for a good portion of the hours of darkness. Few step outside expressly to study the night sky. My walk along the Cornish cliffs made me think that perhaps there was a report I could bring back from this abandoned field. Was I tired of the urban landscape? Not really. Riding my bicycle through glass canyons painted with reflections, beneath bridges on which the windows of silver trains are strung like brightly coloured beads, I wouldn't have said so. But I was also looking for the real night, not the man-made one, however much it had engaged me all these years; the night that was bigger than people and that dated from before their presence on the planet. Particularly those, almost as bright as day, when the earth was bathed in the unearthly phosphorescence we call moonlight. For countless millennia humankind has lived in step with the cycles of the moon, planting crops, wooing lovers and gathering harvests according to its celestial clockwork. It is scarcely more than a century since this connection was decisively broken, since we turned our back on the sky and our faces towards the brilliantly illuminated interiors of our own homes. I resolved to make a note of the lunar calendar, so that I would be aware of when to expect moonlit nights and make sure to walk abroad in them as much as I could. I would grow familiar with the nocturnal sky, so long the true traveller's calendar and compass, that to me was as illegible as a page of Braille to a sighted man. I would look to those artists that had succeeded in capturing the essence of moonlight before it had been so nearly erased from our brightly lit world.

I have always found something attractively perverse about artistic works that portray the hours of darkness, something that seems contrary to a universal guiding principle. Painters, sculptors, artists of all kinds seek well-lit studios and sunlight, not the 'pale fire' that Shakespeare wrote of in *Timon of Athens*, snatched by the moon from its flame-headed, blazing cousin. After all, moonlight does not *reveal*, in the straight-ahead, visual sense; it transforms, changing colours and contours in its shape-shifting light. Artists who have chosen to portray the moon have seen it either as a symbol or an opportunity, its presence a gateway to another visual universe. I hoped that if I re-established a lost connection with the moon, a connection still written into my genes, and spent time in its alchemical light, I too might learn to read the world in a different way.

What follows therefore is an account of a fragmentary journey, dictated by the moon's phases, as subject to prevailing weather conditions as to my own personal circumstances. It is as much a record of moonlight encountered between the pages of books, evoked on canvas, by a camera or in music as it is a nocturnal travelogue. 'Night,' wrote Kenneth Clark, 'is not a subject for naturalistic painting.'* Moonlight, similarly, is a subject almost universally regarded as off-limits to contemporary writers, too kitsch, debased and sentimental to be worthy of serious consideration. This alone would seem to make it a subject worth exploring.

* Kenneth Clark, *Landscape into Art* (London: John Murray, new edition, 1976), p. 103.

PART ONE
Syzigy

A Three-Dog Night by the River

The moon is said to be in *syzigy* when she
is in conjunction or opposition with the sun.

*Falconer's New Universal Dictionary
of the Marine,* 1815 Edition

By afternoon it has clouded over and turned bitterly cold. The
sky releases a fine drizzle that feels as if it may turn to snow. It
has been a heavy week and I feel exhausted by doing simple
chores; it seems enough to get to the end of a shopping list,
wheeling my bike along the street from the farmers' market to
the grocery store. I haven't made any special plans for observing
the full moon even though it falls on a Saturday, but over the
preceding days I have been aware of a subliminal sense of antici-
pation. Coming home in the evenings beneath the waxing moon
I have looked upwards and reminded myself that I have an assig-
nation. But now it seems that we are set to have one of those
nights when the city is shut in beneath a lid of low-lying cloud
that bounces the sulphurous light of the street lamps back down
to us, so that we are condemned to simmer in our own electronic bouillabaisse. Mentally I have already let go of this night,
written it off, resigned to spending the evening in front of a
televisual window on the world rather than beneath the sky.
Once our son is in bed we sit down to watch a DVD. A Chinese
film, it is set in a neon-lit landscape of fast-food joints, subways,
bars, sweatshops and tiny apartments, an almost entirely nocturnal world that never shows the night sky. Some of the chase

scenes are filmed in a kind of jerking slow motion so that the lights blur and smear and create new colours, becoming themselves the film's primary subject. The motivation of the characters remains obscure; genres are shuffled, the sub-plot becomes the main plot and the main plot seems to evaporate. When it finishes we decide to go to bed. I am standing brushing my teeth by the glass-panelled back door when I notice that my feet are spotlit in a pool of silver. I go outside and find that the sky has almost cleared; the moon is high, shining through a thin cloud cover. The temperature has caused what astronomers call a corona to form; moonlight is being refracted through hexagonal ice crystals in the high cloud, creating a circle around the moon that glints purple and gold. The light spilling out from the house and from the houses on either side over the garden fence extends about eighteen feet along the ground; then the moonlight takes over. The garden backs on to allotments that are not lit at night, creating a shadowland where foxes prowl and screech and moonbeams are not entirely robbed of their potency. The bulk of a climbing rose is grey but the raindrops caught in its leaves sparkle, each a tiny reservoir of mercury. The small fig that grows against the windowless wall of the extension is silhouetted, its bare branches, studded with small hard fruit that failed to ripen in the miserably wet summer, casting sharply defined Japanese shadows on the wall.

I decide to take a midnight walk; I want to get away from the lights, see the moon reflected in the waters of the river, as so many artists before have done. To his surprise the family dog is roused from his basket to accompany me. Traditionally, for aboriginal Australians, the temperature of the hours of darkness is described as being a one-dog night, a two-dog night or, in particularly cold seasons, a three-dog night, depending on how many dogs would have been required to keep a man warm in the days when he would have slept outside, in the bush. For all I know this may be colder than it ever gets in Australia but all I have for company as I set out is a trembling, neurotic whippet that shies at every shadow. As soon as I step out of my front door I realize I will have to walk some distance to re-enter the moonlight. The moon has power in the garden only because it is shielded from the glare of the street lights in the lee of the house; I am now entering a world painted in an orange, sodium glow. Then I notice that in the shade of each parked car a tiny pool of moonlight remains. The street lights project from the edge of the road while the moon is directly above. Moonshine infiltrates between the patches of artificial light; yet it is diluted, robbed of its strength. Those still abroad at this late hour have their heads down, their collars turned up. It is easy to forget the presence of the moon above you when you are distanced, immunized against its touch.

I take the bridge across the river. I have never noticed before how brightly lit it is; completely empty, every inch of it is illuminated, its lights writhing in the water below like burning lanterns. The occasional car swishes by, its headlights outdazzled. What a profligate civilization we are, burning up our resources to light streets that nobody walks down and shop-window displays that nobody sees, pouring light on the empty pavements as a ritual oblation to the god of money. This is the senseless waste of energy through which we rob the world of moonlight. Gratefully I take a path down the steep embankment and drop into the relative darkness on the riverbank. This is what I have been seeking: around a quarter of a mile of path running between the river and a water meadow where the City Council's compulsion to banish darkness and ensure public safety has been curbed.

Within a couple of minutes of leaving the bridge behind, every puddle burns with its own miniature flame. Such reflections have fascinated mankind for countless centuries. Astrologers in the

Middle Ages claimed they were 'scrying the moon', predicting the future by noting the position of the markings on the lunar disc's face (which of course never changed) when its image was observed in standing water. Tonight the river has become a looking glass; the trees along the opposite bank stand on their heads, their reflections photographic negatives from a pre-digital age.

Ahead of me on the path I can see a lamp post, lighting the way into the garden of a waterside pub that given the hour has long since fallen as silent as the Egyptian divinity that gives it, and this stretch of the river, its name. For the ancient Egyptians the sky itself was formed by the gracefully curved body of a female divinity, variously named Nut or Hathor, who touched the earth only with the tips of her fingers and toes and whose belly was girded with stars. This belly dance of stars seems to me a ridiculously beautiful idea. However, Nut was not without her troubles. She fell in love with her twin brother, Geb, the earth god, and married him without the permission of their father, Ra, who was so enraged that he decreed that Nut would not be able to give birth to a child on any given day of the year. According to Plutarch, however, Thoth took pity on her. Playing draughts in a long series of games with the moon, he won a seventy-second part of its light; with this as his raw material he created five extra days that did not belong to the official 360-day Egyptian calendar. Nut wasted no time, giving birth to a child on each of them: Osiris, Horus, Set, Isis and Nephthys. (It is Isis, of course, who gives her name to both the river and the pub I stand between.) I stop, reluctant to re-enter the tangerine smog the lamp emits; at the precise moment I pause, under the mournful, long-suffering gaze of the whippet, who himself has the head of an Egyptian god, it switches off. I walk up to it and watch in amazement as the glow of its orange filament dims and the dark rushes back in from under the trees. There seems to be no particular logic to explain why this lamp should be programmed to switch off at this time while those behind and ahead of me still burn. What it tells me is that every one of these lights shut down or knocked out is another few yards won back for the moonlight. And it comes to me then, in a city that retains so much of its medieval fabric and boasts its own observatory, how wonderful it would be to switch this useless light show off and regain the night sky, freeing ourselves to experience once more the silvery touch of earth's nearest neighbour. Doubtless, negotiation with the earthly powers that decree the night be lit would prove as difficult a game as any Thoth played against the moon. Could those prepared to engage in it hope to win from them some unlit nights, as Thoth won Nut her days? And what might be born when we had created such a space?

A Barefoot Galileo

The nature of the moon has been a subject of conjecture for philosophers and poets from the dawn of written history. That the truth of their speculations could not be verified gave them licence to entertain widely divergent theories, some writers holding a number of apparently contradictory possibilities in balance at the same time. In Plutarch's 'On the Face that Appears in the Orb of the Moon', a cast of characters representing all fields of knowledge both report and satirize a number of 'popular notions that are in everybody's mouth' concerning the moon, whether derived from ancient sources or folk legend. They start by discussing the widely held belief that the face of a man or a maiden is discernible on the lunar disc; they decide that this notion cannot be a mere affectation of sight caused by the moon's brightness, as those with weak eyes are less able to discern its features, meaning the face-like markings have physical existence. At the same time they are under no illusion that the face itself is real. Thus the moon must be something like a shadow-puppet screen or a magic lantern in the sky. Another belief held by the ancients that they discuss and dismiss is that the full moon is a mirror, 'of all mirrors, in point of polish and of brilliancy the most beautiful and the most clear', and that its so-called face is 'only reflected images and appearances of the great sea'. This early link between the moon and water reverses a pictorial tradition later to become significant in Western art, in which water reflects the moon. In addition they mention the idea that the moon is composed of glass or ice and that the light of heaven shines through it, making the moon a lens and moonlight the projected illumination of another world. A magic lantern, a mirror or a lens; it is as though the moon from the earliest times was pointing towards the as yet undiscovered science of optics, urging men to increase the power of their limited vision, calling out *look at me, discover me*.

It was not until the beginning of the seventeenth century that men devised the first instruments that allowed mankind to extend its vision to other worlds. The magnification power of Galileo Galilei's first refracting spyglasses,* constructed variously from lead or strips of wood, covered with intricately tooled leather (for those he wished to present as gifts to potential patrons) or paper, was weak by today's standards. His first attempt, made using standard lenses purchased from spectacle-makers' workshops, gave only a magnification power of 3X. Had he chosen to turn this instrument towards the night sky, the detail he would have been able to observe of the *lunar maria* (large plains on the surface of the moon, visible from earth by the naked eye, formerly believed to be seas) would have been scarcely greater than that visible to the naked eye. Fortunately he did not rest with his first attempt, but strove to improve the efficiency of his 'tubes', using his knowledge of optics to grind and polish the lenses himself. By the end of the summer in 1609 he had managed to achieve a magnification of 8X or 9X, putting him ahead of the competition (instruments that could magnify 3X or 4X had already appeared for sale in Venice). The engine that drove him was not purely a love of science but the single-minded desire to advance his career. Initially, at least, the best way of doing this seemed to be to win the favour of the ruling powers of the Republic. Galileo was a man with responsibilities – he had his sisters' dowries to pay for and three children by his

---

* The word *telescopium* was not coined until 1611, probably by the Greek-born poet and philosopher John Desmiani, during Galileo's visit to Rome.

mistress to support, all on the limited income of a university pro-
fessorship in mathematics. He offered his own instrument to the
Doge of Venice as a weapon to add to his arsenal, the missile
defence shield of its day. 'This is a thing of inestimable benefit for
all transactions and undertakings,' he wrote in a letter to the Doge,
'maritime or terrestrial, allowing us at sea to discover at a much
greater distance than usual the hulls and sails of the enemy, so that
for two hours or more we can detect him before he detects us . . .'

By the end of the same year Galileo had created a telescope
with 20X magnification. This was the instrument with which
he began his voyage of exploration into the heavens. I like to
imagine the moment when he turned his improved spyglass on
the moon and the silent planet swam into the watery orbit of his
eye. Stripped of mystery, obfuscation and philosophical debate,
naked, shivering perhaps through the transmitted trembling of
his hand★ (although he had devised a tripod to minimize this
problem), the moon was revealed to be, what? Much like the
earth; its surface irregular, marked by chains of mountains and
deep valleys, geographical features a man could walk among if
only he could devise a way to reach it. Once and for all the Aris-
totelian notion that the heavens were perfect and unchangeable,
while only the earth was the realm of corruption and decay, was
rendered untenable. Before long, Galileo's vision had reached
beyond the lunar plane and discovered four new stars. Not that
these were, as he explained in his dedication to his book *Siderius
Nuncius* (*The Starry Messenger*) in 1610,

of the common sort and multitude of the less notable fixed stars, but of
the illustrious order of wandering stars, which, indeed, make their

---

★ 'The instrument must be held firm, and hence it is good,' Galileo wrote to
a correspondent, 'in order to escape the shaking of the hand that arises from
the motion of the arteries and from respiration itself, to fix the tube in some
stable place.'

journeys and orbits with a marvellous speed around the star of Jupiter, the most noble of them all, with mutually different motions, like children of the same family, while meanwhile all together, in mutual harmony, complete their great revolutions every twelve years about the centre of the world, that is, about the Sun itself.

By discovering that Jupiter was orbited by its own moons, Galileo dethroned the earth from absolute rule at the centre of the spinning, singing firmament, providing compelling support for a Copernican view of the universe. At one stroke he earned himself international fame and the undying enmity of certain members of the Catholic hierarchy. He was first reported to the Inquisition in 1616 and warned to abandon his heliocentric view of the universe. In 1632 he was reported again for his book *Dialogue Concerning the Two Chief World Systems*, which presents the theories of Copernicus as superior to those of Ptolemy. He was condemned for 'a vehement suspicion of heresy' and had to make a dramatic recantation of his opinions before the inquisitors to save his skin.

In his old age, already blind and held under house arrest, Galileo was visited in Tuscany by another defender of regicide, the young Puritan poet John Milton. Milton himself of course would later go blind, having lost his eyes 'overplied / In liberty's defense', as he himself put it in his twenty-second sonnet, as Secretary of Foreign Tongues in Cromwell's government. The poet also found himself out of step with worldly powers; after the Restoration, a republican in a monarchical age, his books were burned in public by the hangman and he narrowly escaped execution. We have no record of the conversation between the scientist and the poet. Their meeting is immortalized in *Paradise Lost* in a few brief lines, in which Milton writes of Satan's shield, which

> Hung on his shoulders like the moon, whose orb
> Through Optic Glass the Tuscan artist views

> At ev'ning from the top of Fesole,
> Or in Valdarno, to descry new lands,
> Rivers or mountains in her spotty globe.

At first, verification of the worlds opened up by this new technology was limited to those in possession of rare scientific equipment; others had to rely on the accounts of these virtual explorers of the regions beyond the earth. In England, a little over a decade after Galileo's discoveries, Robert Burton, that great accumulator of all knowledge both ancient and contemporary, wrote in *The Anatomy of Melancholy* with characteristic caution that 'they find by their glasses that maculae facie luna, [the spots on the face of the moon] the brighter parts are earth, the dusky sea, which Thales, Plutarch, and Pythagoras formerly taught; and manifestly discern hills and dales, and suchlike concavities, if we may believe and subscribe to Galileo's observations'. It did not take long, however, for Galileo's ideas to percolate through the consciousness of Europe, shifting our understanding of the universe for ever. In the land of his birth, he has made an extraordinary journey since his death, from villain to hero, from heretic to saint.

The magnitude of the shift in his status is brought home to me when I visit an exhibition dedicated to his legacy held at the Palazzo Strozzi in Florence. There I see a copy from the original run of *Siderius Nuncius*, on loan from the Biblioteca Nazionale Centrale; examples of his telescopes; and, most extraordinary of all, a remnant of his physical being, its presence an indication of the reverence he has attained since his death. The severed middle finger from the astronomer's right hand, still pointing upwards, is preserved beneath a bubble of glass at the top of an alabaster reliquary. The finger was separated from his remains by a provost named Anton Francesco Gori when Galileo's body was transferred from its obscure resting place under the bell tower of Santa Croce to a monumental tomb in the nave of the Basilica in 1737. It next fell into the hands of a librarian named Bandini, was passed to the Tribuna di Galileo in 1841 and eventually came to rest in the Museo di Storia della Scienza, now the Museo Galileo, in Florence. The inscription on the base of the reliquary praises Galileo's scientific and moral virtues, exonerating him by implication from the charges of the Inquisition. The finger, withered and twisted with age, is a holy relic. So deeply embedded is man's religious impulse that when religion itself is dethroned we beatify scientists instead.

Even today, when telescopes far more powerful than Galileo's are available for the cost of an ordinary meal in a local restaurant, most of us remain unacquainted with the stars at first hand. I never owned or even looked through an astronomical telescope as a child and I am sure that this is not unusual. In an age when men have devised ships able to carry us across the ocean of space that divides us from our nearest cousin, when they have planted flags, collected rocks and lolloped in the lunar dust, sending back their indifferent holiday snaps to earth, it is clear that most of us remain unimpressed. The first time I observed the moon through any kind of lens was 396 years after Galileo constructed his first telescope, when I stood beneath an ancient plum tree in central France (its fruit a dark constellation shedding overripe asteroids at my feet) and turned a pair of second-hand binoculars on the sky. The full moon floated above the hillside on which I stood and I gave it my considered attention as a student of nature, in the words of *The Starry Messenger*. Through the glasses it appeared very different to the way it did to the naked eye; as far as I could discern it seemed to be made of some kind of ceramic material, possibly punched with holes, lit from within by an internal light source and marked with depressions not unlike purple thumbprints. So this was astronomy! But I was no astronomer; I seemed to be deficient in both equipment and knowledge. The sky was studded with stars but the only constellation I could name with any confidence was the Plough, which as a child I had known as the Frying Pan. I was not the first human that, on being confronted by the book of nature, was able to learn little but the extent of their own ignorance.

My next close encounter with earth's satellite didn't take place until two days before Christmas in 2007. We had accepted an invitation to a seasonal drink with a friend who had recently returned from living overseas, to a house a few doors from our own. The full moon was due to fall on Christmas Eve and I was wondering if I would find time amid social commitments to sneak out of doors and walk beneath its light. At the same time another, nagging voice in my head was telling me to abandon the project altogether, to forget the moon and moonlight and find something sensible to write about. As we left our door I noticed that the weather was perfect for lunar observation, crisp and clear, the nearly full moon riding overhead, ringed with faint cloud. The party had been in full swing since the afternoon, the remains of a meal lay on the table and most of the guests either sat around a fire indoors or stood by a brazier in the garden where they were free to smoke and talk and look up at the stars. We were greeted warmly and introduced to our friend's new companion, a congenial host, who was padding around barefoot with plates of food, drink and logs for the fire. However, I was almost immediately distracted by an object in the corner; the long, dark barrel of a telescope as thick as my arm, standing on a neatly folded tripod. Our host noticed my interest (I have never been good at concealing such things) and explained that he had recently purchased it for thirty-five pounds in a car-boot sale, complete with spare lenses. With faultless hospitality, despite the fact that he had been busy looking after his guests all evening, he offered to set it up in the garden. We carried it out of the back door, along with our bottles of beer; I was a little concerned on account of his bare feet as the ground outside was frozen hard, but he didn't appear to notice. The telescope was assembled swiftly. A fairly cheap Chinese model with a wooden tripod, it must have been several years old, but as it was my first encounter with any such instrument I was deeply impressed. My host bent over the lens, aligned the telescope and then stood back for me to take a look. How can I describe what I saw? The surface of the moon filled my field of vision, seemingly almost within reach. For the first time, like Galileo, I saw the craters invisible to the naked eye upon its surface and individual volcano-like mountains, of the size and definition of the barnacles you might find on the side of a boat. So this is the country moonlight comes from, I thought. I am not superstitious, except in so far as any writer is superstitious about the project they are working on, but I couldn't help finding it extraordinary that a telescope should arrive in the street where I lived at precisely the time when I was wondering whether the moon and its light were a proper subject for my book. A few days later I got a text message on my phone. 'We are sitting in the pub,' it read, 'and wondering whether you would like to borrow the telescope for a while?'

Absorbed by Its Shadows

For a deity that is so often addressed, admired and speculated upon, the moon remains remarkably unresponsive. Only in Lucian's *Icaromenippus* do we glimpse its frustration at being the centre of so much human attention and its wish to be allowed to sail on its way undisturbed, a Garbo of the skies. Menippus, himself frustrated at the lack of information he is able to find on the nature of the heavens, has ascended to the moon by strapping on mismatching but symbolically important wings, one from an eagle and one from a vulture. Just as he is about to leave the lunar surface, having had his fill of diverting himself by looking down at the activities of the people of earth, the moon calls out to him, asking him to bear a message to Zeus for her. She has, she explains, had enough of overhearing the spurious theories of scientists about her nature. 'They seem to have nothing to do but poke their noses into my affairs. They're always wanting to know who I am, what my measurements are and why my figure keeps changing into a semi-circle or a crescent. Some of them say I'm infested with living organisms, others that I'm a sort of mirror suspended over the sea . . .' In short, she wants Zeus to 'rub out those scientists, put a gag on those logicians, demolish the Stoa, burn down the Academy and stop those Peripatetics walking around all the time. Then I might be safe from their offensive calculations.'

Sadly, human behaviour has not improved; today the moon is at risk from more than words. Towards the end of 2009, American scientists crashed a 2,200 kg rocket into the permanently shadowed Cabeus crater near the moon's south pole. The rocket was followed into the crater by a probe, which collected samples from the plume of debris shot upwards from the impact. To the great excitement of NASA scientists, the probe detected water molecules, which may have great implications for the sustainability of any moon colony that is established to mine the moon for its natural resources. The most significant of these is a substance called helium-3, which might be extracted by opencast mining and used to power energy generation back on earth. As many voices are now pointing out, such activities would swiftly destroy the pristine ecology of the moon, unchanged for billions of years. Meanwhile, as scientists analyse their discoveries, the rocket and its attendant probe will remain, joining the growing pile of junk left on the lunar surface by previous visitors. All of this garbage, from abandoned moon-buggies to spacesuits, cameras and even defecation-collection bags, is granted an eternal non-life by the thinness of the satellite's atmosphere. (I suppose we should not be surprised that the American astronauts, commissioned to plant their county's flag, should further mark their territory by shitting on the moon.) It is thought that as long as they avoid a direct asteroid hit or future human development on the lunar surface, Armstrong and Aldrin's footprints could remain visible for hundreds of thousands of years, ready to spook a future Robinson Crusoe washed up on lunar shores.

Today I have come to Modern Art Oxford to see a work by British artist Katie Paterson, in which the moon at last plays an active rather than a passive role, making its own mark on one of the great icons of European culture. Paterson, in a work that effortlessly combines poetry with technology, has translated each note of Beethoven's Piano Sonata Opus 27 no. 2, better known as the 'Moonlight Sonata', into its musical letters, which in turn have been turned into Morse code. The code was then transmitted to the moon using an EME (earth–moon–earth) radio communication system from a 'moon station' in

Southampton, England. The signal was reflected off the moon's surface (a process called moonbounce) and received back on earth at a station in Sweden, 480,000 miles and 2.5 seconds later. However, this was not just a game of interplanetary catch. The music has changed. It bears the imprint of its journey. As Paterson puts it in some accompanying notes in the gallery, 'the moon reflects only part of the information back – some of it is absorbed by its shadows, lost in its craters'.

In the centre of the gallery space stands a solitary Disklavier grand piano, trailing the wires that link it to a computer. Remote, electronic fingers depress the keys, filling the room with the opening section of the Sonata, the movement that Beethoven marked 'Adagio Sostenuto', in which the haunting, impossibly simple melody floats above an ever-changing sequence of three-note clusters. It was this section that earned the Sonata the title 'Moonlight', when the critic and poet Ludwig Rellstab likened listening to it to the experience of gliding across the shimmering surface of Lake Lucerne in a boat at night, surrounded by the spectrally lit mountain landscape. Yet the music we are hearing has undergone a change, an extraterrestrial remix. Parts of the piece have simply been erased on its journey, inserting sections of emptiness where none existed before; spaces that speak of the distance the music has travelled on its journey. Curiously the transformation is rather successful; the construction of the original piece is of a robustness that allows it to sustain such editing. Indeed, it emerges from its lunar encounter in a form that is arguably more arresting to twenty-first-century ears than the original, rather as some buildings only come into their own when seen as ruins. Cultural artefacts gain an aura of authenticity through the patina that time bestows. Unlike works of visual art, however, music that is written down can be created afresh again and again – although the shift in the sensibilities of conductors and orchestra leaders, the increasing loudness of musical instruments and the changing fashions in the manner in which they are played adds a veneer of cultural interpretation, like a thick and discoloured varnish on a painting, over the composer's original intentions. Now, with Paterson's help, the moon has given us a radical rereading of this much-loved work, revealing it for what it is; a piece of musical architecture as brittle as any classical ruin, that crumbles in the fingers like dust, while retaining the power to haunt our dreams.

Across town in the Bodleian Library, I come across another meeting between art, the moon and music. A recent acquisition, it is a rare illustrated autograph of a song by Felix Mendelssohn, decorated by the composer himself with a watercolour of a moonlit lake. 'Schilflied', translated as 'Reed Song', was composed in 1842, to words by Nikolaus Lenan. The lyric begins 'On the lake's unruffled surface rests the moon's fair beam', and it is this scene that Mendelssohn has painted, wrapping his depiction of the lake and its surroundings around and even between the musical staves; the drooping branches of a willow trail over the 6/8 time signature and a stand of trees extends its branches between the bird-tracks of musical notes, brushing against the words *andante con moto*. The whole vista is dramatically lit with the moon itself a white circle against an inky sky. The neutral paper, the ground on which the music is written, provides Mendelssohn with his moonlight effects on the water. Two elusive, ethereal substances that travel through space to reach our senses, moonlight and music, are captured and combined on this sheet of paper, itself one of the most miraculous creations of human civilization. Somehow, Mendelssohn implies, if music can emulate moonlight to the ear, and moonlight can infiltrate music on the page, and if the page itself can both bear the fragile imprint of music and stand in for the brightness of moonlight, then these things are connected. The task the composer has set me is to find out how.

Earthshine

After a blustery start to the month, ten days into February we enjoy a few days of false spring; the wind drops and it is warm enough to sit outside at lunchtime on the deck of a boat perched on a mudbank in the Thames in central London. Cormorants at the tideline hold out one ragged black wing at a time to absorb the unaccustomed warmth and a heron picks its way through the shallow water with the gait of a preoccupied parson, hands clasped behind his back. I sit basking in the sun, looking upriver towards Vauxhall Bridge; the water is dazzling and exhales a golden mist and the span of the heavy bridge, glinting with slow-moving traffic, is resolved into the delicate arc of a wooden footbridge in a Japanese woodcut. I imagine myself with Whistler in the rowing boat sculled by his studio assistants on the river not far from this spot, as he journeyed out on the tide in sun, fog and moonlight, composing the riverscapes that were homages to the effects of light on water. The crescent moon appears, as thin and sharp as a fingernail, as I cycle back through Hyde Park that night. For the next few days we are treated to a display of a phenomenon known to present-day astronomers as 'earthshine' and to the ancients as 'ashen light'; the light of the sun, reflected from the earth, is dimly illuminating the body of the moon, so that a ghost image of the whole of the shaded planet is visible above the bright sliver that is catching the sun's rays. The new moon is 'carrying the old moon in its arms'. It is as though a kohl-painted siren was partly opening one heavy-lidded, gleaming eye to gaze coquettishly down at the earth. The weather changes once more and the night temperatures drop below freezing, with perfectly clear skies. The moon, now waxing fuller, is present during the day, rising above the rooftops by two o'clock in the afternoon against a perfectly blue sky. The cold, dry air is perfect for lunar observation; Mare Imbrium and Mare Serenitas, the two 'eyes' of the face of the man in the moon, are clearly visible without the aid of a telescope; below them Mare Cognitum and Mare Nubium appear towards the terminator line. In the early afternoon the massive craters take on the colour of the sky itself, a delicate, pale blue, as if they really were seas, as their names suggest. This daylight moon, the colour of frost, seems brittle as a wafer dissolving on the tongue. Towards dusk, as the sky fades and the light of the moon intensifies, the lunar seas take on the deep mauve of a bruise.

A little short of a week before full moon some friends come to visit. At around half-past midnight, conversation turns to my current preoccupation. I suggest getting the telescope out and to my surprise someone agrees. At this hour the moon, which travels about the span of an outstretched hand each night, hangs outside my back door, over the garden fence. We fumble at the telescope with frozen fingers, attempting to calibrate it, until a gleam from the eyepiece confirms we have locked into position. Was it this phenomenon, this surprising and sudden brightness in the eyepiece of a telescope, that suggested to Milton the comparison between the moon and Satan's highly polished shield? Like me, my friend has rarely if ever pointed any optical device at the lunar surface and is gratifyingly awestruck at what we can discern. One side of a crater on the terminator line, its edge catching the sun's rays, is sharply defined in shadow; to our imperfect vision its illuminated rim appears almost like a hoop, rising from the planet's surface. We puzzle over what we are looking at, arriving at an interpretation as much by the application of logic as by the evidence of our eyes, much as Galileo did, returning to the party both chilled and dazzled.

Eostre and a Paschal Moon

In 2008, Easter falls very early, on 23 March – the first time it has done so since 1913. Anyone wondering why they are shivering their way through the long weekend has the moon to blame. The general rule for calculating the date of Easter was set at the Council of Nicaea in AD 325: from that date on, it was decreed that Easter Sunday would fall on the first Sunday after the full moon, known as the Paschal Moon, which fell on or after the spring equinox. To complicate things further, the early Church decided that the spring equinox would always be set as 21 March, even though in reality the date shifted slightly each year. This means that Easter can fall as early as the last week of March, when in the northern hemisphere snow might still be falling, or as late as the end of April, when spring is well advanced. Full moon in 2008 falls exactly on 21 March, so that Good Friday and the spring equinox inhabit the same space in the year and Easter is almost as early as it can possibly be (it last fell a day earlier on 22 March in 1818).

This linkage between the Christian festival, the coming of spring and the lunar cycle is rich in both metaphorical and historical resonance. In *De Temporum Ratione*, his treatise on the calculation of time written in the eighth century, the Venerable Bede claimed that the name for Easter came from the Anglo-Saxon deity Eostre, who had been worshipped with feasting at the spring equinox in times prior to his own. There seems little reason to doubt his word; why would he, after all, credit a pagan goddess with the origin of the name of the most important Christian celebration without good reason? If he had been as skilful at looking into the future as he was at looking into the past, it is hard to imagine what he would have made of the transformation that has taken place in the Easter festival of today. Eostre, associated with the growing light of spring, is very much present, something that would have been shocking to one dedicated to the project of Christianizing these islands. Her sacred hare is everywhere, disguised in cartoon clothes as an Easter bunny.

To further confuse the eighth-century cleric, the festival's pre-Christian elements have been skewed by the intervention of capitalism. The eggs, symbols of new life and associated very early on with this time of year, have been touched by its magic wand and changed into chocolate. Instead of being a time when first crops would be planted and the hearth forsaken, when young women would take to the woods and collect the 'holy tide' of water from the brook that had the power to restore youth, Eostre, like Christmas, has become a time of feasting. We would rather wax fat than dance or pray. But perhaps this is not such an irrational response to world events. As the climate changes and water levels rise, it could be that evolution is responding and turning full circle; by gaining extra layers of blubber, the people of the richer nations, sleek as seals, may be getting ready to return to the water once again.

A White Horse and Mammoth Bones

The moonbeams kilter i' the lift,
An Earth, the bare auld stane
Glitters aneath the seas o space
White as a mammoth's bane.

Hugh MacDiarmid,
'The Man in the Moon'

On a Sunday evening in early March, three days short of the full moon, on a day marked by high winds and sudden squalls of icy rain, when thoughts are already turning to the next day's work ahead, I go upstairs to fetch something from the room where we sleep beneath the eaves, like swallows, a rescued roofspace with a dormer window facing south. I pause, with my finger on the light switch. There is a lozenge of moonlight on the floor, bright enough to cast my shadow across the bed when I step forwards. I push the blind up further to see that the skies have cleared and the moon is sailing free in the frosty air. Instantly I am gripped with the desire to shrug off my usual Sunday-evening routine, to forgo a second glass of wine, a TV show, the gentle slide back into the working week. I want to get outside. The moon will do this to you. But I have no wish to walk in the city tonight, searching for surviving pools of moonlight in the shadow of buildings or parked cars. For some time now the idea has been forming at the back of my mind of taking a night walk up on the Ridgeway, the prehistoric highway that runs along the top of the Chiltern Hills, the nearest point to the city perhaps that might escape the patina created by the street lights which turns the sky to beaten bronze. Putting thoughts of my early start on the morrow out of my head, I decide to drive out to the Uffington White Horse, the largest and oldest prehistoric sculpture in Britain, carved into the downland chalk around 3,000 years ago by a long-vanished people for a purpose that still evades us.

I am a great believer in impulsive behaviour, as a way of grasping experiences that otherwise would be missed. However, it has its drawbacks. Consequences will arise out of a lack of planning that will have to be faced in due course. Aware of the lateness of the hour, I leave in a hurry with no clear idea of the route I am going to take. The only map in the car is an out-of-date road atlas, at a scale that makes it impractical for use once off the main routes. The fuel level is also worryingly low, I notice, when I switch on the engine. As we live in a city and have the use of our legs, we use the car very little. We are lucky enough to have a supplier of bio-fuel in the neighbourhood, a viscous yellow liquid made from recycled cooking oil that our diesel car drinks happily, with no ill effects, and this is what we use to power our four-wheeled travel. The sole disadvantage of this fuel, of which the only by-product seems to be a gentle olfactory reminder of the chip shop on stepping from the car at the end of a journey, is that it is sold in large plastic containers rather than from a pump, as the supplier does not have a licence to act as a filling station. The containers have to be carried home and poured into the car on the street. This is really a two-person job, with one person holding a funnel in place and the other lifting the container into position. Although I have a full container in the back of the car, I am hoping I won't have to attempt emptying it into the tank on my own.

Almost as soon as I leave the city, the orange warning light on the fuel gauge comes on. I decide to travel as far as I can on a major road, to save time. The traffic is moving at high speed down the carriageway, forcing me to keep up, although I am not sure where it is I am going. It is darker out here already; moon-light spills in through the window to illuminate the empty passenger seat beside me. I pull off into a side road and study the map; the Vale of the White Horse is marked, spanning quite a large area, as is the village of Uffington, although the smallness of the roads that lead to the village and beyond to White Horse Hill and the creases and marks on the page make it difficult to work out my route. I pull back out on to the main road rather too close to an approaching truck that ignites a wall of white lights and blasts me with its powerful ship's foghorn. A few miles further on I decide to take another turning to the left; although the village mentioned on the sign isn't on my map, the lane at least seems to lead in the right general direction. After wandering this way and that between high hedges, I find myself back at my starting point, rejoining the main road a mile or so further on. Wisps of cloud are visible in the moonlit air; I am growing anxious that my whole expedition will turn into farce and that by the time I reach my destination the moon will have disappeared. I take another turning and after meandering through the lanes for what seems an age, I see a signpost to Uffington. I drive through the silent and apparently deserted village, listening to a programme on a local station about a visit to the area from an Argentinian accordion player, and take the road to White Horse Hill. The steep escarpment looms above me, its bulk a shadow against the sky. I pass the conical mound of Dragon Hill, where local legend has it Saint George slew the dragon, its spilled blood the reason for the bare chalk patch on the hill's summit where no grass will grow, and find a gateway in which to leave the car. Once I have killed the engine and the tango music dies away, I hear the wind. It is bitterly cold; snow is falling in other parts of the country and news of its passage is borne here on the gusts that buffet the stationary car. Beyond the gate, a steep bridleway climbs the side of the hill. Many feet have worn a deep groove in the turf, exposing the chalk that lies just beneath the surface of these downlands, making them a potential blackboard for our Bronze Age ancestors. In the moonlight, the path's whiteness is extraordinarily bright and the grass on its banks glitters with reflective droplets of moisture. During the day, and especially at weekends during the summer, this hill is covered with walkers and picnickers who come here to fly kites, run their dogs, fly pestilential petrol-driven planes that pollute the silent air with their mosquito whine, examine the White Horse and enjoy the view. At ten o'clock on a Sunday night in early March, I have it to myself. I walk swiftly uphill in an effort to get warm and when I turn back, the walls of the valley below White Horse Hill are lit up in the moonlight. This deep-sided, enclosed coomb is known as the Manger; legend has it that the Horse leaves the hill under cover of darkness and wanders here to graze. It is too early for its slopes to have greened up; I can see the wind moving through the long, straw-coloured grass, so that the whole valley seems to shimmer. Up on the hilltop, 850 feet or so above the plain, the works of man are reduced in scale. Human settlements light up the sky in the distance. Swindon blinks and glimmers to the west, its orange lights an outpouring of molten lava, and a train snakes across the flatlands like a brilliantly coloured millipede. I turn my back to face the hill. Here, the moon is the only source of light. It is bright enough for me to see the blue of the sky; the molehills that punctuate the turf are the colour of blood-sausage, specked with fragments of luminous chalk that have been turned up by their worm-loving architects. I find a path and follow it to the White Horse itself. The relief carving is the work of a prehistoric avant-garde. On paper, the line of each limb would be a mere brushstroke, such is the economy and sophistication of its styling, the whole design unreadable to those standing near it or even those who cut its lines through the skin of the hill to expose the skeleton beneath. For the Horse, if that is what it is (although it has been known as such for a millennium at least, there have always been those who maintained that it is a dragon, or some other mythic beast), can only be seen and visually comprehended from a viewpoint across the plain: as if the people supervising its creation were able to stand far off and direct the cutting, or fly upwards to gain a vantage from where its design could be apprehended. These were the artistic skills used by the painters of baroque ceilings in Neapolitan churches, which look perfectly in perspective from the ground but close up (to those with ladders or the keys to hidden stairways) are hideously distorted. The ability to calculate the effect on the eye of the angle of vision and of distance, so highly prized in seventeenth-century Europe, is here projected by prehistoric artists across a measure of miles.

The sweeping lines of the Horse's form, maintained and kept clear of grass today as they have been for numberless centuries, glow in the gloom like the mammoth's bone in MacDiarmid's poem. Those approaching across the plain 3,000 years ago on a moonlit night would have seen it, etched on the hillside in negative – god, totem or tribal insignia, we cannot say. Was its visibility by moonlight partly their intention? Prehistoric peoples in Europe had been closely calculating the moon's cycles for many millennia before the Horse was carved on this downland turf. A piece of bone discovered in the Dordogne in France, dating from the Cro-Magnon period 25,000 years before the birth of Christ, is etched with a serpentine design of two complete cycles of the moon's phases, providing a handy and accurate pocket lunar calendar. After the ages the bone spent undiscovered in the earth it spent further years in equal obscurity in a glass cabinet in a museum in Paris. No one took the trouble to attempt to decipher the scratches and grooves in its surface, as no one believed primitive cave dwellers capable of sophisticated notation. The White Horse hides from no one, yet its meaning and purpose remain a mystery. Perhaps after a certain number of centuries have elapsed, all that civilizations can hope to leave as a trace of their passing are one or two really good riddles to keep future generations puzzling, until their efforts too are obliterated in the drift of time.

The wind has grown colder, its teeth sharper; my forehead, which had felt pierced by needles, is growing numb. Running down a bank in deep shadow, I stumble and momentarily imagine breaking a leg up here and freezing, in sight of the winking lights of distant towns, while the villagers of Uffington watch television behind closed curtains. Nothing so dramatic happens: the sense of isolation the hill creates at night is an illusion, even if it is one I am grateful for. All I need to do is feed my beast of burden its ration, a distillation of a thousand drunken takeaway meals, and it will leap forward, eager to carry me out of here. Somehow I manage to prop a full container on my knee, hugging it in a greasy embrace with one arm while holding the funnel in place with my other hand. Some of the fuel is lost, whipped out of the funnel's mouth by the wind, a twenty-first-century offering to the spirits of this place, but enough glugs into the tank to get me home – a journey that, following a more direct route, seems to take no time at all.

Fear of the Dark

I believe that men are generally still a little afraid
of the dark, though the witches are all hung and
Christianity and candles have been introduced.

Henry David Thoreau, *Walden*

I'm thinking again about my dentist's poster and the way the night sky has been painted over by the glare of our permanently lit streets. At the station, my eye is attracted to the front page of a newspaper, not one I would normally pick up by choice. It is dominated by the headline RETURN OF THE BLACK-OUT, its wording resonating with a readership old enough to recognize the reference to the Second World War. I buy a copy to read on the train. It seems that, to the newspaper's fury, certain councils are proposing to turn off street lighting between midnight and five in the morning, in a bid to save money and lessen carbon emissions. A typical sodium street light, we are told, costs between twenty and forty pounds a year to run and many councils are responsible for up to 100,000 lights, so savings on both economic and ecological fronts would be considerable. But this is not a newspaper renowned for campaigning in favour of green issues. Sure enough, their self-appointed role as guardians of law and order means they are entirely against such moves. Their invective is charged with the usual undercurrent of apoplectic rage.

A reporter has been dispatched to a housing estate in Hampshire where an experiment is under way in which the lights are turned off at night (or, as the paper puts it, the council have 'pulled the plug on street lighting after midnight for 1,000 residents without warning'). The reporter manages to locate a local willing to go on record with her unhappiness over the situation. 'It is now pitch black after midnight,' she tells him. 'The big concern is that it will encourage vandalism and burglary. For many people, particularly those who live on their own, it is very intimidating . . . It is a criminals' haven.' Inside the paper the article continues, beneath the headline MARKET TOWN GOES BACK TO THE DARK AGES. Having already made a connection with the front-page headline to the war years, sacred territory to the readers of this newspaper, this second headline cleverly links the turning-off of street lighting to the pre-industrial, pre-Enlightenment era. At the flick of a switch, it implies, these local politician busybodies propose to undo five centuries of progress. The Dark Ages *would*, on occasion, have been a time when it was frightening to go outside at night. No policemen on the streets, robbers lurking in the forests eager to redistribute the hard-earned savings of the prosperous to the undeserving poor, mischievous faeries abroad in the moonlit fields and hedgerows . . . They're not suggesting we go back to *that* state of affairs, surely?

This fear, this shunning of the night, is by no means a new phenomenon. It is possible that man evolved the habit of sleeping in safe, secluded places as a response to the danger of attack from wild animals during the hours of darkness. Light has had a supernatural importance since prehistoric times. In Jewish and Christian theology, God separated light from darkness shortly after creation and human beings have been attempting to extend light's dominion ever since. The search for a means of lighting the interiors of houses has been a test of mankind's resourcefulness and ingenuity for millennia. The glow of the hearth fire was long ago supplemented by the light of bundles of resinous

sticks, of rushlights made from rushes dipped in animal fat, or
by foul-smelling tallow candles. Lamps fuelled by the oil of
grape pips, flax or olives emerged in the countries bordering the
Mediterranean. For the prosperous in northern climes there was
the clear and very expensive light of the beeswax candle. In an
indication of mankind's ongoing hunger to turn night into day,
a particular breed of whale was engaged in hazardous and bloody
pursuit across remote oceans to obtain the rose-coloured liquid
wax found in its forehead, in order to fuel the whale-oil lamps
that graced the parlours of the ladies of New England.

The march towards a thoroughly lit world continued apace.
The residues of long-vanished forests were excavated, their
vapours tapped, their liquid excrescences pumped to burn with
ever-brighter brilliancy. Towards the end of the nineteenth century, gas and then electric street lighting was laid on as a public
service in developed nations, rolling out into the twentieth,
until cities from the air became flashing, blinking circuit-boards,
permanently connected. Strangely, crime did not disappear.
Muggers, whores, panhandlers, card cheats and drug dealers
all seemed to relish the free illumination that turned the street
into their showrooms, perfect spaces in which to advertise their
wares and do business. They were spotlit players, gyrating on a
stage; their very visibility drove away the legitimate bystanders
and pedestrians, who would have preferred, and felt less threatened, not to know what was going on.

Despite the doubt surrounding its efficacy in reducing crime,
comprehensive lighting of the streets remains a totem for those
seeking public order, including the editors of the newspaper I
picked up at the station. 'The Government-backed blackouts
have provoked anger from police leaders and motoring organ-
izations,' the article goes on to claim. A spokesman from the
Police Superintendents' Association steps forward. 'Good street
lighting reduces crime,' he suggests, in tones some way from

anything that could be described as 'anger'. 'It makes people feel safe and it reduces the risk of road traffic accidents. I would need to feel confident that the environmental savings were being balanced against the impact on local crime.'

The feature is illustrated with three photographs. The first is captioned *9.30: Now You See It: In the evening this street is well lit by street lamps.* The next reads *12.35: Now You Don't: The lights go out at midnight, leaving residents in the dark.* It is interesting to compare the two images. In the first, the colour of the suburban street recalls a fizzy orange glucose drink that used to be given to British children when they were ill and that has more recently rebranded itself as a sports tonic. The effect is of daylight seen through a pair of cheap plastic sunglasses. In the second photograph there is still a strong glow above the rooftops from neighbouring areas that have escaped the blackout, but higher in the sky the stars are clearly visible. So are the houses, a path and the street. There is no way that this equates to the 'pitch black' mentioned by the interviewee; anyone stepping beyond the halogen glare of their porch security lighting and letting their eyes adjust for a minute or so would have no problem navigating the neighbourhood. The photographer has taken the second shot from a little further back, or the picture editor has cropped it differently, so that a tree and some shaggy grasses on the verge come into view, as if threatening forces of nature were moving in under cover of darkness. The third photograph is of the embattled resident, a smartly dressed woman in early middle age, smiling somewhat warily at the camera, above the caption *Older people are feeling insecure.* Does her expression indicate she already feels she has been manipulated into saying more than she really means? Does she know that her words, once they have been regurgitated from a reporter's shorthand notebook, will no longer sound like her own? 'It is absolutely pitch black,' she insists again, in the box beneath the photographs, in a peculiar contradiction of the visual evidence. 'We are more concerned about crime than anything else . . . This is a very middle-class residential area . . . There are quite a lot of older people here and they are feeling insecure.'

Different newspapers employ different triggers to maintain a loyal readership. The trademark technique of this particular example is the peddling of fear – or, as they would put it, speaking up for 'the needs and fears of ordinary people'. 'We are more concerned about crime than anything else,' their interviewee had said, a resident not of some strife-torn inner-city ghetto but of a 'very middle-class residential area' in the suburbs, where crime rates are presumably low. All the recent surveys in England report that crime is falling, while at the same time fear of crime is increasing. The genius of the author of this article is to combine this deep-seated fear of crime with our primal fear of darkness. Even where there isn't any crime, people lie awake at night worrying about it. And even when there isn't really any darkness, to the intimidated and elderly, who spend long periods shut in their houses being told by people on their televisions it is dangerous to go outside, it appears pitch black. Why does it seem so dark? *Because they have so many lights on!*

Meanwhile the message of the night sky, an illuminated manuscript a dweller in the Dark Ages could read as easily as his descendants read a newspaper, is erased by a generation too frightened to go to sleep without leaving a lamp burning beside them.

Darkness and the Desert:
An Islamic Moon

(He is) the cleaver of the daybreak. He has appointed the night
for resting and the sun and moon for reckoning. Such is the
measuring of the All-Mighty, the All-Knowing.

Qur'an 6.96

Cycling home from work one evening in September down the
brightly illuminated Cowley Road I turn off down a street
named after a haemophiliac son of Queen Victoria, to enter a
different city. The street lights and the lights in the houses are all
off. Shopfronts are dark; here and there a window glows with
candlelight. The whole neighbourhood has been blacked out by
a power cut. The sensation is like diving from a hot, sunny riverbank into a dark, tree-shaded pool. In a city, 'darkness' can only
ever be relative, but it is astonishing how much difference turning off the lights has made. The moonless sky overhead is
studded with stars, the streets bathed in a long-vanished chiaroscuro. Our house has become a centre for dispensing candles to
neighbours who usually have no need of such things. My son
and I decide to go out for a walk to enjoy the unaccustomed
appearance of the surrounding streets. We are in the last few
days of Ramadan, the holy month of daytime fasting for Mus-
lims, leading up to the first appearance of the crescent moon,
signalling the beginning of the new month and the feast of Eid.
New moons are spoken of in the Qur'an as 'signs to mark fixed
periods of time for mankind', part of the *Ayat* or evidence of

revelation, and so they remain for countless millions in our dazzling, twenty-four-hour world. Tonight, technological failure
has restored some of the night's power. Groups of men are making their way to the mosque, their white trousers glowing in the
shadows. There is a subdued air of expectation in their murmured conversation. 'This is the day when the Qur'an was born,'
a neighbour tells me. It is known as Al-Qadr. Many people sleep
at the mosque during the last few days of the fast, while the
earth is wrapped in what the holy book describes as the mantle
of the night and a quarter of the world's population wait for the
appearance of the crescent moon.

Islam places great importance on the hours of darkness. Born
in a hot, desert climate, it honours what the cool hours of the
night reveal, either through dreams or in discussion by the light
of the moon. Muhammed's first revelation came as a vision in
his sleep and dream interpretation was widespread in the Muslim world many centuries before Carl Jung. More than 600
renowned experts in such matters are listed by the twelfth-
century chronicler al-Hasan ibn al-Husayn al Halal in his book
The Generation of the Dream Interpreters. One scholar, Fatema
Mernissi, has written of the distinction between the attitudes of
Islamic and Western civilization towards night and darkness,
suggesting that the West's fear of Islam, and of the dark, may
have its roots in a suppression of the unconscious.★ She focuses
on the concept in Arabic culture of *samar*, a term for which there
is no equivalent in northern languages. '*Samar* is one of the
Arabic language's magic words,' she writes, 'that weaves together
the sense of "dark colour" with the pleasure you get from opening up to the mysterious "other", all the while being stimulated

★ Fatema Mernissi, 'Seduced by "Samar", or: How British Orientalist Painters Learned to Stop Worrying and Love the Darkness', in *The Lure of the East:
British Orientalist Painting* (London: Tate Publishing, 2008), pp. 33–9.

by the moonlight.' In this world-view, the night becomes a creative space and a source of inspiration, rather than something to
be feared, as it so often has been in Western cultures. According
to the Islamic, lunar calendar, the day begins at sunset. Of
course, in the desert, far from any other source of light, the
moon is particularly glorious; so much so that the Hadith (Book
12, no. 770) records the Prophet used the full moon as a metaphor for the appearance of Allah to the faithful in the last days.
'The people said, "O Allah's Apostle! Shall we see our Lord on
the Day of Resurrection?" He replied, "Do you have any doubt
in seeing the full moon on a clear (not cloudy) night?" They
replied, "No, O Allah's Apostle!" . . .' He said, "You will see
Allah (your Lord) in the same way."'

The moon, then, in Islam, is an instrument by which time is
measured and parcelled out to humankind by the 'cleaver of the
daybreak'. Its rhythms are immutable, eternal, its course through
the heavens fixed. Only once is it suggested these things could
be interrupted, even by the 'All-Mighty'. 'The hour of Doom is
drawing near and the moon is cleft in two. Yet when they see a
sign, the unbelievers turn their backs and say, "Ingenious sor-
cery!"' (Qur'an 54.1–2.) This verse gave rise to the story in the
Hadith that the Prophet, to prove the validity of his mission to
a questioner, ordered the moon to split into two. The moon
came down to the top of the Kaaba and circled it seven times.
Then it floated down to Muhammed, entered the right sleeve of
his garment, exited from the left, descended and divided into
two, one half appearing in the eastern sky and one in the west.
Eventually the two halves were reunited.

As is well known, differences in temperature between night
and day in the desert are extreme. The sun is clearly the source
of the burning heat of day – might not the moon be the source
of the chill of night? A verse in the Qur'an, describing the
reward in Paradise that awaits believers, would seem to suggest

so: 'Reclining in the Garden on raised thrones they will see neither the Sun's excessive heat nor (the Moon's) excessive cold'
(Qur'an 76.13). The moon, then, in this interpretation, is a
generator of cold just as the sun is of heat, moonlight the illumination that spills from a fridge door opened in a silent kitchen
at night.

The great African and Arabian deserts are a challenge to the
European visitor not only in terms of their extreme climate but
also in their appearance. To eyes accustomed to the intensely
managed, colourful landscape of the north they are essentially
formless and therefore threatening, rather as the endlessly inter-
woven abstractions of Islamic art seem to question the figurative
tradition in Western culture. Do deserts not deceive the unwary
visitor with mirages by day, as well as bring visions in the darkness? Antoine de Saint-Exupéry crash-landed in the Sahara
more than once and, in an incident that formed the core of his
book *Wind, Sand and Stars*, narrowly escaped dying of thirst
before being rescued by passing Bedouin tribesmen. On the
occasion of one such unscheduled landing he records in the
book, a moonlit night spent beneath the canopy of the sky
brought a new understanding of his relationship to the planet
that was to inform much of his subsequent writing.

Forced down once more in a landscape of deep sand, I was waiting for the
dawn. The golden hills offered up their luminous slopes to the moon, and
others rose up in the shadow to its frontier with the light. In this deserted
factory of darkness and moonlight there reigned the peace of work in
abeyance and the silence of a trap, and I fell asleep within it.

Waking in the middle of the night, opening his eyes on the sky,
'that hatchery of stars', with no physical object by which to
ascertain a sense of distance or scale, he experienced intense
vertigo, until he was reassured by the sensation of gravity pin-
ning him to the sand dune on which he lay.

I felt the earth propping up my back, sustaining me, lifting me, carrying me within nocturnal space. I found myself adhering to the planet, held by a force like the force that pins you to a wagon on a curve, and I found joy in this excellent rampart, this solidity, this security, as I sensed beneath my body the curved deck of my ship.

For Saint-Exupéry, the 'deserted factory of darkness and moonlight' he found waiting for him when he came down in the desert produced an insight as powerful as any prophetic vision. As a European, he had to fall from the sky to discover it. For Moses and Muhammed, along with countless other prophets, the desert was an accessible resource, part of their native landscape, a place of solitude and revelation. From the beginning of time, we seem to have felt the need to measure ourselves against something infinitely vast, whether it be the wilderness, the ocean or the darkness. This inbuilt impulse remains, although we are hemmed in on every side. For this reason alone, a walk beneath the night sky would seem at least therapeutic, and perhaps essential.

Mussolini, the Madonna and Moonlight

I am travelling to a hilltop city in Tuscany that has been dedicated, since medieval times, to the Virgin Mary, so often portrayed in Western art standing on the crescent moon. My official reason for coming is an invitation to attend the opening of an exhibition at the contemporary art museum, but I also have a line from Antal Szerb's *Journey by Moonlight* ringing in my head: 'Who knows if I will ever get to Siena if I don't go there now?' From the trip I have bartered for myself a day of freedom on which I intend to visit as many museums and churches as I can, as well as walk the city's streets and sit in its famous squares. I am travelling alone. The airport I arrive at is named after Galileo Galilei, whose telescope first brought the moon within reach. Outside, a train is waiting at the platform and I remember to validate my ticket in the yellow machine before I board. Nobody watching could possibly know how often I have rehearsed this simple action in my mind, or the satisfaction it gives me, once achieved. One of my main reasons for agreeing to attend, apart from loyalty to the artist whose work is being shown, is this: the countryside rolling past the windows of the train as I cross the plain outside Pisa as far as Empoli, where I will drink a cup of bitter espresso and board another train towards Siena.

It is early summer. The mountains one sees from the outskirts of Pisa are blue, their intricate silhouettes cut out against the sky as if with a jigsaw. An elderly man, dressed in faded trousers and dusty boots, is hoeing between the rows of vines, his dark brown skin hanging loosely over his belt like a jacket.

Maize that has self-seeded along the sidings has already grown to waist height and the small green waterways, filled with recent rain, are choked with reeds. For a resident of a country where the rail network resembles the sclerotic arteries of a lifetime chain-smoker, the trains in Italy are astonishingly cheap and efficient. Like much of the nation's infrastructure, they were a beneficiary of modernization carried out during the rule of Benito Mussolini, when punctual trains were held up as a totem of fascist efficiency; indeed the station itself where I will disembark, at Siena, is a piece of Mussolini-era modernism. Perhaps these visible signs of the fascist legacy, remaining long after its idiocies and atrocities have faded from the public mind, partly explain why a name that was once only uttered *sotto voce* is now more often being spoken openly, with pride. It is the first time I have been in Italy since Silvio Berlusconi won a second term, along with a list of allies that included Mussolini's granddaughter. I have been struck by the way in which Italian colleagues have reacted as if something momentous and tragic had occurred; almost as if they feared their country was returning to the politics of the 1930s. There is talk of a different kind of dictatorship, of a country controlled through a stranglehold on the media, a drip-feed of soap operas and tabloid polemics that is poisoning the nation.

Mussolini had an intense but problematic relationship with the moon. As a child of the barren Romagna hillsides, which grew more revolutionaries than vines, and of a crowded house where his blacksmith father's broad leather belt was a regular instructor, Mussolini proved difficult to educate, changing schools frequently during his childhood. Alessandro, his father, a socialist who mixed Marx with Italian nationalism and anarchism, bequeathed to his son a taste for revolutionary insurrection, a dislike of authority (other than his own) and an ability to shuffle political ideologies that was to stand the young man in good stead. But there was another figure in Mussolini's early childhood who remained a profound influence; he was schooled in lunar lore by an elderly woman known by the nickname La Vecchia Giovanna, regarded by many as a witch. Her beliefs went beyond the usual country knowledge concerning the planting and pruning of crops according to the moon's phases. For her, the planet was a powerful and sometimes malevolent force, its light not so much a source of illumination as a dangerously potent agent of change. Despite his bullish, macho swagger and his eulogies to Order, Hierarchy and Discipline, the antithesis, surely, of rural superstition, an important element in Mussolini's psyche was shaped by these ancient beliefs. An embarrassingly fawning biography of 1925 by one of his mistresses, Margherita Sarfatti, makes no attempt to airbrush these peculiarities out of the picture. 'He is an adept at interpreting dreams and omens and in telling fortunes by cards,' the author tells us. 'He can explain too why oxen allow themselves to be led by women and why the front paws of a hare are so short.' Other peculiarities were less like party tricks than debilitating phobias. He was frightened, for instance, of those he believed had the power of the evil eye and did all he could to placate them; he would never sit down to dinner where there were thirteen guests. In particular, he was convinced of the dangers of falling asleep where the light of the moon could fall on his face; blinds remained drawn even in the most sweltering Roman summers. It was as if he thought that, like Endymion, he risked becoming bewitched, his energy and virility sapped away as he lay tangled in a cobweb of moonbeams. Or did he think that moonlight could change the colour of the skin? As the poet Giacomo Leopardi noted in a journal entry, such beliefs were not uncommon among country people.

Moon fallen in my dream. Moon which according to our peasants makes the skin black, so that I heard a woman jokingly advise the company sitting in the moonlight to put their arms under their shawls.*

Mussolini was, after all, a son of the Catholic Church, despite the oedipal vigour with which he denounced it in his early, socialist phase; the Church that had invested the Madonna, the female principle, with cosmic power, attributing to her many of the qualities associated with moon goddesses from religions that had preceded Christianity. Textual justification for this reading of Mary's role, absent from the Gospels, could be found in the Book of Revelation:

A great and wondrous sign appeared in heaven; a woman clothed with the sun, with the moon under her feet and a crown of twelve stars on her head. (12:1)

If this remarkable figure is read as a personification of Jesus's mother, then her subsequent deification has a biblical foundation. From the Egyptian Isis, variously goddess of wisdom, fortune and the moon, she inherited the name Stella Maris (Star of the Sea). Among the wider Catholic community her titles included Mother Moon, Queen of Heaven, Moon of our Church. Many early Christian writers compared her relationship with God to that of the moon with the sun; acting as a mediator, she gently reflects back the intolerably bright light of divinity to mankind, illuminating the otherwise impenetrable darkness that confounds and misleads the human heart. In this way, long-established veneration of the moon and the prayers of those seeking its blessing on their fields could be redirected towards the Virgin. In all this there is an echo also of the mother's position within the traditional Italian family and the wider

* From Giacomo Leopardi, 'Arguments of Idylls', Opere 336, *Canti*, trans. J. G. Nichols (London: Oneworld Classics, 2008), p. 297.

culture: patient, sinned against perhaps, yet venerated as the source of life and the bestower of good things, of nourishment both physical and emotional; the maternal moon to the father figure's dangerously hot sun.

For the flag of the new Italy, Mussolini resurrected the insignia of Roman authority, adding to the *tricolore* the fasces – the bundle of rods or twigs bound around an axe. This axe, the labrys, dated back as a religious symbol to ancient Crete, its sickle-moon-shaped blade derived, according to some, from a prehistoric cult of the moon goddess. Mussolini was well aware that for his supporters, fundamental symbols, carefully selected, had a potency unmatched either by the totems of the left or the principles of the Enlightenment. Respect for traditional social and religious values lay closer to the hearts of a significant section of the population than concepts such as democracy, freedom of speech or equality under the law. 'If by "Liberty" be meant the right to spit upon the symbols of Religion and of our Native Land and of the State,' he told them, 'very well. I, as Head of the *Fascisti*, declare that this "Liberty" shall never come into existence . . . Fascism throws the noxious theories of so-called Liberalism upon the rubbish heap.' With his belief in supernatural portents and the potential of the moon to rob him of his power, Mussolini can appear to us now as in some ways closer to a king in a Shakespearean tragedy than a twentieth-century leader. One can only ponder what elaborate plot the intelligence services of his enemies might have dreamed up, had they been aware of Il Duce's secret weakness. Did moonlight play a part in his eventual downfall? Did he leave the blind open one night and wake in terror, bathed in the cold phosphorescence he had for so long tried to avoid? What we do know for certain is that he died after being captured by Communist partisans while attempting to cross the Austrian border, disguised, humiliatingly, as a German soldier. His body, along with that of his mistress, Carla Petacci, was taken to the Piazzale Loreto in Milan and strung up by the heels from one of Marinetti's 'shining, humming globes', the street lights that his Futurist supporters hoped would banish moonlight from the city for ever. This character, who in life had dealt symbols as fluently as a Tarot player, became in death a mute hermetic symbol, the Hanged Man, beneath the unpitying eye of an electric moon, exposed to the blows and mockery of the crowd.

The day after the opening I find myself standing in a tree-shaded square that offers from its benches a panoramic view of ridges and valleys of terracotta tiles. It is obviously a favourite place for the old people of that *contrada* to come and sit in the late afternoon, as the swifts wheel and scream above, engaged in their aerial *palio*.* From here they can escape the shadows of the narrow backstreets and the tourist hordes in the main ones, and survey the rooftops of their city, keeping a lookout for the weather approaching from the distant hills. The clouds are magnificent: the same Renaissance clouds I have seen in countless paintings during the day as I have moved with the crowds of sightseers from cathedral to museum, from town hall to crypt. Just as Antal Szerb writes in *Journey by Moonlight*, Siena 'undulate[s] over several hills in the shape of a happy-go-lucky star'; its extraordinary cathedral hovering over the city, 'like a towered Zeppelin, in the livery of a pantomime zebra'. This afternoon the sky is having an argument with itself; different weather fronts are colliding, creating an architecture of towers and castellations hundreds of feet high. Suddenly the sun is extinguished and the gravel of the square hisses with rain. Umbrellas blossom, like black peonies. The elderly ladies who have been sitting on the benches retreat as swiftly as their arthritic

* The biannual horse race run around Siena's Piazza del Campo.

knees will allow beneath the trees, and as even that shelter begins to be penetrated by the assault from the skies, allow themselves to be helped by their younger companions towards home.

I dodge into the open door of a church that stands on one side of the square. Once inside I find myself the sole visitor, my only company an elderly man in the dark blue blazer of the custodians of Siena's treasures. Even though this place is no longer used for worship, the paintings and frescoes have retained their aura in a way that is seldom possible once works are removed from the place of their commissioning and purpose to a sterile museum. I am particularly attracted by a crucifixion that is surrounded by painted *trompe l'œil* pillars that are partially obscured by a pile of grey plastic chairs. (This also I have seen and loved in Italian churches; paintings lit by flickering strip lights, on walls running with damp, leant up on makeshift trestles or set in recesses so deep in shadows that they hang, brooding, in a midnight of their own, their mystery restored.) The altarpiece is a Perugino, the only work by him in Siena, dating from his later period of which art historians are somewhat dismissive (although they seem to me to be so drunk on riches as to be careless of minor masterpieces like this one). In any case, I am not complaining; for this moment, with the silence within the church intensified by the rain thrumming on its outer walls, the painting grips me. The artist has made no attempt to depict a lifelike event; this is an elaborate ritual, not an execution. The baying crowds have gone, as have the Roman soldiers and the blazing heat of a Palestinian afternoon. At the foot of the cross are gathered the three Marys: the Virgin, the ex-prostitute, and the wife of Cleoplias. Also present are a small cluster of saints: Jerome, Augustine (who gives his name to the order who founded this church), Monica and John the Baptist. A pelican has made its nest at the summit of the cross and is stabbing itself in its breast to nourish the three young ones that are clamouring for sustenance, beaks agape. Jesus's mother has laid her cheek in the palm of one hand in dignified sorrow; the other is placed, fingers spread, across her womb, as if she is remembering the act of giving birth to the man on the cross before her. The others are lost in prayer or meditation, in the attitude of people contemplating a crucifix on the wall of a cell rather than an agonizing death. Jerome is naked to the waist, clutching a stone in his hand, a relic of his desert vigil. John the Baptist, dressed in animal skins, looks directly at the viewer, motioning towards the cross with an *I told you so* gesture. Angels hover, collecting in goblets the blood that drips from the lacerated hands, while disembodied cherubs, mere faces surrounded by wings, dart around the cross and above the tops of the trees. But what interests me most is the landscape in which the scene is set and the sky that enfolds it. Above the arms of the cross, in one of the most ancient configurations in Christian iconography, are a sun and a moon, the sun on the left of the painting and the moon on the right. This motif, seen as early as AD 586 in the Rabbula Gospel, one of the earliest known Syriac illuminated manuscripts, recurs right through the medieval period and the Renaissance, into the early sixteenth century. So ubiquitous was the theme that no one during the period thought to write down what it meant. One interpretation is that the moon, associated since classical times with corruption and impurity, represents the human, mortal side of Christ's nature that must die, and the sun represents the divine. It is also worth remarking that throughout the Jewish scriptures, the sun and moon represent the cosmic order, established by the Creator; the sun is appointed to govern the day, we are told in Genesis, and the moon, the lesser light, the night. Both are part of the celestial clockwork that marks off the seasons. David is promised in the Psalms that his line will be 'established forever like the moon, *the faithful witness in the sky*'. This order is disrupted only at times of great crisis. When Joshua

led the Israelites into battle against the Amorite kings on the
road from Beth Horon to Azeka, he called on God to halt time
to allow him to fulfil his purpose:

> O sun, stand still over Gibeon,
> O Moon, over the valley of Aijalon.
> So the sun stopped still
> And the moon stopped,
> Till the nation avenged itself on its enemies.
> (Joshua 10:12–13)

It is hard to know what natural phenomenon gave rise to this
legend. The biblical account tells us that the halting of sun and
moon was accompanied by a hailstorm of such violence that it
cut down more of the Amorites than fell to Israelite swords, further indication of divine favour. Did some extreme climatic
event create an extended twilight at noon, in which Joshua's
army was able to wreak carnage on the Amorites in Old Testa-
ment fashion?

In Perugino's painting, sun and moon are held in balance with
one another like scales, as though the whole cosmos could be
tipped one way or another in the battle between good and evil,
sin and redemption, flesh and spirit. The artist has intensified
the power of this imagery by representing both of the heavenly
bodies in semi-eclipse; the sun is ringed with fire, the moon's
surface partially obscured by a purple disc. Behind the cross is a
simple rural scene, not unlike the view from the train as it noses
its way among the green and wooded valleys on the approach to
Siena. The landscape seems to tremble in suspended animation,
much as it does during an eclipse, when birds fall silent and cat-
tle lie down to prepare for night. It takes a moment to notice
that there is not a bird (apart from the pious and allegorical
pelican), an animal, a worked field or a human dwelling in sight.
The crucifixion is taking place, then, in liminal territory, at a

moment that is neither night nor day. (If sun and moon are nature's clock, during an eclipse the world in some sense exists outside time.) The heavenly bodies are both stopped in their celestial tracks, as they were once before at a time of crisis; this time the war is not waged with swords or hailstones, but blood dripping into a cup, while the faithful witness hides her face.

Returning down a hill to my hotel that night, exhausted after a day in which it seems I have gazed into the faces of several hundred Madonnas – Madonnas *dolente*, Madonnas *del Voto* and Madonnas with Large Eyes (for, as an official noticeboard tells me in the Museo Civico, the Virgin Mary is 'Queen and Patron of our city')* – I look back towards Siena's stacked streets and see a crescent moon floating above the rooftops. Earlier in the evening it had been pale as ice; now it has taken on the gold of a Duccio Virgin's halo. A little owl is questing overhead, its cry piercing the evening sky. A group of men standing on the corner break off from their conversation and one of them answers the owl with a whistle, once, twice, and then turns back to his friends. The bird loops around our heads once more, and again the man answers its call, in polite acknowledgement. Owl, moon and city seem joined in equilibrium. To an outsider, a traveller passing through, there is no suggestion here of the political turmoil I have heard so much about. Is the future of the nation itself held in the balance? Are we really to witness the deposition and resurrection of the Hanged Man? Only time will tell whether the moon will be called upon to rescue Italy from another dictator's grip.

* The relationship between the city and the Virgin dates back to a votive promise made on the eve of a battle between Siena and Florence, from which Siena emerged victorious. In gratitude, Mary was symbolically presented with the keys to the city.

Extollagers in the Valley of Vision: Memory, Moonlight and Samuel Palmer

HARVEST MOON. It is remarkable that the moon, during
the week in which she is full in harvest, rises sooner
after sun-setting than she does in any other full-moon
week in the year. By doing so, she affords an immediate
supply of light after sun-set, which is very beneficial
to the husbandman, for reaping and gathering
in the fruits of the earth.

*Falconer's New Universal Dictionary
of the Marine*, 1815 Edition

Thoughts on RISING MOON with raving-mad splendour of
orange twilight-glow on landscape. I saw that at Shoreham.

Samuel Palmer, written on the outside
of a portfolio, 1860

It is not so very long ago that many perfectly sensible people
believed each one of us was touched, for good or ill, by the
influence of particular stars and planets and that this influence
played a large part in shaping our destinies. Whatever we may
think about this (and it is extraordinary the extent to which a
world-view based on astrology survives into the age of radio
telescopes and space exploration), some biographies do seem to
betray a lunar influence. The Victorian painter Samuel Palmer's
life was marked from its beginning by the moon's imprint. His
obsession can be traced back to his earliest memory, of an event

that took place when he was three years old. He stood one night with his nurse, a woman named Mary Ward, looking out of the window. The moon cast the shadows of the branches of an elm tree on to a white wall, where they swayed to and fro in the night breeze. As he watched, fascinated by the sight, Mary recited some lines by Edward Young, from the extensive poem *The Complaint, and the Consolation; or, Night Thoughts*:

> Fond man! The vision of a moment made!
> Dream of a dream, and shadow of a shade!

For some reason these lines, evoking the transitory nature of human existence, combined with a vision of a transcendent, unchanging spiritual reality in nature revealed by the moonlight, had a remarkable effect on the fledgling artist. It may seem a strange couplet to recite to a three-year-old, but perhaps he was a strange child – ideas about child-rearing have certainly changed since Palmer's day. Mary, whom the artist described as a 'simple country-woman', seems to have been an uncommon nurse; she was certainly a confidante for Palmer until her death. The poem remained a touchstone, as it was for many in that era; with its championing of death as a state superior to life ('*Death* but entombs the body; *Life* the soul'), it spoke to those of a visionary disposition who felt frustrated with the everyday. Translated into German in 1760, it became a strong influence on a generation of Romantic artists and poets. Crucially, it reconciles scientific discovery with Romantic yearning. Young realizes that more and more revelations about the nature of the universe will come from astronomical observation and prays for an open mind to be able to absorb them. Rather than pointing to a rationalist explanation of the cosmos, they merely reveal the greatness of God's creation. As he puts it in 'Night 9', 'An undevout astronomer is mad.' The night is the time most suited to prayer, when the devout can meditate on the mathematic glories of the skies. At the centre of Young's vision is the moon.

> Night is fair Virtue's immemorial friend;
> The conscious Moon, through every distant age,
> Has held aloft a lamp to Wisdom, and let fall
> On contemplation's eye her purging ray.

In England, William Blake was an admirer, creating illustrations for the poem in a deluxe four-volume edition commissioned by the bookseller Richard Edwards in 1795, although only the first volume was eventually published. Both Blake and, at a later date, Palmer seem to have taken on Young's idea of a 'conscious', proactive and beneficent moon, its potency undiminished by the increasing knowledge science was bringing of its physical nature.

But we left the child and his nurse at the window; a moment that Palmer later identified as the wellspring of his artistic life, as different elements of the Romantic sensibility, the visual and the literary, fused within him. The experience never left him, becoming his yardstick of transcendent spiritual glory, so that seventy years later he would write, 'I never forgot those shadows and am ever trying to paint them.'

The results of his efforts can be found in the most unlikely places. The Prints and Drawings Room at the Ashmolean Museum in Oxford is down a set of backstairs from the first-floor galleries, through a door controlled by an entryphone; it feels as though it is deep in the basement, although natural light, the level of which can be controlled by blinds, still comes through its subterranean windows. I am here to see some of Palmer's works on paper that feature the moon, as well as a notebook dating from 1856, written partly by Palmer and partly by a pupil of his, the tea and coffee heiress Louisa Twining, who was later to become a philanthropist of note. The notebook itself is fragile; I am told that I cannot wear gloves to protect it, as the art historian sitting opposite me does, who is looking through a large glass at some drawings by Rembrandt; gloves make it difficult to turn the pages. I am sent somewhat sternly down a windowless corridor to wash my hands, a ritual of both physical and psychological preparation for the task ahead. The corridor has an uneven floor and plain wooden chairs abandoned at its corners as if in the past silent watchers of the type that patrol the galleries upstairs invigilated even this remote place. Many institutions are honeycombed by such unloved, in-between spaces, underground or behind the scenes; they have their own charm for the wanderer who chances upon them as places both in which to reflect and momentarily disappear.

The notebook dates from a difficult period in Palmer's mid-life when it had become clear that his youthful 'visionary' work would never gain wide critical acceptance in his own era. The young Palmer had begun his training as a seventeen-year-old, taken up by the older painter John Linnell, who encouraged him to sketch statues in the British Museum, rescuing the young prodigy, as Palmer put it, from 'the Pit of Modern Art'. But Linnell also took Palmer when he was nineteen to meet William Blake, whom they found at his house in Fountain Court near the Thames, 'lame in bed of a scalded foot', sitting up working on his illustrations to *The Divine Comedy*. Blake provided the young artist with an inspiring model of a man who remained unwaveringly faithful to his vision, however little favour it found with the world, supporting himself as and how he could. Although Blake was in the last years of his life when the two met, it is clear that Palmer regarded him both as a prophet and a genius. As he recalled in a letter to Blake's biographer Alexander Gilchrist: 'In him you saw at once the Maker, the Inventor; one of the few of any age; a fitting companion for Dante. He was energy itself, and shed around him a kindling influence; an atmosphere of life, full of the ideal.'

Another living inspiration was the poet John Keats, a favourite with Palmer's friends and hardly older than they were. But, as befits a man so at odds with the modern world, the greatest literary influences on his work were from the past: Milton, Virgil and John Bunyan. Milton appealed to him particularly for the way in which he combined a deeply religious world-view with close observation of nature. In the flyleaf of his copy of Milton Palmer noted those passages from the poet's rendering of Psalm CXXXVI and from *Paradise Lost* to do with the moon and the effects of moonlight:

> The horned moon
> . . . Amongst her spangled sisters bright
>
> . . . . the moon, rising in clouded majesty
>
> Full-orb'd the moon, and with more pleasing light
> Shadowy sets off the face of things . . .

Had not Milton intimated that the present world might be nothing more than a shadow of the world to come in heaven? This spiritual reality was what Palmer was trying to capture; a state hinted at, perhaps, when night fell and moonlight transformed the landscape.

In 1827, a small legacy from his grandfather allowed Palmer to move with his family to the village of Shoreham in the Kentish countryside. Here, in the sheltered valley of the River Darent, surrounded by thickly wooded hills, he found a place seemingly untouched by the modern world, protected by its geography from the suburban creep of stockbroker villas and not yet connected to London by the railway. (He would have agreed with Thoreau when he wrote, 'We do not ride upon the railroad; the railroad rides upon us.') If being exposed to the extraordinary force field that was William Blake at the age of nineteen was formative in confirming in Palmer the call to penetrate beyond the surface of things and try to render the essence of what he saw, in Shoreham he felt he had found his subject. It is for the works from this period that he is most celebrated today. *Coming from Evening Church*, painted in 1830, is perhaps the best-known among them. It shows a group of villagers, ranging in age from young children to ancient, long-bearded prophets, processing solemnly from a church beneath a huge, yellow moon that has risen above the hill almost to the level of the cross on the top of the church spire; the whole scene is lit by its glow. It is an extraordinary work, the paint applied so thickly as to be almost sculptural, mixed with various glues, gums and sugar to avoid cracking; a miniature moonlit world, sealed behind copious layers of varnish.

The public did not warm to Palmer's visions of Shoreham during his lifetime, and fewer and fewer of his paintings were accepted for exhibition. By extreme measures of economy (he allowed only one candle once darkness had fallen) he managed to remain in the village for seven years, staying on after his father and brother had returned to London, with only his old nurse, Mary Ward, for company. His letters reveal an almost daily battle with self-doubt and depression. He was further shaken by the agricultural disturbances in support of the Reform Bill of the early 1830s, when poverty-stricken farm labourers set hayricks on fire, demanding the right to vote. During the election of 1832 he campaigned against what he saw as the rising tide of anarchy and in support of the Tory candidate, declaring in a pamphlet that the nation's decision would herald 'Existence or Annihilation to good old England'. There was no place for an extended franchise in the medieval past he aspired to; in truth, there was a reactionary strand in Palmer's Romanticism that put him out of sympathy with his neighbours who apparently had no desire to inhabit Virgil's *Eclogues*. Whether it was these events, his growing loneliness or simple poverty that persuaded him to abandon Shoreham and return to London, what is certain is that for the rest of his life he looked back at this time with longing, aspiring

with mixed success to the artistic achievements of his rural exile.
With the birth of his first son, Palmer had to resign himself to the
fact that teaching would play an essential part in the support of
his own family for some time to come.

The notebook is of a type available from stationers to this day,
with lined pages and a marbled cover. When it is placed before
me I am at first disappointed by how much of the written material is by Louisa and not Palmer himself. However, she was a
dutiful pupil and his voice is clearly present in the notes she
made of the lessons he gave her in watercolour painting –
earnest, pedantic, slightly eccentric, but above all deeply serious
about the craft he was trying to impart to her and about the art
of truly seeing what was before one's eyes.

   The lessons begin with exhaustive lists of colours – Gamboge,
Indian Yellow, Cadmium Yellow, Raw Umber, Yellow Ochre –
with notes on combining them and colour wheels to show how
they relate one to another. 'Much of the <u>mystery</u> in drawing from
nature,' Louisa writes, her underlining conveying the emphasis of
her teacher, 'consists in the relation that one colour bears to
another, & what we think pure colour is not really so.' Elsewhere
there are direct, practical hints on tackling the landscape. 'Remember the difference in outline between the grand form of a distant
Wood (or in middle distance) and the forms of bushes or brush-
wood. Intricacy with form and drawing the great difficulty with
landscape . . . Raw umber again over distant fields, then blue
again. Ultramarine for final blue often very fine . . .'

   Palmer was a firm believer in a formal training for those he
taught. The simplified shapes and archaic figures that populated
his idealized, medievalist landscapes were not the result of a lack
of technical ability or ignorance of the great masters. Rather
they originated in a complex and sustained belief system that
saw nature as the handbook of a beneficent creator. All his pupils,

whatever their level of achievement, were put to work practising drawing techniques and sketching still-life objects to learn the subtleties of shading – Palmer's own demonstration of such exercises, sketches of an egg and of geometric shapes accompanied by notes, are included in the notebook and are the main object of attention for those scholars that have studied it, simply because they are by the hand of the master rather than the pupil. Nevertheless, however vital he thought such groundwork, it was but a preparation for the more important truth he wanted to convey. As Louisa notes, perhaps cautioning herself against impatience to be let out of the studio into the wider world: 'This careful copying is the best preparation for drawing from nature . . . When you look at a view you will be able to refer all to something in your own mind and understand it.' The artist needs to be able to decipher the book of nature, just as the mystic does; in Palmer's case, of course, the two were much the same. The most important lines in the notebook for understanding Palmer's attitude are included both in a version transcribed by Louisa and in Palmer's own hand, the master's free and expansive after his pupil's studious holograph.

Drawing from Nature
It may be divided into two parts
Accurate imitation of the material
whether near or distant, extensive or contracted
like drawing one's face in the glass with a faithful
rendering of all the parts

Catching its EXPRESSION and securing
what affects and charms us.
OR
It may be stated thus
No 2 is the end
No 1 the means

To put it another way, when Palmer looked at nature, he saw himself – which is perhaps both his strength and weakness as an artist.

The series of ink drawings I have come to see date from 1825, the year following Palmer's first meeting with William Blake and his falling under the enchantment (there seems no other word) of Blake's woodcut illustrations to Virgil's *Eclogues*. Of these, Palmer wrote enthusiastically in a notebook, 'There is in all such a mystic and dreamy glimmer as penetrates and kindles the inmost soul, and gives complete and unreserved delight, unlike the gaudy daylight of this world.' To achieve his own glimmer, Palmer evolved a technique for his drawings, working in pen and dark brown ink and brush with sepia mixed with gum, coating all in varnish, the gum and varnish creating a raised, three-dimensional effect, the whole as seen through bottle-glass. In *A Rustic Scene*, a ploughman places a yoke across the shoulders of an ox in the foreground, lit by a waning crescent moon and the first rays of dawn. An heroic figure, he stands between two worlds; the night, symbolized by the moon, a time of mystic revelation, and 'the gaudy daylight', a time fitted for work and the rational explanations of science. The landscape has been organized, firstly by agriculture but secondly by the artist; the vegetation is groomed and manicured into pattern and line at least as closely as the thatched roof that stands in the background; the curls on the brow of the ox and the turf he stands upon are microscopically observed, yet the trees growing on the hills are resolved into exotic blooms in a botanical hot-house. If it is an idealized world Palmer is depicting, it is one exploding with fecundity, the mystic lunar rays from above catching the exposed bands of chalk on the distant slopes. This is the first in a series of works inspired by the Darent Valley at Shoreham.

The circle of Palmer's friends that called themselves the

Ancients, who had taken to gathering at Blake's house in Fountain Court (in their parlance 'The House of the Interpreter'), were frequent visitors to the secluded village. They often walked the landscape Palmer christened 'The Valley of Vision' after dark, singing and reciting poetry to each other by moonlight. The group included the artists Edward Calvert and George Richmond and the engraver Welby Sherman. Even the group's lodestar, Blake himself, blessed the valley with a visit the year Palmer moved to Shoreham; his presence must have confirmed for the young artist that he had correctly interpreted his calling by moving to the countryside in his search to capture the 'soul' of the landscape. To the villagers who came across the group at unexpected times, walking through woods or moonlit fields, reciting mysterious incantations as they went, they were the Extollagers (a rustic word for astrologers), divining the future from the stars.

Palmer and his friends consciously set themselves apart from what they saw as the depraved values of their age and looked back to an imagined Gothic past. For Palmer, moonlight was a gateway to this spiritual realm, a gateway that perhaps also led, through that powerful first memory, to his childhood, a time before the loss of his mother, who died when he was thirteen years old. He wrote in 1827 to his friend Richmond of 'the moon, opening her golden eye, or walking in brightness among innumerable islands of light', that could 'not only thrill the optic nerve, but shed a mild, a grateful, an unearthly lustre into the inmost spirits, and seem the interchanging twilight of that peaceful country, where there is no sorrow and no night'. He was aware that outside the valley, with the spread of street lighting and industrialization, the night sky was on the retreat. His son, writing years later of his memories of Shoreham, described the way people 'toiled on till the harvest-moon gilded their faces and the hungry owl gave them shrill warning of his supper-time . . . and the moon herself bore little resemblance to the pallid, small reality we see above us nowadays. She seemed to blush and bend herself towards men (as when she stooped to kiss Endymion . . .).' Perhaps this was the state that William Blake wrote of in his poem *Vala, or The Four Zoas*, a manuscript of which belonged to John Linnell and that may have been known to Palmer:

> There is from Great Eternity a mild & pleasant rest
> Nam'd Beulah, a soft Moony Universe, feminine, lovely,
> Pure, Mild & Gentle, given in mercy to those who sleep.

For Palmer, was the 'feminine' moon linked to the half-remembered embrace of the mother taken from him at the point at which he was emerging from childhood? In another work from the Shoreham series of drawings entitled *Late Twilight*, a shepherd in the foreground lies in slumber, supported on the backs of his sleeping flock, a complete union of a man with his calling that is perhaps symbolic of Palmer's immersion in his role as artist. Or is he more closely identifying with the solitary, contemplative figure in the fields, keeping watch beneath a crescent moon; the moon that has kept step with him throughout his creative life, its light gilding his shoulders as a plump bat flies overhead?

Dark Adaption and the Eye
of the Beholder

One day a friend's child comes back from school with a new fact she is eager to share.

'Mum,' she asks, 'did you know the moon affects water?'

'Oh yes?' her mother replies, encouragingly.

'Yes. That's why you can't help looking at it, because your eyes are full of water.'

Maybe the kid had something. It is true, after all, that our bodies, like the earth, are two-thirds sea and one-third land; and it does seem as if humankind has been unable to tear its eyes from the moon since the beginning of recorded time. For a similar period, people have been fascinated by the way in which its light changes the world into something else entirely, reacting at different times and in different cultures with enchantment, mystification or terror. Why do things look so different by the light of the moon? The answer lies not so much in the external world, in the qualities of moonlight itself, as it does in our own bodies. Many of moonlight's most magical effects are caused by the internal mechanisms of the eye; to begin to understand what is going on we have to learn something of the workings of this extraordinarily sensitive organ, which can 'see' with varying degrees of effectiveness in conditions as widely different as bright sunlight and an overcast, moonless night, lit only by the dimmest glimmer of stars. It is therefore necessary to adopt the language of science for a paragraph or two. I make no apology for this; the distinction between scientific and non-scientific language is a false one in any case, as the science of the eye, dealing as it does so closely with subjective experience, reaches into the territory usually claimed by poetry, and poets and novelists themselves have proved accurate scientists of vision. Some of this research into the workings of the eye and the brain remains theoretical. I do not have the equipment or the knowledge to test it empirically; therefore I intend to put it to an even more rigorous test, the test of literature, and at the same time, conversely, put literature to the test of science.

The sun, we are told, is around 30,000 times brighter than the moon. The unit of measurement used to calibrate such statements is the intriguingly named foot-candle; direct sunlight ranges from 5,000 to 10,000 foot-candles and moonlight is equivalent to 0.02 foot-candles. Yet it is only when brightness levels are reduced to 0.003 foot-candles that the human eye is finally defeated and can no longer distinguish any feature in its surroundings. A moonlit night will provide plenty of illumination for the nocturnal wanderer, although he or she may find the world altered in unexpected ways.

To begin at the beginning: the eye, as we all know, is a lens system, which focuses light entering the eye through the cornea on to the retina through a crystalline lens. The transparent cornea is the 'window on the soul' that allows our interaction with the world outside our own bodies. The lens is made up of dead cells that cease to be connected to the body's blood supply when a baby is still in the womb, although it continues to grow and become thicker, rather in the manner of hair or fingernails. Though relatively rigid, like the lenses in the eyes of our piscine ancestors, it can be bent by the ciliary muscles in order to focus on objects at varying distances. The space between the lens and the retina is filled with a substance known as the aqueous humour ('your eyes are full of water') in which ghostly objects sometimes appear to float because of the shadows they cast. The retina itself is packed with receptors, which convert light into electrical signals, transmitting them along nerve fibres to the brain, where they are interpreted as vision. (Another well-known fact: because the cornea is curved it bends the light it receives, displaying images on the retina upside down, like a camera; the brain corrects the images, turning our world the right way up again.) In fact, a neuroscientist will tell you, the patterns of light that fall on the retina do not correspond with our mental image of the universe. The brain learns to see by building on experience, differentiating between millions of signals, many of which are essentially the same, making all kinds of assumptions as to what they might mean. This then is the visual 'reality' most of us rely on for so many of our activities: light bounced off objects around us and projected upside down on to the backs of our eyes, translated into electrical signals and unscrambled by our brains.

The retina is a complex part of the eye; as early as 1834, the biologist Gottfried Treviranus demonstrated that it contained two different types of photosensitive cells, called cones (or bulbs) and rods. To oversimplify for a moment, cones are the cells used for daylight vision; sensitive to red, green and blue wavelengths, they allow us to see detail and colour. Rods are primarily responsible for night vision; extremely sensitive to light, they are not able to discern colour or provide as much detail as their daylight cousins. Treviranus's discovery led the anatomist Max Schultze to propose what was known as a *duplex retina*, operating at two different levels: one bright and sensitive to colour, the other duller and monochromatic; one functioning in daylight, the other by moonlight. In fact, this analysis is not strictly accurate; both types of receptor operate in low lighting, down to a level measured as 50 per cent moonlight, beneath which the eye switches to rods alone to provide solely what is called scotopic vision. Most people venturing abroad by the light of the moon would be experiencing mesopic vision, an intermittently effective blend of signals from both types of receptor, a transitional state of interconnection and slippage between two systems; between, in effect (as, for sighted people, so much of our world is made up of visual information), two worlds.

What is actually happening in the eyes of these night wanderers? The mechanisms by which the eye copes with differing levels of light vary. The best known is a physical one, the dilation and contraction of the pupil. This pinhole aperture in the middle of the iris can increase in size from 1.5 to 8 mm, multiplying the amount of light that reaches the retina. This is a fairly rapid process (although we have all experienced the temporary blindness that results when walking from bright sunlight into a dark interior). It can also be triggered by the appearance of an object of desire or the imbibing of various types of narcotics (in other words, by intoxication, whether chemical or sensual). For effective night vision, more complex processes are required. Light-sensitive chemicals known as photopigments in the rods and cones react to light, creating electrical activity that is conducted by nerve fibres to the brain. Photopigments are decomposed by light; the brighter it is, the faster and more completely they are broken down. For a few moments we can be 'blinded by the light', as the saying goes. The contrary experience we know as 'our eyes becoming accustomed to the dark' is caused by the regeneration of the photopigments, a process called dark adaption. The cones take five to seven minutes to adapt, while rods can take anything from half an hour to a full day, or even longer, to achieve maximum night vision. Night pilots wear sunglasses if they are going outside in sunshine during the day, to speed up the adaption process after take-off. The rods are remarkable in their hunger for light; when it is at its most scarce they do not give up but spontaneously unite into bundles of up to 100 at a time, so that several very weak stimuli can be combined into one signal strong enough to be read by the brain. We are used to denigrating our night vision in comparison to that of nocturnal mammals and birds; in fact, humans can detect light that is a billionth of the strength of daylight – the equivalent of the flame of a single candle seventeen miles away.

What does all this have to do with the peculiar qualities of moonlight? As we have established, cones are sensitive to colour; rods are not. If you sit in a garden as dusk falls you will notice the colour leaching out of the flowers; the eye's sensitivity to greens and blues is enhanced, while its sensitivity to red decreases, a reversal of daylight vision known as the Purkinje shift. Just as in a black-and-white photograph, the lack of colour visible by moonlight makes the architectural structure of the landscape more apparent. Goethe discovered this while visiting Rome in 1787.

Nobody who has not taken one can imagine the beauty of a walk through Rome by full moon. All details are swallowed up by the huge masses of light and shadow, and only the biggest and most general outlines are visible. We have just enjoyed three clear and glorious nights. The Colosseum looked especially beautiful . . . This is the kind of illumination by which to see the Pantheon, the Capitol, the square in front of St Peter's and many other large squares and streets . . .*

It would be entirely wrong to think that Goethe, as a leading figure in the German Romantic movement, was uninterested in the science of vision. On the contrary, he is often credited with being instrumental in the emergence, in the first half of the

* Johann Wolfgang von Goethe, *Italian Journey*, trans. W. H. Auden and Elizabeth Mayer (London: Collins, 1962), entry for 2 February 1787.

nineteenth century, along with Maine de Biran and others, of a modern understanding of perception; his *Farbenlehre* (Theory of Colour) was widely disseminated and influenced a generation of artists. In his world-view there was no division between the artistic and the scientific: the Swiss geologist Horace Bénédict de Saussure and the English scientist Luke Howard, who devised the first classification of cloud formations, were as much Goethe's heroes as any literary giant. He was also a friend and champion of Jan Purkinje, the Czech scientist whose experiments on human vision, often made on his own eyes, were remarkably ahead of their time. Goethe himself was equally at home making sketches of the landscape, collecting geological specimens or proposing theories about the origins and development of plants. A century later and on a different continent, Thoreau was a man of similarly wide-ranging interests, from radical politics to literature, philosophy and farming methods. He brought his keen eye to bear on the visual appearance of the nocturnal world in his essay 'Night and Moonlight'.

The leaves of the shrub-oak are shining as if a liquid were flowing over them. The pools seen through the trees are as full of light as the sky . . . All white objects are more remarkable than by day. A distant cliff looks like a phosphorescent space on a hillside. The woods are heavy and dark. Nature slumbers. You see the moonlight reflected from particular stumps in the recesses of the forest, as if she selected what to shine on.

As light fades in the New England woods, Thoreau's eyes switch from photopic (cone) to scotopic (rod) vision. White and silver features assume a new importance by moonlight as he loses the ability to discern colours in his surroundings. Many other writers have attempted to describe these subtle effects. In his novel *As a Man Grows Older*, first published in 1898, twenty-five years after Thoreau's essay, Italo Svevo describes the moon rising over the sea in the Bay of Trieste.

Certain objects whose outline had become more distinct could rather said to be veiled in light than illuminated by it. A snowy brilliance overspread it, motionless, while colour slumbered in a shade of secret immobility even on the sea, whose external movements one could just discern in the silver play of water on its surface; colour was lost in sleep. The green of the hills and all the many colours of the houses were darkened, while the light which saturated the outer air was suspended in white incorruptible purity, inaccessibly removed from contact with the objects of our vision.

Nature slumbers; colour sleeps. Water reflects the sky. Moonlight appears to obscure almost as much as it reveals, selecting arbitrarily what to illuminate. Ruskin, for whom the eye was the portal to the soul, described similar phenomena in a diary entry written during a visit to the Alps in 1844, where he had an incandescent lunar encounter amid the dramatic alpine scenery.

I never was dazzled by moonlight until now; but as it rose behind Mont Blanc du Tacul, the full moon almost blinded me: it burst into the sky like a vast star . . . A meteor fell over the Dôme as the moon rose: now it is so intensely bright that I cannot see the Mont Blanc underneath it; the form is lost in its light.

Far from illuminating the physical world, the moonlight Ruskin observes is partially erasing it, hiding one of its most majestic features and refocusing human attention on the heavens. Several physical and visual stimuli, as well as his own aesthetic sensibility, may be combining to cause this moonlit epiphany. In dim light the eye relies on contrast to be able to differentiate between objects, which can be distinguished only if they are lighter or darker than their background. The snow-covered slopes of Mont Blanc might well thus disappear into each other, vaporizing in the moonlit air, itself sparkling with suspended ice crystals. Ruskin speaks of being 'dazzled';

perhaps, consciously or unconsciously, his language is conditioned by the moonrise Keats describes in *Endymion*:

> And lo! From opening clouds I saw emerge
> The loveliest moon that ever silvered o'er
> A shell for Neptune's goblet: She did soar
> So passionately bright, my dazzled soul
> Commingling with her argent spheres did roll
> Through clear and cloudy, even when she went
> At last into a dark and vapoury tent –

The sudden emergence of the moon from behind the mountain, with all the attendant reflection from the surrounding snowfields, might have caused a condition in Ruskin's eyes known as flash blindness. The very gradual adaptation of the rods to dark conditions can be undone in a few seconds' exposure to a bright light; this is why pilots are trained to avoid looking directly at explosions or spotlights while flying at night, or at least to keep one eye covered when they do so.

The American novelist Nathaniel Hawthorne placed a description of moonlight at the beginning of his novel *The Scarlet Letter*. He knew Thoreau, as he proudly asserts in his 'introductory' to the book. He was one of those who beat a path through the woods to meet that most-visited of solitary men, where they spent time 'talking . . . about pine-trees and Indian relics in his hermitage at Walden'. Perhaps they also discussed the owl-haunted nights the philosopher was accustomed to spend beside the pond. The long and digressive scene-setting introduction to *The Scarlet Letter*, in which Hawthorne gives an exhaustive account of the life of a Surveyor of the Customs in Salem, seems at first glance to bear little relation to the novel itself and has sometimes been published on its own. It does contain, however, a striking vignette of the novelist, struggling with a torpor that today we would call writer's block, sitting in a parlour lit only by the glowing embers of a coal fire, with the light of the moon streaming through the casement.

If the imaginative faculty refused to act at such an hour, it might well be deemed a hopeless case. Moonlight, in a familiar room, falling so white upon the carpet and showing all its figures so distinctly – making every object so minutely visible, yet so unlike a morning or noontide visibility – is a medium the most suitable for a romance-writer to get acquainted with his illusive guests.

He goes on to list the furniture in the room and moonlight's effect upon it.

All these details, so completely seen, are so spiritualised by the unusual light, that they seem to lose their actual substance and become things of intellect. Nothing is too small or too trifling to undergo this change and acquire dignity thereby. A child's shoe; the doll seated in her wicker carriage; the hobby horse – whatever, in a word, has been used or played with in the day is now invested with a quality of strangeness and remoteness, though still almost as vividly present as by daylight. Thus, therefore, the floor of our familiar room has become a neutral territory, somewhere between the real world and fairy-land, where the Actual and the Imaginary may meet, and each imbue itself with the nature of the other.

The scene provides an intimation of the world of the imagination into which Hawthorne will be launched by the discovery, among piles of discarded papers and other rubbish in a storeroom at the Customs House, of the Scarlet Letter. Why do the mundane objects he describes, although vividly present, seem 'invested with a quality of strangeness and remoteness'? It seems to be their loss of colour, above all, that injects mystery into the scene. Light employs such a vivid palette to paint the backs of our eyes, as it bounces off the objects that surround us, that its absence signifies entry to another realm. Outside the window of the train on which I am writing these lines, the rust-brown and silver rails, purple buddleia, ochre bricks, myriad greens of trees and bushes on the railway sidings make up a visual symphony of great complexity that is nevertheless accepted by my senses as everyday reality. Moonlight, as effectively as any psychotropic drug, can unsettle the senses and create a feeling of displacement. Like a drug, it triggers real physiological changes in our bodies, which in turn change our perception, offering escape from the routine banality of existence. Significantly, the lighting conditions that Hawthorne describes as ideal for creative action and the stimulation of fantasy result not from moonlight alone but from a combination of moonbeams and glowing embers. The dim firelight, which will provide sufficient illumination for the cones in his eyes to operate, albeit at a low level, is a necessary element in the scene.

It throws its unobtrusive tinge throughout the room, with a faint ruddiness upon the walls and ceiling and reflected gleam from the polish of the furniture. This warmer light mingles itself with the cold spirituality of the moon-beams, and communicates, as it were, a heart and sensibilities of human tenderness to the forms which fancy conjures up. It converts them from snow-images into men and women.

The physical warmth of the fire produces light which in turn allows the eyes to perceive colour; these differing properties allow Hawthorne to speak of the 'warmer' light of the fire and the 'cold', spiritual light of the moon. Warmth and colour attach us to the physical world, while moonlight allows us to step beyond it, to a place where the normal laws do not apply. At the same time as it is associated with physical warmth, colour is also often connected with human empathy and emotion. In *Lord Jim*, Conrad states that 'There is something haunting in the light of the moon. It has all the dispassionateness of a disembodied soul, and something of its mystery.' For painters of moonlight scenes, as well as writers, the challenge was always to compare and contrast these two lights, the warm and the cold, the human and the dispassionate, by including a light source, whether it be a fire on a beach around which fishermen are gathered, a blacksmith's forge, a lantern or an active volcano, setting off the icy qualities of the light falling from the night sky.

Hawthorne's moon is essentially benevolent, a muse bringing refreshment to the writer's imagination. It has, however, penetrated the shelter of the writer's home, entering through the aperture of the window, precisely as Mussolini and countless others throughout history have dreaded. Since prehistoric times, men have withdrawn to caves and shelters to escape the dangers and lawlessness of the night; yet the moon, as night's agent, reaches out its silvered fingers to infiltrate their defences. In countries as far apart as Greenland, France and Australia, young girls have been advised to close their curtains against the full moon lest they get pregnant; in England, in what is perhaps a folkloric euphemism, looking at the moon through glass is said merely to bring bad luck. In either version, the entrance of the moon into human habitation undoes something, whether virtue, security or good fortune.

Such superstitious fears certainly haunted the early years of Walter Benjamin, growing up in pre-war Berlin, who described waking up in a moonlit room in his essay 'The Moon'.

My sleep became unquiet, cut into pieces by the coming and going of the moon. When she was in the room and I awoke I was unhoused, for my room seemed willing to accommodate no other than her.

Like Hawthorne, Benjamin described the effect of moonlight on the fixtures and fittings in his room, but to very different effect.

The first thing my glance encountered were the two cream-coloured bowls of the washing utensils. During the day it never occurred to me to find fault with them but in the moonlight the blue band that ran around the upper part of the tumblers disturbed me. It looked deceivingly like a piece of material that was worming its way in and out of a seam.

Night after night the young Benjamin is terrorized by this nocturnal invasion. Getting out of bed to drink water he experiences auditory hallucinations, as if every sound he makes is a repetition. He is terrified that on returning to his bed he will find himself still stretched out, sleeping there. Waking, he becomes aware of a question that seems to hover in the room.

Perhaps it was poised in the folds of the curtain that hung before my door to keep out the noise. Perhaps it was only a remainder of many past nights. Finally, perhaps it was the other side of the strangeness that the moon diffused in me. It went: why is anything in the world, why is the world itself? I thought with astonishment that nothing in the world required me to recognize its existence.

For Benjamin, the influence of moonlight extends beyond the nocturnal stage of his bedroom, casting even the daytime world in a different light and calling all its values into question. Describing these sensations from the perspective of adulthood in the early 1930s, moonlight undermines even his mission as a writer, which he here summarizes as 'to recognize the existence of things' (what more precise description could there be?). The climax of the strange little story recounts a dream in which the moon invades the daylight sky above Berlin, heralding an apocalypse that unmakes the world. Benjamin's family, all gathered as if in an old daguerreotype, fall from a balcony and are crumbled to dust: 'The cone that the moon had shaped in coming sucked everything up. Nothing could hope to come through it unchanged.' Even though he manages eventually to escape from this nightmare into wakefulness, Benjamin is left with the sensation that ultimately the vision of the dream will never leave him: 'The horror with which the moon imbued me seemed to nest itself eternally and hopelessly within me.'

As Theodor W. Adorno pointed out in the 'postface' he wrote to the posthumous publication of Benjamin's stories, the memories contained within *A Berlin Childhood* were written under the darkening shadow of the Hitlerian Reich, blending its approaching horror with mourning for all that had been irretrievably lost. The modernist moon of Benjamin's dream, in the description of which he combines prophetic, biblical imagery with a terrible prescience about the fate of the German-Jewish bourgeois culture he describes, is somehow far more chilling than the moonlight in any nineteenth-century Gothic tale. Yet it is fitting that the moon, which has played such a part in the art and literature of the nineteenth century, should be the instrument that sweeps it away. It is as if in Romanticism, with its turbulent emotional range and its nationalistic undercurrents, German culture laid the seeds of its own destruction. Appalling as this apocalyptic moon is, like the child at the beginning of this chapter the young Benjamin cannot help looking at it, as though it exerted its pull on the inner springs of his consciousness. As the writer that he will become, he has no choice but to recognize the existence of something that is dedicated to eradicating existence itself.

The Path of Totality

On a Thursday evening in August I am cycling home from the station along my usual route when my eye is caught by a stall that has been set up on the pavement. Two people, a young woman and an older man, are standing in front of a table festooned with handwritten placards, bright yellow and dense with text. At first sight I take them for religious zealots of the kind whose inner promptings are too complex to allow them to condense their message into a few words. As I get nearer I realize that they are calling out something, but all meaning is lost in the traffic noise. It is only as I draw abreast that I can hear them clearly: 'Get your solar-eclipse viewers here – be ready for the solar eclipse.' This is what their placards are advertising – not the end of the world, but the temporary obscuring of the burning star that gives it life. I pull up hurriedly. Behind me the traffic has stalled and a group of men in a low-slung car who have read the placards call out to the young woman, 'Is it a real eclipse, love?' 'There is a partial solar eclipse tomorrow morning at nine-thirty,' she replies patiently. She explains that the moon will pass across the sun, casting a shadow across a section of the earth, but that from our latitude we will only be able to observe it using these special viewers; no effect will be visible to the naked eye. 'Oh, it's not a real one then,' the man says in a bored voice, and guns his motor as the traffic inches forwards again. She shrugs good-naturedly. I am making mental calculations. At about nine-fifteen in the morning I am usually cycling through Hyde Park in London, on my way to work. If I wait there a few minutes, equipped with my goggles, I should be in a perfect spot to observe the eclipse. 'How much are they?' I ask the man who has wandered over to take care of me. 'Three pounds. Two pounds if you are a student.' 'Oh, I don't think he's a student,' the young woman says, smiling. 'Why not?' I ask, somewhat offended. 'Well, are you?' she replies, challengingly. 'Maybe not, in the official sense,' I concede. 'Oh, I'm one of those unofficial students too,' says the man, handing me my glasses in a plastic pack, together with a leaflet printed on paper that is the same yellow colour as their placards. I pay the full amount and cycle home, delighted to know that once again the moon is intervening in the affairs of men and that by pure chance I have found out about it in time.

I read the leaflet as the train draws into London the following morning. For several million people in the world, it tells me, this eclipse will indeed be 'real'. The moon's circular shadow (or *umbra* in astronomer's Latin) will race across the earth's surface at a speed of up to 2,000 miles an hour, along a trajectory known as the path of totality, within which the eclipse will be total. On this occasion, the shadow's journey will begin over the islands of north-east Canada at their sunrise, passing over the northern tip of Greenland and the Arctic Ocean, then crossing Novaya Zemlya and Siberia (at noon local time), touching the western tip of Mongolia and finishing in central China at sunset. Although this vast shadow, almost 200 miles across, will have traversed nearly half the planet, it will have taken a mere three hours to do so. On earth, progress is less rapid. Predictably, with the cosmological timetable giving added urgency to my schedule, my train is delayed by the usual catalogue of disasters – points failure here, a faulty engine that has to be shunted into sidings there – and I am getting nervous that I will miss the eclipse entirely, or have to observe it precariously holding on to my cardboard goggles as I lean out of a moving carriage. I imagine the headline: RAILWAY ECLIPSE

WATCHER BEHEADED BY LOCOMOTIVE. Events occurring overhead cannot be held back for my benefit; yet the inexorable movement of the planets is not mirrored on earth, where our own circulation systems are subject to all kinds of delays and misfortunes.

Eventually we edge into the platform and I rush to unlock the bicycle that waits for me in the racks. I race through the backstreets and enter Hyde Park from Bayswater Road, near Marble Arch. The first thing I notice is a group of about a dozen people gathered on the grass, huddled together and bent double; together in silhouette they form a many-legged porcupine, its spines formed by the telescopes and powerful camera lenses they are crouching over and pointing at the sky. They, in turn, are being filmed by a TV camera crew. I cycle across the parched grass towards them and lean my bike up against a tree. One or two turn to greet me. The group is almost exclusively composed of bearded middle-aged men, I can't help noticing. Why the unusually high proportion of beards, I wonder? Perhaps they are needed to keep faces warm through the long watches of the night, or shield them from harmful gamma rays emitted by distant stars. In any event they are very friendly and not at all averse to answering the questions of an ignorant stranger. They tell me that what we are about to witness is a 'significant' eclipse – the moon will cover around 13 per cent of the sun's visible surface. The moment approaches and the TV cameraman is getting restless. 'Assume your positions, please, gentlemen,' he instructs us. 'Look through your telescopes, or look up at the sky and, *please*, look interested.' We *are* interested, but have to remember to appear so, so that our lives during the minutes of the eclipse make better television. I stand back a little, out of the camera's range. I don't feel like spending these few moments of planetary conjunction feigning interest for an unseen audience; the effort to do so might erase the genuine interest I feel. I don my eclipse viewers, along with several others not using more specialist lenses; together we look like a hastily assembled cinema audience from the 1950s, watching a monster-movie through 3D spectacles. The leader of the astronomy group has been lined up for a live interview as the eclipse begins. Right on cue, as he starts to speak and we train our eyes upwards, a dark cloud appears in the bright blue sky and blocks out all sight of the sun; a chill wind begins to blow, sending crisp packets and paper cups swirling around our ankles. The TV presenter laughs in exasperation, muttering something about the bloody British weather, and asks the astronomer he is interviewing to go again. 'Try to sound *really* excited,' he says. 'Let us know why you're here and why it matters.'

From behind my goggles the sky is completely black; then the cloud shifts and I can see the sun, glowing dimly but clearly through the black polymer – and its top rim has been eaten away as the moon shoulders its way in front of its bigger cousin. Gradually, the bite out of the sun's circumference increases, until a friendly astronomer tells me that the eclipse has achieved its maximum size. He offers to let me look through his solar telescope, directly at the sun. The image of the turbulent star is inverted, its missing section now at the bottom of its fiery wheel. I can clearly see what the man tells me is a filament, a jet of even hotter gases arcing out from its surface, reaching into space like a tendril. The moon is a purple eyelid, for once obscuring rather than reflecting the seething furnace in the sky upon which we all depend.

Adrift on the Iapetus Ocean

The light pouring down from the moon is of little value
in the arena of our daily existence. The area that
it uncertainly illuminates seems to belong to
a counter earth or a contiguous one.

Walter Benjamin, *A Berlin Childhood*★

Darren Almond is a twenty-first-century artist to whom moonlight is as important as it was to any nineteenth-century landscape painter. Like them he has spent many nocturnal hours perfecting his craft. Unlike them he does not employ oil paint, watercolour or a brush. The tool of his trade is the camera. By using extremely long exposures he unlocks a visual world of colour in the moonlit landscape that lies outside our limited optical range. For a decade he became what he called in one interview 'a follower of the moon', going to work when others retired to bed, stepping out into a world devoid of people and waiting for an image to accumulate over time as moonlight poured in through the shutter of his camera. The results are extraordinary.

On a cold Saturday afternoon in January I set out to walk with friends from Hackney in east London down to Shoreditch to see an exhibition of Almond's *Full Moon* photographs. Art and its attendants – the artists, their collectors and the dealers who speculate on their creativity, along with the service indus-

★ Trans. Mary-Jo Leibowitz, from *Art & Literature* no. 4, Spring 1965.

try that supports them, from journalists and broadcasters to PR people, chefs, studio managers, art handlers and the young women who sit behind the desks in the marble-floored art showrooms – have changed this area of the city more profoundly than any government regeneration scheme could hope to do. They have led a Bacchic dance along its tired old streets and dusty squares, and at the sound of their revelry long-empty warehouses have come back to life, their interiors transformed in muted monotones, sucking in the light through huge windows that open on to grey skies and strangely silent backyards. With the arrival of these shrines to art and money come the bars and nightclubs, the loft apartments and the crowds of pilgrims in search of a cultural moment that has already passed into the realm of myth. The direction of the tide of money in this city has changed from west to east over the last thirty years in a way that anyone transported from the late 1970s to the present would scarcely have credited.

Almond is also interested in time travel, but on a larger scale. The exhibition that we have come to see, 'Moons of the Iapetus Ocean', takes its title from the sea that separated England and Scotland 400 million years ago. This is time measured not in the rearrangement of bricks and concrete, of social demographics or property prices, but in the shift of massive mineral substrata, of tectonic plates – a movement too slow to be tracked by conventional clocks, invisible amid the clamour of our frenetic, distracted lives. The moon itself does not appear in most of the photographs on display in the muted twilight of the gallery's interior, but its influence is everywhere. The scenes Almond captures are lit by an unearthly light that has transformed the colour palette of the landscape; this is the light that Sylvia Plath describes in her poem 'The Moon and the Yew Tree' as 'the light of the mind, cold and planetary'.

Almond's photographs transport us to clifftops on the wilder reaches of the British and Irish coastline and to the unpopulated lochsides and gorges of its interior. At first, their subject seems to be rock formations themselves – the perpendicular rock stack at Yesnaby, the glistening black cliffs at Rossan Point – but they also tell the story of the relationship between the moon and the sea. In the unenclosed oceans of the world the rising and falling of the tide occurs twice a day as the great masses of water come under the influence of the gravitational pull of the moon. As William Falconer explains in his *Universal Dictionary of the Marine*, first published shortly before its author's disappearance at sea in 1769: 'About every six hours the waters of the ocean extend themselves over its shores: this is called the flux or flood; in this state they remain a short space of time, after which they retire or fall back, and this is called the reflux or ebb tide.' When the moon and the sun are opposite each other, resulting in a full moon, the gravitational pull on the earth's oceans is at its greatest, causing a surge in the deep water lying offshore. Two days later, these unstoppable forces deliver the high tide. Or, as Plath puts it in her poem, the moon, 'White as a knuckle . . . / It drags the sea after it like a dark crime.'

The combination of moonlight and long exposure in Almond's photographs transforms breakers on the shore into drifts of snow lit from beneath, or molten, white-hot metal. Out to sea, the action of currents or underwater reefs is clearly traced in luminous, swirling lines, making explicit the hidden pull of the tides and the sea's response to the moon's unending call. Almond's ocean, with its lactating rocks wreathed in mist, recalls another marine milkshake. In Hindu mythology, the moon (Soma) was born when the gods and demons, in a temporary alliance, using the snake Vasuki as a rope and the mountain Mandara as a stick, churned the sea of milk. First to emerge from the boiling liquid was Surabhi, mother of all, followed by Varuni, goddess of wine. Parijata, the tree of paradise, was revealed next, followed by the moon, which Siva immediately grasped to wear as a jewel on his forehead. The moon, originally associated with a plant (soma), is the source of the nectar of immortality that the gods feed on.

Another creation myth in the Hindu scriptures places the moon at the centre of human consciousness. The Aitareya Upanishad, written between the sixth and fourth century BC, tells the story of the origins of Fire, Wind, Sun and Moon. Once they had come into being, they asked Atman, the creator, where they should live. At first he offered them a horse, but they rejected it. Then he suggested they take up residence in a cow, but again they refused. Finally Atman brought a human being before them and they accepted. 'Fire became speech and entered the mouth. Wind became breath and entered the nostrils. The Sun became sight, and entered the eyes . . . The Moon became mind, and entered the heart.' As Jules Cashford argues in her encyclopaedic study *The Moon: Myth and Image*, the sun is therefore associated in this kind of thinking with outward vision and the hours of daylight; the moon with the inner, intuitive vision that comes during the hours of darkness. In an echo of the Upanishads that stretches across two and a half millennia, the sun illuminates the world while the moon, just as in Sylvia Plath's poem, supplies the light of the mind.

August Beach Moon, Normandy

From the clifftop in Cartaret the sea is silent, its voice stolen by the wind, which whistles, shouts and tussles, catching at my sleeve, inviting me to a bar-room brawl. It is eleven-thirty at night. The moon itself is hidden behind a cloud as black as squid ink, but from its secret location it is backlighting the sky, creating a dramatic stage set worthy of any Renaissance master. A glimmer of moonlight leaks out, silvering a stream that snakes across the sand as I descend the cliff path. At its foot a restaurant is still open for trade, spilling light and laughter on to the beach. I do not begrudge them their enjoyment; only the night they have stolen with the floodlight that illuminates tables on the terrace outside where nobody sits, rattling forlornly in the wind. The tide is at its lowest, half a mile out, and just on the turn. I want to venture beyond the reach of the lights, to walk off the warm fuzziness of the wine I have drunk with dinner and the weight of food in my belly, to escape the confines of this small and cosy French seaside town and meet the moon at the sea's edge.

First I must cross a small desert that is still faintly lit by the lights of the road. Looking down at my feet I see jet streams of sand flying across the beach surface in an ankle-level sandstorm. It is like watching a speeded-up film. A lighthouse beam that rakes across the beach is congested with flying yellow grains that sting the face and get in the eyes. A few hundred feet from diners sitting framed behind glass, like creatures in an aquarium, I am in a place that is wild and strange. If I stand still my shoes become covered with a fine layer within a matter of seconds. Seaweed disgorged here by a recent storm is vanishing beneath sand drifts; individual fronds have become intricate sand sculptures while the lumpen piles are disappearing more gradually; in the dim light they look as though they are floating in some frozen creek, ice-bound. Beyond the dry part of the beach, where the sea seldom reaches, the sand has been shaped into hummocks and runnels by the retreating tide. It is easier to walk here. Ghostly wading birds are making use of what light remains to chase crabs that have been brought in with the seaweed. They glow quietly in the shadows and then make little runs, their heads jabbing; occasionally one is blown off its feet in the teeth of the wind and tilts wildly this way and that in the air before coming to land again. I can hear the sea's roar now, although it is still far off. Without warning the moon emerges, at first ringed with haze and then clear, oval-shaped, tinted with lemon, a few days short of full. Each hillock of sand is now an alp, capped with reflected light. The sea is black and silver; at the tideline I watch it running in along the lines it has carved for itself, at ninety degrees to the shore, the first channel flowing left to right, the next right to left. I squat down in the moon's path to get as close to eye level as I can with the tide it is sending me. The wind is stippling the incoming fingers of water as it runs and its surface breaks up into a thousand shards of light. I can see the waves themselves beyond the shallows, heaving and crashing, slopes of jet topped by foam. I look behind me, a little nervously; I need the moon to alert me to where the water is headed, seeking out its circuitous route inland, betrayed by its shimmer – I don't want to have to wade home. Turning away from land once again, I see that the moonlight has made a road across the sea, catching the phosphorescent foam of each wave top and leaving the valleys between them in deep shadow.

This is the scene that so many painters have tried to capture, competing with each other to best portray the nocturnal beauty of the Bay of Salerno, say, or of a Venetian lagoon. Studying the original makes me more aware both of their art and their shortcomings. I have seen a small Van Gogh landscape in which the leaves of poplars seemed to tremble in a breeze, but I have never yet met a painting that could evoke this stinging, tangy wind, the waves' thunder, or the ever-shifting drama of this sky. I walk for half an hour or so at the advancing sea's edge before I decide the time has come to turn back if I want to make it home without mishap. As I leap a newly filled channel I notice something at my feet. It is a large jellyfish, washed in by the rough seas of the night before, glowing quietly on the sand like a translucent crystal skull. I prod it gently with my toe and find it surprisingly firm and resilient. Bending closer I can see the moon reflected in its mysterious, pale body, the same moon whose gravitational pull has delivered it here, like a message from the stars. I am not an expert in the identification of such creatures, but from the transparency and shape of its body, or bell, it could be a Moon Jellyfish (*Aurelia aurita*). Their sting is said to be mild, a mere kiss from the unexpected. I hope it is alive, but have no way of knowing. If I had time I would stay and wait for the tide to reach it; I would like to see it lift off once more, like a spaceship heading home (perhaps then I could establish its identity – Moon Jellyfish only have short tentacles). But the encircling tide is reaching out its arms to enfold me; I don't want to be lassoed by its embrace. So I turn my back on both the moon and its messenger, and climb the cliff path back to the electric, street-lit world.

Immaculate Conceptions
and Transparent Moons

Considering the moon is visible in the sky so much of the time it is remarkable how long it took for the first naturalistic paintings of it to emerge in Western art. Long after painters were able to render in meticulous detail a human eye, or a distant landscape, they persisted in portraying the moon in ways other than it would have appeared to the most casual observer. Why was this? It is almost as if the sheer weight of misguided theories as to its nature and the myriad legends and symbolic associations the moon had accumulated over the centuries served to obscure its face, preventing accurate observation.

As we have already seen, the tradition of associating the Virgin Mary with the moon in painting was well established throughout the Catholic world during the Renaissance. Above all, the conjunction of Mary and the moon was associated with the idea, supremely difficult to render in paint, of the Immaculate Conception – a complicated doctrine which asserted that at the moment at which Mary was conceived in the normal human way, her soul was washed clean of original sin. (Doesn't a little of this semi-divine status adhere to every Catholic mother?) In many paintings within this tradition, the Virgin is represented balanced on a crescent moon, usually inverted as if it were a miniature boat in which she could cross the heavens.

In seventeenth-century Seville, however, a different pictorial tradition emerged from the studio of Francisco Pacheco, one of the most influential artists of the period. He left behind a treatise on painting, *Arte de la pintura*, published posthumously in 1649, in which he spells out his template for portrayals of the

Immaculate Conception: 'The moon, although it is a solid globe, I take the liberty to make clear and transparent above the nations; the moon high above, clearer and more visible, with its points facing down.'

Remarkable examples of this transparent moon exist, painted by artists following Pacheco's instructions, including two of his most famous pupils, Alonso Cano and Diego Velázquez. Called 'the Michelangelo of Spain' for his achievements as a sculptor, Cano was a remarkable painter as well as a trained architect. If this extraordinarily talented man had a fault, it seems to have been his ungovernable temper; in an argument with a potential purchaser, we are told, he dashed a sculpture of a saint to the ground, smashing it to pieces, an act of desecration for which he could have faced the flames. He was also accused of murder, a slur that hung over him for years, even though it was refuted; the victim was his wife. In an age when artists needed the diplomatic skills and manners of an ambassador to ensure they retained the patronage of both Church and state, such a volatile temperament was not an advantage. His paintings and sculptures, in complete contrast to his fiery nature, exude a transcendental serenity. His *Immaculate Conception* was painted on his return, after turbulent years spent in Seville, Madrid and Toledo, to his home town of Granada, where it graced a stairway for many years in the Franciscan convent. Cano's Virgin stands, eyes modestly downcast, on an impressive full moon. Full or not, it is a diaphanous object that, while capable of supporting the weight of the Madonna and the heads of several disembodied cherubs who peer out from beneath the robes at her feet, is more like a Moon Jellyfish than a moon, transparent enough to allow sight of the landscape behind it. It is clearly a metaphorical object, just as the moonlit landscape below it is a metaphorical landscape, carefully populated with symbols associated with the Virgin: an enclosed garden (*hortus conclusus*), a ship, a tower, a fountain, a city, a temple, a palm tree; each element of the composition prescribed in the litany – and approved in Pacheco's treatise.

Diego Velázquez's treatment of the same theme in his *Immaculate Conception*, now in the National Gallery in London, was painted when he was around nineteen years old and a recent graduate from Pacheco's studio. Once again, Mary stands on a transparent moon, its upper half filled with light, its lower half disappearing into the landscape. Although her hair is blonde and her skin doesn't seem to have known the fierce sun of the southern Spanish plains, she has the broad face of a peasant girl in her early teenage years (Pacheco recommended in his treatise that the Virgin should be portrayed as a girl of about thirteen years old). In fact, part of the startling effect of both these paintings is the contrast between their mystical trappings and the obvious reality of the models that posed for them. Although Velázquez's model is lost in contemplation, her fingertips barely touching in an attitude of prayer and her gaze on the earth below, and although she is crowned with a diadem of stars, it is easy to imagine her dropping her pose and filling a jug at the symbolic fountain beneath her feet, laughing with her companions. She has been frozen temporarily in the attitude of a devotional statue, removed from the normal activities of life by the painter's spell; but to ensure devotion from her flock she depends on the artist's skill in revealing her humanity.

These transparent moons, symbolic of divine intervention in human affairs (was not the whole Church calendar regulated by the lunar cycle?), are delicate as thistledown, as if constructed of their own light. Immaterial as they are, they form a bridge between the physical and spiritual worlds, constructed by artistic sleight of hand. Velázquez has paid great attention to the Virgin's robes; while her blue cloak billows gently behind her, its curves echoing the massed clouds that boil in the sky with the energy of a cosmic event, her red dress falls in stiff folds, hiding the surface on which she stands. In this way, without having to resort to a cluster of putti as Cano does, the artist avoids confronting the problem of how a young woman's physical, load-bearing feet would be supported by something that appears no more solid than mist.

Let's Murder the Moonlight!
Futurists and the Moon

The linkage between the advance of modernity and the retreat of the moon was made explicit at the beginning of the twentieth century by that great hymn-writer for all things modern, the Italian Futurist Filippo Tommaso Marinetti. Marinetti, who described himself as 'the caffeine of Europe', was a master polemicist, his diatribes in praise of speed, mechanization and urbanism and against the stultifying baggage of Italian history and culture the fuel that launched the Futurist project into orbit. Every generation of the avant-garde is compelled to destroy what has gone before; without such clearing of the ground there can be no forward progress. But Marinetti was the only one bold enough to try to rearrange the cosmos itself. In 1909 he wrote:

A cry went up in the airy solitude of the high plains, 'Let's murder the moonlight!' Some ran to nearby cascades; gigantic wheels were raised, and turbines transformed the rushing waters into magnetic pulses that rushed up wires, up high poles, up to shining, humming globes. So it was that three hundred electric moons cancelled with their rays of blinding mineral whiteness the ancient green queen of loves.

For Marinetti, the moon was everything Futurism was not. Ancient, associated with romance and superstition, linked traditionally with harvest and the female principle, it was on his hit list of cultural objects to be torn down and destroyed. Electricity was the new, masculine source of illumination that would light the heroic thrust into the industrial age, gobbling up the night in the same way that new factories and dockyards were

consuming the countryside. While Italy had lagged behind the
other nations of Europe in the first industrial revolution based
on iron, steel and coal, remaining largely an agrarian society, it
had huge natural resources to exploit in the torrents that cas-
caded down from the Alps, the very 'rushing waters' Marinetti
wrote of; its vast hydroelectric projects were the envy of the
world. Marinetti did not despise the night; the hours of darkness were a time of adventure, of freewheeling discussions and
wild drinking parties, of careering rides through the city in
powerful motorcars and of the sepulchral, upturned faces of the
crowds, seen literally in a new light. As the painter Umberto
Boccioni announced in the lecture he gave at the Circolo Artis-
tico in Rome in 1911, what interested the Futurists was 'Night
life, with its women and men marvellously bent on forgetting
their daytime life; the panting factories that incessantly produce
wealth for the powerful; the geometrical city landscapes enam-
elled with gemstones, mirrors, lights; all of this creates around
us an unexplored atmosphere that fascinates us, and into it we
fling ourselves to conquer the future!' By reprieving nocturnal
hours from the clutch of darkness, like Dutch engineers reclaim-
ing fertile farmland from the sea, the bringers of electric light
had created a new world where anything was possible. 'We have
been up all night, my friends and I,' begins the Futurist Manifesto, 'beneath mosque lamps whose brass cupolas are bright as
our souls, because like them they were illuminated by the
internal glow of electric hearts.'

In this enthusiasm for electricity, Marinetti was reflecting
a widely felt excitement. The Electrical Exhibition in Paris
in 1881 attracted over 750,000 visitors, more than 8,000 a day
gawping at the 159 different lamps on display. Giacomo Balla
was so overcome by the Palais d'Electricité that was a feature of
the Paris Fair of 1900 that he not only depicted it in a painting
but also named his two daughters in memory of the experience –

the girls were called Luce and Elettricita. In 1909 he painted *Street-Lamp – Study of Light*, a depiction of one of the lamp posts that had just appeared on the streets of European cities. The arrow-like particles that radiate outwards from it render the crescent moon in the top right-hand corner of the picture weak and ineffectual, an undercooked and discarded croissant from the table of a boulevard café.

Although Marinetti and Marcel Proust were born within five years of each other and inhabited the same city of Paris for a period, it is hard to imagine two more contrasting sensibilities: as unlike as espresso and lime-flower tea. On the one hand the poet of velocity and violence and on the other the reclusive dreamer within his cork-lined room. If the Italian had a soul lit by an electric heart, as he claimed, Proust's spirit was fed by the moonbeams that fell in the fictional garden at Combray, 'like broken staircases of white marble', lighting Marcel's way as he retraced the walks he had taken in childhood. 'Literature has up to now magnified pensive immobility, ecstasy and slumber,' Marinetti wrote in his manifesto, as if consciously skewering Proust's literary ambitions in a few well-chosen words four years before the publication of the first volume of *À la recherche du temps perdu*. 'We want to exalt movements of aggression, feverish sleeplessness, the double march, the perilous leap, the slap and the blow with the fist.'

Both Proust and the Futurists celebrated transformation; the Futurists sang of the effect on the city of electricity, while Proust was content to hymn that most ancient alteration on summer nights, when 'the moonlight striking on the half-open shutters would throw down to the foot of my bed its enchanted ladder'. Its potency was not restricted to the world of child-hood, or to the countryside. A great city could be changed as easily as a child's bedroom when 'the pavements of Paris [were]

glistening beneath the moon'. Seated in his carriage on fine and
frosty nights, driving down the Parisian boulevards and seeing
the moonbeams 'fall between his eyes and the deserted street',
Swann thinks 'of that other face, gleaming and faintly roseate
like the moon's, which had, one day, risen on the horizon of his
mind, and since then had shed upon the world the mysterious
light in which he saw it bathed'. Moonlight in the external
world is a metaphor for the change that has been wrought
within him. The seduction of his heart has taken place almost
without him noticing; the power balance in his relationship has
shifted and the truth of his condition is revealed not in the clear
light of midday, but through the lunar X-ray the moonlight
provides of his emotions.

In Greek mythology, the beautiful shepherd Endymion was
similarly ensnared by the moon when he was least able to resist.
The moon goddess Selene fell in love with him as he slept and
begged Zeus to grant her the power to keep the young man in a
deep, unending slumber so that she could descend from the
heavenly realm and embrace him at will. In the painting *Diana
and Endymion*★ by Pierre Subleyras in the National Gallery, the
goddess, her arrival trailed by a train of tangled clouds, cradles
the youth's moonlit, sleeping form, gazing avidly into his face
and tracing the line of his cheek with a finger. The masculine
strength implicit in his torso is rendered powerless and vulnerable, an image that both evokes a deeply seated male fantasy and
stands as a warning to their sex. This was the very enslavement
that Marinetti despised and that in his eyes lay at the heart of
Mediterranean culture; the myth of the Latin Lover that diverted
virile males from effective action, persuading them to spend
their vigour uselessly in the arms of moonlit seductresses.

★ Selene's identity later became subsumed within that of the Roman hunt-
ress Diana.

Proust himself, the hypochondriac, bisexual, nocturnal dandy, frequenter of aristocratic parties and duchesses' salons, with his lustrous, self-barbered black hair and pale, Semitic features, eating his favourite asparagus in the Ritz with his fingers without removing his white gloves, was hardly heroic material in the Futurist model. Yet, like Marinetti, his art was to make him the toast of modernists throughout Europe, an inhabitant of the front pages of newspapers, the talk of the town. The two men even shared a patron. In 1910 Marinetti's crusade to convert the world to Futurism arrived in London, where he subjected guests gathered at the house of Sydney and Violet Schiff to a noisy, impassioned performance. His earnestness was too much for the Italian tenor Caruso, who put on a false nose and rolled around on the floor beneath the piano. Schiff was an early translator of Proust's novel and one of his most constant admirers. It was he who staged the famous party at the Majestic Hotel in Paris in 1922 to which Proust was invited, along with Picasso, Diaghilev, Stravinsky and James Joyce.*

In the Paris of today the *grands magasins* on Boulevard Haussmann remain illuminated all night. Parisian streets in the early hours may be as deserted as those that Proust's hero drove down in his victoria, but they hold little mystery for the eye of the observer, their dark corners penetrated, their pavements no longer glistening, but scrubbed clean of moonbeams as efficiently as they would be of silvery fish-scales at the close of market-day.

---

* This gathering is captured in Richard Davenport-Hines's *A Night at the Majestic: Proust and the Great Modernist Dinner Party of 1922* (London: Faber & Faber, 2006), to which I am indebted.

The Agency of the Night

I recall
My thoughts, and bid you look upon the night.
As water does a sponge, so the moonlight
Fills the void, hollow, universal air –

Percy Bysshe Shelley,
'Letter to Maria Gisborne'

The urge to travel is self-perpetuating and can never be satisfied. It seems to have been handed down genetically, a residual trace perhaps of vast prehistoric migrations undertaken by our distant ancestors. As we hurl ourselves forward, fuelled by a compressed version of the distant past, we are, we now realize, in danger of erasing our future. But eighteenth-and nineteenth-century travellers, in at the beginning of the carbon age, shared with us less obvious, psychological after-effects of making journeys. The problem lay not in setting out, but in returning.

Londoners leaving the landscape of Italy and finding them-selves once more in the streets of the city that William Cobbett christened 'the Great Wen' – swollen, oozing, bisected by a foul-smelling river – might well have felt a touch of the post-holiday blues. The docks, factories and foundries of this small nation were, it was true, supplying the furthest reaches of the largest empire the world had ever seen. Its scientists, astron-omers, engineers, chemists and geologists were at the forefront of European scientific advances that every week seemed to reveal new wonders. Yet travel makes one aware of the deficiencies as well as the comforts of home. There are certain things that cannot be inserted into life even through the most furious activity: sublime beauty, for instance, or a classical past. What in London could compare to walking across Piazza San Marco in Venice by moonlight, a scene almost as popular with artists as an erupting Vesuvius? As Giuseppe Pavanello wrote in *Italy by Moonlight: The Night in Italian Painting 1550 to 1850*, 'The nocturnal vision of Venice is connected with the sublime and the Romantic predilection for mystery and dreams: in the darkness, barely illuminated by the ambiguous light of the moon, the city is transformed, and assumes the appearance of a unique phenomenon of nature.'

The German Romantic painter Friedrich Nerly was one of those who tried to capture that 'ambiguous light'. In his painting *Die Piazzetta in Venedig bei Mondschein* (1842), the golden moon appears around the edge of the Doge's Palace, throwing a dazzling trail on the lagoon. Moonlight strikes the column topped by the Lion of Saint Mark halfway up, casting its shadow across the square, where groups of well-dressed promenaders walk and speak together. In the foreground of the scene, among the arabesque shadows of the porticos of the palace, stroll two men in Moorish dress, symbols perhaps of the city's far-reaching trading routes and historic connection with the Islamic world. Deeper in the shadows, three cowled figures in dark robes add a more sinister note. The piazza was historically, after all, not just a place of social exchange. The space between the two columns that formed a gateway to the city was a special one, allocated on the one hand for the playing of permitted games of chance and on the other for dealing with those who had in some way gambled and lost – by public execution.

There was no greater champion of the beauties of Italy, its landscape, art and architecture and what he called the 'blue Italian weather' than Percy Bysshe Shelley. Moreover, his 'Ode to Naples' is infused with the optimism he felt at the signing of a new constitution by the Bourbon King Ferdinand IV. A spark of hope at last, after the crushing of the Parthenopaean Republic and the subsequent butchery of the poets and intellectuals that had been its figureheads, a rout made doubly horrible in that it was orchestrated by an English admiral, Horatio Nelson.

In his 'Letter to Maria Gisborne', the poet addresses his absent hostess, who is 'In London, that great sea, whose ebb and flow / At once is deaf and loud', while he resides in her house at Leghorn in Tuscany. While it may not be as physically beautiful, he implies, London contains within its depths its own treasures, in human form. Among the band of mutual friends and co-conspirators he lists in the poem are his father-in-law, the unjustly imprisoned radical William Godwin; Coleridge, who 'sits obscure / In the exceeding lustre and the pure / Intense irradiation' of his mind; and Leigh Hunt, a happy soul and 'the salt of the earth', 'without whom / This world would smell like what it is − a tomb'. Ironically it was to meet Leigh Hunt on his arrival in Italy that Shelley made the journey along the Tuscan coast in the small boat he had built himself, and in which he had never before ventured into the open sea. After spending several happy days together the friends separated and Shelley set out on the return journey to where his wife, Mary, was waiting, by her own account full of ominous foreboding. The boat, along with the poet and his two companions, vanished in a storm.

In the 'Letter', Shelley is caught in the archetypal English conundrum; he loves the natural world and needs to spend time in it to refresh his poetic muse, yet the city is the crucible of innovation and creativity, the home of genius. Outside its boundaries he will always be to some extent in exile. So his poem is a bridge between two worlds. Though he and Maria Gisborne are apart, they are united by having friends in common. And what else?

> I recall
> My thoughts, and bid you look upon the night.

Though separated, the distance between them is as nothing compared to those travelled by the wan moon, that 'Climbs with diminished beams the azure steep', or by the clouds,

> Piloted by the many-wandering blast,
> And the rare stars rush through them dim and fast: –
> All this is beautiful in every land.

This theme, of a protagonist set apart and yet united with what he has left behind by the moon in the night sky, is a universal one. It is not clear why the sight of the moon fills exiles with nostalgia for their homeland, but as a theme for poetry and art this sensation transcends borders. It was certainly as central to Japanese culture in the nineteenth century as it was to the European Romantic tradition. One of Hokusai's best-known prints, *Nakamaro Gazing at the Moon from a Terrace*, depicts a young nobleman sitting apparently lost in thought on a terrace, gazing out at the moon above the sea, ignoring the Chinese servants who are offering him food. The print illustrates the story of Nakamaro, who at the age of sixteen was sent on an expedition to China, charged with finding out the secret of calculating time. The legend has it that the young lord was welcomed, but was not allowed to return home in case he was a spy. Forced to remain in China he served the Emperor, rising to the rank of a regional governor, never escaping the melancholy of separation from his home. Another version of the story has it that the suspicious Emperor laid on a feast for Nakamaro on a terrace; when he fell asleep, overcome by wine, the Emperor's servants removed the ladder, imprisoning Nakamaro there. In this

version, when he awoke in the moonlight and realized his fate,
he bit his thumb and wrote the poem for which he is famous in
blood upon his sleeve:

> When I look upon Heaven's plain I wonder:
> Is that the same moon that rose
> Over Mount Mikasa in Kasuga?

Shelley is unequivocal: whatever the daytime differences
between the two countries, the night sky is as beautiful in London as Italy. And yet the eyes are torn away from it by the
distractions of the local scene.

> But what see you beside? – a shabby stand
> Of Hackney coaches – a brick house or wall
> Fencing some lonely court, white with the scrawl
> Of our unhappy politics; – or worse –
> A wretched woman reeling by, whose curse
> Mixed with the watchman's, partner of her trade,
> You must accept in place of serenade –

The eternal heavens are replaced by the details of the specifically
drawn modern city, complete with taxicabs, graffiti, drunken-
ness and political unrest. In contrast, Shelley, secluded in Tuscany,
is surrounded by 'a chaos of green leaves and fruit', where fireflies
'flash and glance', their lustre dimmed in full moonlight but
bright beneath the trees – a magical world Gisborne knows well.
Once again, the gulf between their two situations, temporarily
bridged by the poem, seems immense. And then comes a moment
of particular transcendence:

> a bird
> Which cannot be the Nightingale, and yet
> I know none else that sings so sweet as it
> At this late hour; – and then all is still: –
> Now – Italy or London, which you will!

Shelley's nocturnal caroller came to mind in a different city, on the other side of the Atlantic. For reasons to do with my work, I often visit New York in late May or early June, staying with friends who live in a brownstone in a leafy street in Brooklyn. I am not the only seasonal visitor. For two weeks at this time of year a bird sings at night in a tree outside the house, its song echoing through the streets between midnight and two in the morning. We stand on the stoop one night listening to it after seeing off some visitors; its song is a complex sequence, each call of which is repeated three or four times, varying from musical trills to cartoon sound effects and avian-DJ samples from the songs of other birds. The raised voices and sirens on Grand Street have quietened down and a yellow moon, broken neatly in half, rises above the roofs of the houses opposite as we listen. Brooklyn, with its parks and its trees, is home to many birds; blue jays, house finches, doves and red cardinals regularly visit the backyards where grey squirrels use the overhead power lines as a freeway.

One early Sunday evening I walk down to Fort Green, where the cafés and sidewalks are thronged with people enjoying the early-summer sunshine. Outside the door of a boutique, the one that used to belong to one of Bob Marley's daughters, or daughter's daughters, I don't remember which, a small group has gathered. A hawk, a young peregrine, probably from a nest on Brooklyn Bridge, is sitting on the sidewalk, its head swivelling as it follows passers-by with its yellow eyes. It has backed itself up against a wall beneath the overhang of the front window of the shop and it is holding one wing behind it, as if hiding it from view. A woman is already on her phone, calling Animal Welfare, when a ragged man walks up.

'Anybody got a perch?' he asks. 'Got a bit of stick for it to sit on?' And he bends down unsteadily, taking a long look into the yellow eyes that look right back, unblinking.

But this interference is not welcomed by the small crowd. 'What you wanna mess with it for?' another man asks, his sunglasses pushed to the top of his shaved head, his biceps glistening in the sun where he too holds a phone to his ear.

'OK, OK,' the ragged man says, raising his hands as though to shield himself from the threat implicit in the questioner's voice. 'Just trying to help,' and he shuffles on his way. I watch for a while as Brooklyn gets itself organized to deal with the miniature-bird-care crisis. The hawk couldn't have crash-landed in a better spot. So absorbed have I become in this avian psychodrama that I am late for my next appointment, at the Metropolitan Museum. Fortunately I have come to see only one work, a crucifixion attributed to Jan Van Eyck, said to contain the first accurate representation of the moon in Western culture. I have seen the painting in reproduction of course; what I am immediately struck by, once I have run up the wide, stone staircase and located the gallery that contains it, is both the smallness of the actual work and the intricacy of its intensely naturalistic detail.

The etiolated body of Christ on the cross, its sinews and veins straining beneath the skin, is no bigger than the page of my pocket notebook; the waning half-moon that hangs in the sky behind the cross of the thief to his left, the size of my fingernail. Unlike the unnatural eclipse-light in the painting by Perugino that I saw in Siena, this crucifixion takes place in the natural light of late afternoon. The three crosses are surrounded by a throng of onlookers dressed in contemporary Flemish clothing. A soldier in a lush green costume and fur-trimmed hat thrusts his spear between the Saviour's ribs; his victim's mouth is open in agony, while the thief to Jesus's left has broken the rope that bound his waist to the cross, his body contorting in a spasm that echoes the curve of the moon. The execution seems to be an everyday occurrence for the locals; richly attired merchants enjoy a joke, seated on horses that paw the arid ground. Behind the hill on which the crosses stand can be seen the roofs and gables of an intricately rendered Flemish city. Snow-capped mountains rise in the distance and a river winds past a hill topped with a castle. Scholars have pointed out that these different landscapes – arid, fertile, mountainous – could not exist in one geographical location, any more than the waning gibbous moon could occupy the position in the sky in late afternoon that Van Eyck has given it. His world is a collection of details, each finished to a high degree of naturalism but not assembled into something slavishly imitating reality; or, as Scott L. Montgomery has written, in his magisterial book *The Moon and the Western Imagination*, 'Each of his paintings is a kind of *Kunstkammer* [cabinet of wonders] of precisely rendered observations from various places.' As Montgomery points out, Van Eyck has turned a thousand years of iconography on its head by positioning the moon not above and to the right of Christ's head but below the cross-beam of the thief's cross, at the extreme right-hand edge of the painting. His moon has stepped out of its ordained position, both in terms of tradition and reality. Whether or not it has lost any symbolic potency by doing so, it has at least been recognized; its face, complete with *lunar maria*, observed and accurately recorded for the first time.

If the young hawk received a kind reception when it was blown off course and on to a Brooklyn pavement, the night-singing bird is not so warmly welcomed by all the Borough's residents. As the city heats up and grows humid and mosquitoes begin to make their presence felt after sunset, there are many of the opinion that it is already hard enough to sleep without this crazy midnight vocalist sounding off. On the internet, bloggers from Brooklyn seek information about the bird's identity, asking for suggestions of how to scare it away. One even threatens to blast it from the tree if it keeps up with its relentless song. An ornithologist from the Audubon Society posts a notice, explaining that what people are hearing is a young male mockingbird, seeking a mate. Close your windows, or sleep in a different room, he urges. Once the bird has mated it will cease singing. Perhaps if we could all think back to how we behaved when we were young and courting, we could cut the bird some slack?

Whatever songster it was that Shelley describes hearing in his poem it wasn't a mockingbird any more than it was a nightingale. Nevertheless, through the agency of its music, of poetry and of the night, with its attendant , stars and scudding clouds, he describes the way the nocturnal world and its inhabitants take possession of the city. As the Brooklyn mockingbird reminds us, they are still working at this transformation today, despite all the barricades modern man erects against them. For a few hours at least, the streets become a landscape as otherworldly as any a returning traveller will have met with on their wanderings far from home.

PART TWO
Tsukimi

Beyond the Gateless Gate:
September Kyoto Moon

The autumn moon inspired my heart with a desire to see the rise
of the full moon over Mount Obasute . . . There was another man
filled with the same desire, my disciple Etsujin, who accompanied
me, and also a servant sent by my friend Kakei to help me on the
journey, for the Kiso road that led to the village was steep and
dangerous, passing over a number of high mountains.

Matsuo Bashō, *A Visit to Sarashina Village*

I

In Japan the autumn moon that falls on the fifteenth day of the
eighth month of the old Japanese lunar calendar is the most
important of the year. It is also considered the most beautiful.
For more than a thousand years its arrival has been observed and
celebrated in the autumn moon-viewing festival known as Tsukimi (named after the goddess of the moon, Tsuki-Yomi). The
festival, along with a love of moonlight in general, is among the
many cultural features imported from China during Japan's
Heian period (AD 794–1185), when moon-viewing platforms
became a feature of ornamental gardens, and courtiers, both
male and female, would write poetry by the light of the moon.

During the Edo period, when the capital of Japan moved from
Kyoto to present-day Tokyo, the warrior and merchant classes
began celebrating Tsukimi, and farmers combined it with their
own harvest festival rites. Taro roots (*sato-imo*) were prepared as

offerings, giving the full moon another name, *imo meigetsu*. In modern-day Japan, Tsukimi is very much a family event. While the Chinese see a hare in the moon, preparing the drug of immortality for its mistress, Japanese children see a rather cute rabbit, pounding rice. In Japanese, the words *mochi-zuki* mean both 'to pound rice' and 'the full moon' – the ideographs are different but the sound of the words is the same. During the festival, rice is pounded into paste and made into dumplings or 'moon-cakes', a meal shared with the lunar deity. Moon-cakes and an arrangement of at least one of the seven ornamental grasses of autumn are traditionally placed on a lacquer tray in a window as an offering at the point where the moon's light is most likely to enter the house.

Tsukimi is not an exclusively Shinto festival; it also lies at the heart of one of the most meaningful seasons in the Buddhist calendar. The spring and autumn equinoxes are known to Buddhists as Higan and are seen as a time to meditate on the impermanence of human life, mirrored in the changing seasons. The Chinese ideographs for Higan literally translate as 'the far shore', that place on the other side of the Sea of Nothingness spoken of in Indian Buddhist scriptures. During the seven days of the autumn equinox, Buddhists congregate at temples to meditate and to hear teachings and readings from the *Dharma*. Buddha is said to have been born at full moon; in Buddhist iconography the final lunar phase has come to represent enlightenment.

As I read more about the part the moon has played in Japanese literature, art and culture, I am gripped by the idea of seeing the autumn moon rise over the sacred land of Japan. How could any journey in search of moonlight be complete without it? In an apparent confirmation of my desire, a funding body I have applied to without much hope of success sends me a cheque and the trip becomes possible. So it is one evening at the beginning of September that I am searching feverishly through books on Japan when the doorbell rings. The new moon at this time of year in the Islamic calendar marks the beginning of Ramadan and my Muslim neighbours have arrived, having broken their fast, bearing gifts of food. It feels as though the whole world is keeping step with the cycles of the moon and I just hadn't noticed.

The Tsukimi has provoked many journeys, although mostly within Japan itself; the most famous of these have been made not by aeroplane but on foot. Good examples are the travelogues of the seventeenth-century poet Matsuo Bashō, composed in *haibun*, a combination of prose and haiku. At the beginning of *A Visit to the Kashima Shrine*, he quotes a poem written by a near contemporary from Kyoto on the beach at Suma, a famous beauty spot in the Bay of Akashi, before introducing his own journey.

> Crouching under a pine
> I watched the full moon
> Pondering all night
> On the sorrow of Chūnagon

Having for some time cherished in my mind the memory of this poet, I wandered out on the road at last one day this autumn, possessed by an irresistible desire to see the rise of the full moon over the mountains of the Kashima Shrine.

On his journey, Bashō has two travelling companions:

One was a masterless youth and the other a wandering priest. The latter was clad in a robe black as a crow, with a bundle of sacred stoles around his neck and on his back a portable shrine containing a holy image of the Buddha after enlightenment. This priest, brandishing his long staff, stepped into the road ahead of all the others, as if he had a free pass to the World beyond the Gateless Gate.

How much preferable it sounds, to set out by boat and then on foot (they decide against hiring a horse because they want 'to try the strength of [their] slender legs'), as if one had a free pass to the world, rather than in the belly of a gas-guzzling, carbon-spewing plane, weighed down by conflicting emotions. It is commonplace to feel fraught at the beginning of a journey. There are loved ones and responsibilities that all have a hold, making leave-taking difficult. On many levels I find it hard to justify the trip, even to myself. Last-minute worries about my itinerary – will it really be possible to change planes in Amsterdam in forty-five minutes and still stay connected with my suitcase? – combine with rising excitement and the extra coffee I drank at Heathrow to raise my heartbeat.

Flying eastwards, time accelerates and night falls swiftly. I cannot sleep at the beginning of a journey. I read some Bashō. The lights are switched off and my neighbours settle down to watch movies, or drape blankets over their faces, sitting immovable as statues. Two very young children keep up an almost continual wailing. After four hours or so I get up to take a walk. At the back of the plane, near the galley, a window remains with its blind undrawn. I look out, to see the moon riding above the wing. We have risen above the clouds that have sat over Europe for the last few weeks, into clear air. The cloud tops beneath us are gilded silver.

Back at my seat I close my eyes and attempt to sleep but, just as I enter a state of drowsiness where images of airports and the movies I have watched combine with echoes of Bashō, I find myself composing a haiku instead. Sleepily I try to follow the conventions that have been accepted for the last 350 years or so: that the haiku should be set in the present; that only seventeen syllables should be used; that only one poetic image should be evoked; and that reference is made to one of the four seasons. A further requirement it was culturally unnecessary to state in seventeenth-century Japan was that the haiku should be composed in Japanese by someone of great refinement and sensitivity, rather than a dehydrated, absurdly tall *gaijin* sky-traveller; this last I am unable to fulfil.

> Above the clouds
> An autumn moon
> Our travelling companion

It's no use. I watch a film, drink some orange juice, take another walk. The window by the galley now has its blind pulled down, like an eyelid covering an eye, or so it seems to my semi-feverish brain.

> This plane flies with its eyes shut
> Trusting the autumn moon
> To guide it

I land at Kansai after one hour's sleep and head for the platform for Kyoto. Once the train arrives, before anyone can board, the arms of the seats must be dusted, the floor vacuumed and the rubbish bins emptied by an army of immaculately uniformed cleaners; at the flick of a switch the seats rotate to face in the direction we will be travelling. As we skim smoothly through the developments that lie between Osaka and Kyoto I am impressed by the way agriculture goes on right in the middle of town. These are not hobby-allotments, or the workers' gardens of Germany, but small farms, with earth in the building-lot-sized fields banked up for irrigation in the middle of housing projects and miniature rice paddies, complete with their ancient cultivators in conical straw hats, next to car parks. I have been reading an article on the plane about how far Japan is ahead of the West in facing the 'demographic time bomb' of a steeply ageing population. Perhaps the view from the train offers an example of a way forward for us: our increasing numbers of old people could retire from public life and, like Roman senators, become urban farmers, staying fit and active, using land made available by the economic downturn, making some money and providing local communities with fresh food. Government could compulsorily purchase office buildings standing empty and raze them, clearing the land for agriculture. Those looking after the land could receive a basic wage, saved from government budgets through the health benefits of such toil and the change in the national diet, to top up their earnings from the sale of produce and their pensions. Such a way of life in the 'third age' would seem to offer the best of both worlds: contact with nature that is usually available only to those living in the countryside, and close proximity to all the amenities offered by a city. After a day's work in the fields, our farmers could wash the earth off their hands and go for a drink in their favourite bar, watch a football match at their team's home ground or catch a movie at the cinema, all at special, discounted farmers' prices.

There is nothing like an impractical, utopian dream to raise the spirits. However, I have other things to consider. Deciding where to see Tsukimi is something to be planned carefully. In Junchiro Tanizaki's *In Praise of Shadows*, his defence of traditional Japanese aesthetics against the onset of artificial lighting, the process is fraught with problems.

This year I had great trouble making up my mind where to go for the autumn moon-viewing. Finally, after much perplexed head-scratching, I decided to go the Ishiyama Temple. The day before the full moon, however, I read that there would be loudspeakers in the woods at Ishiyama to regale the moon-viewing guests with phonograph records of the Moonlight Sonata. I cancelled my plans immediately. Loudspeakers were bad enough, but if it could be assumed they would set the tone, then there would surely be floodlights too strung all over the mountain.

It was at Ishiyama Temple that the Heian-era courtesan Murasaki Shikibu began writing *The Tale of Genji*, the world's earliest-known novel, on the night of the full moon in August 1004.

Hiroshige, one of Japan's most famous masters of the landscape woodblock print, depicted just this location in the work *Autumn Moon at Ishiyama*, a series of prints published around 1834 and surely known to Junchiro Tanizaki. The temple is nestled among trees and rocks on a mountainside that is rendered in different shades of grey, with the cliff face at its peak catching the light of the full moon, which hangs above in a deep blue sky. Moonlight spills on to the waters of the lake and moonlit mists almost erase Mount Hira in the distance, which is pale grey against a lower sky tinged with yellow. The poem incorporated into the print reads:

> At Ishiyama, the moon casting light on Lake Niho
> Is no less than at Suma or Akashi.

By the 1930s, when Junchiro was writing *In Praise of Shadows*, Japan's enthusiasm for bright lights and amplification in public spaces had already transformed the night. His resigned abandonment of Ishiyama as a destination is spurred by a memory of another ruined moon-viewing, when he and his friends took out a boat on the lake at the Suma Temple. To his chagrin, the trees around the lake's edge were hung with garish lights in five colours. 'There was indeed a moon,' he comments wryly, 'if one strained one's eyes for it.'

My own search is urgent as I have limited time. I have discovered one temple, in the town of Arashiyama just outside Kyoto, which is advertising full-moon celebrations on the three days of the holiday weekend (Tsukimi falls on Sunday, the day before the actual full moon). Daikaku-ji was originally the country residence of Emperor Saga, but it was converted into a Shingon Buddhist temple at his command in the year 878. It is situated next to a small lake, originally used for boating by the Emperor and his courtiers, and also contains some fine painted screens. The temple's website gives more details of the celebration.

Osawa-no-ike is the oldest artificial pond in Japan. Under the Sagano moonlight, it is a beautiful sight to behold.

The Kangetsu-e ceremony originated in the time when Emperor Saga played with nobles on the boats in the Osawa pond.

At a moon-viewing party, we observe the harvest-moon. On this day, we launch a dragon-headed boat and a bird-headed boat in the pond and hold tea ceremonies. Koto music is played, which recreates the ambience of the Heian period.

The website goes on to list events taking place that include a full-moon Buddhist ceremony, along with Buddhist teaching, traditional music performances and the boat launch. It does not sound as if the event would meet with the approval of a purist like Junchiro, but I find the unashamed mix of spiritual and blatantly commercial activity rather appealing. The schedule is preceded by the ominous words: 'It is possible to be rained out.' This is my particular dread: to have crossed the world to see the moon, only to find it obscured by clouds. I would not be the first to have set out on such an expedition only to be frustrated by the weather. In *A Visit to the Kashima Shrine*, Bashō experiences similar frustrations. His party arrive at Kashima by boat, after a short rest in a stinking fisherman's hut and a journey downriver in bright moonlight. However, it starts to rain shortly after they disembark and it soon becomes obvious that viewing the rising of the full moon will be an impossibility. Good traveller that he is, on hearing that a revered priest is living in seclusion in the neighbourhood Bashō decides to give up on the moon and ask if he can seek shelter in the priest's house. At least he might learn something there to his spiritual benefit.*

---

* Bashō wore the black robe of a priest for this journey, but, as he put it, was 'neither a priest nor an ordinary man of the world . . . for I wavered ceaselessly like a bat that passes as a bird at one time and for a mouse at another'.

The tranquillity of the priest's hermitage was such that it inspired, in the words of the ancient poet, 'a profound sense of meditation' in my heart, and for a while at least I was able to forget the fretful feeling I had about not being able to see the full moon. Shortly before daybreak, however, the moon began to shine through the rifts made in the hanging clouds. I immediately wakened the priest, and with other members of the household followed him out of bed. We sat for a long time in utter silence, watching the moonlight trying to penetrate the clouds and listening to the sound of the lingering rain. It was really regrettable that I had come such a long way only to look at the dark shadow of the moon, but I consoled myself by remembering the famous lady who had returned without composing a single poem from the long walk she had taken to hear a cuckoo.

Any journey undertaken to view the full moon, whether by a twenty-first-century traveller or a seventeenth-century Japanese monk, is liable to end in disappointment. At such times I will have to take my consolation from Bashō.

The weather, at least on my arrival, seems perfect – I have exchanged the sodden English skies for a brilliant arc of blue and a heat and humidity that, combined with my lack of sleep, have me wandering the streets in a trance. I am staying in a *ryokan*, a traditional inn, in a backstreet in the Hagashiyama district of the city, where every corner seems to reveal an extraordinary temple or shrine, each of which acts as a portal into a different world. These range from the smallest – a simple glass case at the edge of the street in which a figure of the Buddha sits meditating in front of a golden full moon, accompanied only by a vase of white silk lilies – to the massive shrines and temple complexes set in elaborate gardens that are among the glories of Japan. Nothing prepares the first-time visitor for the experience of stepping through the *torii*, the gateway to a Shinto shrine, hung with the sacred rope of straw and zigzag flags of white paper that act as lightning conductors to attract the presence of the spirits. Having first picked up a copper or bamboo ladle and poured cool water over your hands and rinsed your mouth, there is something strangely moving about approaching the central shrine of such a place to find it empty, devoid of images, a warm breeze perhaps blowing some of the first maple leaves to fall around your feet, the bell rope hanging down and swaying gently, which you pull, after throwing a coin in the box, the bell making a small sound like an old tin kettle struck by a thrown pebble, enough merely to gain the attention of the wandering spirits, as you bow and clap your hands together twice as you have seen others do. I will learn on my trip that such places are the death knell to any tightly planned itinerary; entering one can be like falling through a hole in time.

One temple in particular I want to visit is Ginkaku-ji, popularly known as the Silver Pavilion, with its famous garden of raked and sculpted white and grey sand, designed to be seen by moonlight. Arriving at my *ryokan* I had been cheered to see that there was a small reproduction of the garden hanging over the low door to my room, like a blessing on my journey. Rather than take a bus I decide to walk through the foothills, beginning with a visit to the Kodansha Shrine, a Buddhist temple complex a mere ten minutes from my door. I have it almost to myself in the heat; a solitary man sits reading a newspaper in the shade of the massive gateway, his cap laid beside him, silhouetted against the brilliant greens and golds of foliage and the white light reflected from the gravel and the stone lantern in the courtyard beyond.

I am intrigued by the sounds that emanate from the trees around me: in a strange reversal of the natural environment I am used to, the insects sound melodic, like birds, and the birds sound mechanical, like wooden football rattles. In fact, the challenge for the new arrival is to work out which of the choristers in the trees have feathers and which have antennae and long, articulated back legs. I have arrived in Japan at the beginning of the cricket-singing season, much celebrated by Japanese poets. The male bell crickets – it is only the males that sing – serenade their prospective partners just as birds do and their appreciative audience has not been confined to their own species. Inhabitants of medieval Japan went out to the fields to capture fine specimens so that they could enjoy their songs at home. I stir myself to go and buy a postcard of the main shrine at Kodansha, taken at night, with the gold Buddha image it contains lit up and a full moon sailing directly overhead in an indigo sky. It is an apt reminder of my objectives at a time when I am in danger of merely finding a place in the shade, sitting back and enjoying the invisible orchestra that surrounds me.

I set off into the hills without a map and only a vague sense of the direction of Ginkaku-ji; I am in no hurry. In a backstreet I meet an ancient taxi driver with a kind, creased face and wearing a cap and white gloves and ask him for directions. He has some words of English. 'Straight,' he says, gesturing with one gloved hand, 'scramble, then right.' I take him to mean I need to climb higher before taking a right turn, while knowing deep down this can't be correct. After I have 'scrambled' for some minutes I reach the crest of a hill where I meet a man carrying a dog; he is walking up to a shrine that has an apparently endless avenue of orange *torii* over a flagstoned path leading off into the woods. We exchange greetings. When he puts the dog down – it is a bushy-haired, dachshund-like animal – I realize with a shock that it has lost its back legs, and that these have been replaced by small wheels. It seems quite happy as it trundles up the sacred path, sniffing at this and that, as dogs will. I try to take its photograph when its owner's attention is elsewhere but at the moment I press the shutter the dog rolls behind a pillar, leaving me holding an image of the empty path in my palm, as if the mutant creature is just one more apparition haunting these hills. Perhaps

he is related to the laughing fox spirits, whose images protect
these shrines. They can possess a person, entering beneath the
fingernails; at one shrine in the city I have seen two guardian fox
effigies that have been enclosed in wire cages, as if to stop them
escaping and making mischief.

At Ginkaku-ji, my solitary journey is over, at least temporarily.
We are not yet in holiday season; the heat of August has not dis-
sipated and there is the threat of autumn rain in the air. Yet I
join crowds of sightseers trooping up the long path between the
towering camellia hedges that lead us, as if blindfolded, to the
entrance. This Zen temple was established in 1482 and is set
within one of the most famous of all Japanese gardens. Ashikaga
Yoshimasa, the 8th Muromachi shogun, originally built this
place as a retirement villa, and as a kind of architectural and aesthetic response to the more famous Kinkaku-ji, or Golden
Pavilion, built by his grandfather Ashikaga Yoshimitsu. While
the elaborately gilded Golden Pavilion hovers like a vision above
water, the Silver Pavilion is famed for its dry Zen garden, its
sculpted gravel landscape coming into its own by moonlight.
European gardeners are known to create beds of flowers with
pale colours and night-opening blossoms to take advantage of
the moon's presence, but only the Chinese and Japanese seem to
build the moon into the hard architecture of a garden's design in
this way. A bed of white sand behind a bamboo fence is pains-
takingly raked into patterns said to resemble waves; at one point
it is formed into an almost impossibly perfect conical mound
with a flattened top. This is thought by some to resemble Mount
Fuji, the most sacred and most portrayed of Japan's volcanoes.
(A less romantic explanation is that the cone evolved from the
leftover sand generated by raking the wave patterns.) I should
have arrived here early, before the garden had lost its shade;
instead I followed the elusive fox spirits into the hills. Now, in
early afternoon, the sun has emerged from behind a cloud and

the sand is so bright it is almost impossible to look at. The shadows of the fence against the brightness are stark, almost three dimensional, and the sand itself, which is more like fine gravel than the sand you would find on a beach, is revealed in all its granular detail, like unrefined sugar. If nothing else, this is a perfect example of the differing effects on our visual world of the light of the moon and the sun. I move a little way away from the glare and view the garden from the other side of the small lake, against a background of pine trees and maples whose leaves are just beginning to turn. The inverted image of the mysterious moon-volcano floats on the surface of the green pool, among reflections of small bushes and carefully placed rocks, which frame it in a miniaturized landscape. A slight breeze on the water disturbs its liquid silhouette, rearranging it in the horizontal lines of a mountain in a Hiroshige print.

The woods and walkways of the extensive grounds of the temple give respite from the sun and also from the crowds. On one side they rise steeply up a hillside known as Tsukimachiyama (Moon-Waiting Mountain). Guests attending Ashikaga's moon-viewing parties would wait for the moon to show itself above the hill; at its highest point it would be reflected in the pool at the foot of the torrent known as Moon-Washing Cascade that descended from the summit. Green-and-black-striped dragon-flies jet along the course of the streams that run between steep mossy banks and then ascend vertically, joined in conjugal ecstasy, towards the canopy. The mosses beneath the trees are different shades of luminous green: a series of wooden trays displays dozens of examples, each separately labelled. They are categorized under three main headings, helpfully translated into English:

The Inhabitants of Ginkaku-ji
Moss the Interrupter
Very Important Moss (like VIP)

The moss provides a perfect habitat for wildlife: I watch for a few minutes as the lizard known as Nihon-Tokage,★ with its green-and-yellow-striped body and a bright blue tail, its armature gleaming in the sun, surfs the lichen waves beside a path, dropping out of sight to emerge with a mouthful of still-fluttering wings. This particular moss variety has star-shaped nodules that seem to echo in minute form the foliage of the pine trees beloved in Japanese gardens. It would not surprise me to learn that it has been selected for this reason. It is just the kind of attention to detail that strikes the visitor in such a place. Elderly women in white gloves kneel and remove individual blades of grass from a mossy bank to preserve its uniform smoothness: silent gardeners overhead in the pines trim the trees' foliage needle by needle, ensuring perfection.

The world resolves into visual compositions; strangely, the effect extends beyond the hushed precincts of gardens and temple grounds into the busy streets of the city. At one moment during my stay, perhaps walking home from Ginkaku-ji along the Philosopher's Path, perhaps while observing a flight of cranes across a flooded rice paddy from a Shinkansen Bullet train, or perhaps while eating cold soba noodles on a hot afternoon beside a river, I think to myself, *I will never complain about my life again*. I know this statement is unlikely to be true, even as it forms in my mind, as I have a talent for dissatisfaction; nevertheless the impulse that gives rise to it feels like a special gift.

II

At two o'clock the next morning I hear rain pattering on the tin roof of an adjoining building. It sounds like someone typing a

★ A Japanese five-lined skink.

script that does not include being able to see the moon. By the time I get up the rain has stopped but the sky is partially covered with threatening-looking clouds. I have established the nature of my quest with the woman who runs my *ryokan* and she has recommended that I choose the Shimogamo Shrine for observing the ceremony, situated at a famous beauty spot in the north of the city where the Takano and Kamo rivers meet. She rings the shrine and establishes that on the night of Tsukimi there will be a Japanese classical music performance and various other activities going on. It is clear that she has a loyalty to this temple and is mildly annoyed (beneath a veneer of impeccable courtesy) that I am suggesting travelling elsewhere for the ceremony. I am worried by the sky, however – with a day to go before Tsukimi all the signs are that, like Bashō, I will have made my journey only to find the autumn moon invisible. At least Daikaku-ji Temple begins its Tsukimi celebration this evening; if I go there tonight I double my chances of a successful outcome.

The temple is situated in a small town to the west of Kyoto called Arashiyama, on the Hozugawa River. A popular destination with Japanese tourists, the town is nestled in a valley beneath the wooded foothills of Mount Arashiyama. It is famed for its long, wooden bridge called Togetsukyo (literally 'Crossing the Moon Bridge') and the bamboo groves that climb its hillsides, as well as the many temples it contains. Bashō visited Arashiyama, and Hiroshige depicted its river and its cherry blossoms in a print in his series *Famous Views of Kyoto*. The practice of making journeys to see displays of blossom or maple leaves, of observing the autumn moon in scenic spots or attending snow-viewing parties, was already well established by the beginning of the nineteenth century. Official restrictions on travelling within Japan were circumvented by combining such trips with religious pilgrimages to revered shrines, which were permitted. Thus in Japanese culture the religious and the aesthetic impulses are combined with a love of the natural environment, as they have been since the beginning. In *The Records of a Travel-Worn Satchel*, Bashō wrote that 'all who have achieved real excellence in any art possess one thing in common, that is, a mind to obey nature, to be one with nature, throughout the four seasons of the year. Whatever such a mind sees is a flower, whatever such a mind dreams of is a moon.' The journeys undertaken to observe natural phenomena created a market for prints of particular scenes which Hiroshige and Hokusai, among many others, did their best to supply, much as eighteenth- and nineteenth-century European artists catered for aristocratic tourists by painting scenes of Rome and Venice.

Crossing the Moon Bridge spans the wide, shallow river that flows between heavily wooded conical hills, reminiscent of so many woodcuts, with Mount Arashiyama looming in the background. I walk its span, retracing the footsteps of the young men of Arashiyama, who upon reaching the age of twelve are encouraged to make the same journey, never looking back for fear of leading a life marred with bad luck. Beneath the bridge a cormorant, dressed somewhat raggedly in black like a wayfaring priest, sits on a rock drying its wings in the sun, just as they do on mudbanks in the Thames. Arashiyama is one of the few places in Japan to still have a community of men licensed to engage in *ukai* (cormorant fishing), working the river in flat-bottomed boats similar to the ones depicted by Hiroshige. On summer evenings they tout for tourists to accompany them from landing stages by the bridge, lighting fires in metal baskets at the prow of their boats to attract the fish. The *ukai* season (whether in pursuit of fish or tourists, I am not sure) ends around the time of the autumn solstice; tonight might be one of the last nights of the year on which it would be possible to take such a trip. Under normal circumstances I would have been fascinated to watch the leashed birds with metal rings around their long necks being sent overboard to dive for fish, only to be hauled back on board and forced to disgorge their catch, a perfect Marxist metaphor for the alienation of labour (on the part of the cormorants rather than the fishermen). Tonight, though, I have an appointment with the moon.

The streets in the north of the town are quieter than in its bustling centre but this evening the pedestrians I encounter all seem to be moving purposefully in one direction, with an air of quiet excitement: towards Daikaku-ji. I pause briefly at the magnificent Sagashakado Buddhist Temple; the main buildings have closed for the night but I walk around its courtyard, trying to imagine myself back into the tenth century, when this place was the mountain villa of Minamoto Toro, the model for Prince Genji in Murasaki's masterpiece. The place is eerily quiet, the sliding panels in front of the altar have been closed. Smoke still rises from the stubs of incense sticks in a free-standing brass censer in which a grey, volcanic cone marks the day's worship, a Bodhisattva's ashtray. A monk, walking quickly along a path to his residential quarters, observes me without apparent interest as I leave.

In the street, security men are waving illuminated batons guiding coaches to their parking spots and the trickle of pedestrians approaching Daikaku-ji has turned into a crowd. I stand in a queue between ropes, marshalled by cheerful monks, without being sure of what it is I am queueing for. Eventually I receive a small and rather beautiful green ticket, printed with red and black characters. It does not cover entrance to the temple, for which there is another charge. I put it away carefully, trusting that its use will become evident later. It is still light as I find myself in the great courtyard. Benches covered with red cloths have been laid out and people are eating picnics while watching a performance of koto music that is relayed throughout the temple precincts by loudspeakers. Along the shores of the lake, behind more ropes, a group of cameramen have set up their lenses pointing to the sky where the moon is scheduled to make an official appearance. Food stalls are doing a roaring trade in noodles and teriyaki, and chilled beers and soft drinks are dispensed from ice-filled dustbins.

I finally discover the purpose of the mysterious green ticket, which admits me to a tea ceremony at the Shrine of the Five Great Vidyaramas. A moon-viewing platform is built on to the eastern side of the shrine, overlooking the lake. Tables have been laid out where I join other ticket-holders for a serving of green tea and a special moon-cake, served by kimono-clad wait-resses. The dragon-headed boat and the bird-headed boat glide across the water as promised, poled by young men dressed in white and full of trippers who have booked in advance (a long and orderly queue has formed at the landing stages). An ampli-fied commentary from within the boat is audible at the shoreline. I join the crowds around the edge of the lake, where I sit on the steps of a wooden pavilion as darkness begins to gather among the trees, scalding my mouth on deep-fried shrimp and vege-table dough balls that have been cooked before my eyes. A group of children are playing an elaborate game of hide and seek among the long grasses at the water's edge; in their excitement they are prepared to overlook my all too obvious foreignness. They sit beside me in the shadow of the eaves and we all collapse in laughter as their pursuer walks past without looking up and discovering our hiding place. Once I have eaten I stroll around the perimeter of the lake. Families have brought large water-proof tablecloths on which to sit and eat and observe the sky in the time-honoured way. Students from a local art college have been commissioned to create vast electrically lit paper lanterns and sculptures along the path. With this barrage of lights and the clouds that still partially cover the sky, the moon is going to struggle to make its presence felt here. Still, it is an occasion of great cheerfulness. I ignore Junchiro Tanizaki's disapproval from beyond the grave; with apologies to his ghost, I am enjoying myself.

I return to the temple and remove my shoes to follow the wooden walkways that lead from one building to another, their boards polished smooth by countless feet. Away from the crowds I come across a raised red-and-gold pavilion that is vibrating with the chanting of a group of monks. Screens have been rolled back to reveal the ornate interior of the shrine, its gold images and heavy lamps gleaming. The six monks all appear to be in their early twenties. Dressed in black, white and mustard-coloured robes, they give themselves with complete concentration to the task. Their voices are perfectly in rhythm so that the words they repeat are percussive in their intensity. We are in the engine house; the sound of the chanting is a well-oiled motor turning over, keeping the temple afloat. Or perhaps the temple is a hive and the monks are bees. Every so often one of them strikes a small bell and they pause, clap twice and bow and those assembled all stand in silence until the chant begins again. Then, at a signal I do not notice, they stop and walk off down a pathway in single file.

Back in the courtyard I search for the guest of honour. As the sky darkens, the moon emerges through a light mist, above a low bank of cloud. It looks fractured, like a broken plate, then like a thin slice of onion bubbling in oil. Only a few people seem to notice its arrival among the general busyness and after a minute or so it disappears again. A few minutes later, I look up at the sky once more, just as the full moon steps out, like a bashful actress on to the stage, from behind a curtain of mist and rain clouds, sailing up into the clear sky, a perfect golden orb. A man standing next to me applauds softly, reverentially. A younger man takes a photo on his phone and shows it to his girlfriend

(I am beginning to think that nothing in Japan exists until it has been recorded in this way). I too lift my camera and pluck an image from the sky of the moon above a temple roof. It seems the most appropriate way to join with the homage being paid on this night by a people who still celebrate the moon's arrival and the light it brings in one of the most technologically advanced nations on earth.

In the courtyard, on a raised dais, senior monks assemble; they include one very elderly man in a red robe who I take to be the abbot of the monastery, who has to be helped up the steps. He waves a thin stick, like a wand, over an offering of the fruits of the harvest arranged at one end of the platform, facing the point in the sky where the moon is hanging. The chanting has started again, this time accompanied by a large drum, emphasizing its hypnotic, rhythmic quality. Next to the platform stand a line of women dressed in white kimonos trimmed in red, hands folded demurely. When the ritual is completed and the monks get down from the platform, they walk across the courtyard to a gate in the wall, accompanied by their female attendants. Without ceremony, the oldest monk slips away through the gate. Those who remain are surrounded by a surging crowd of well-wishers, cameras and phones held aloft. One of them, who appears to be master of ceremonies tonight, suggests good-naturedly that rather than filling up their memory cards with images of unphotogenic monks, the assembled crowd should be taking pictures of their beautiful kimono-clad attendants; without further encouragement these ladies line up obligingly in a carefully posed group. Dapper in their ceremonial robes of purple and gold, the jocular monks disperse as the cameras begin to flash in earnest, speaking easily with those who still press forward to pay their respects.

At the edge of the lake the food stalls, their sweating cooks lit up by lanterns as they ladle, fry and pour, take on a medieval appearance. Children still run in and out of the shadows, their screams of laughter adding to the general hubbub. Reluctantly I take my leave, aware of the long bus ride back to the city and the strict curfew in place at my *ryokan*, emphasized in many urgent notices taped up at the front entrance. A senior monk is walking along the street that leads to the temple, thanking the ticket-collectors and security guards, who seem to be competing with the depth of their respectful bows. He graciously acknowledges my appreciation also, with an amused inclination of the head. During my long wait at the bus stop I am accompanied only by the moon, which for a few hours at least will grace a cloudless sky; the same moon celebrated by Bashō and Lady Murasaki, shining now on the empty streets of Arashiyama just as in a few hours it will shine on the streets of Paris, London and New York.

Cats' Eyes and a McDonald's Moon

I rise the next morning with the residual glow of one who feels that they have been, at least for a moment, in the right place at the right time. It is gently but persistently raining, meaning that any celestial events tonight in Kyoto will be invisible. A good day, I decide, on which to take my leave.

I am heading almost as far south as you can go in mainland Japan, to Kagoshima, in Kyushu. An unpretentious, bustling city nearly 1,000 kilometres as the crane flies from Tokyo, Kagoshima is not usually high on the tourist itinerary. The seat of the Shimazu clan, who ruled the area from the twelfth century until the Meiji Restoration 700 years later, it was permitted to trade with the outside world throughout the period of Japan's seclusion policy, during which the nation's rulers otherwise forbade contact with foreigners. It was through the Port of Kagoshima that much Western technology, particularly artificial lighting, first entered Japan. If Kyoto represents the ancient, pre-Edo kingdom and is the perfect place in which to explore the place of moonlight in Japanese culture, Kagoshima is its antithesis, the birthplace of the luridly lit night sky synonymous with the contemporary Asian city.

Situated at the extreme southern edge of Japan and exposed to attack from the navies of other nations, the city's encounters with Western culture were not always peaceful ones. As if it did not face enough threats from outside, Kagoshima is situated next to its own active volcano. Sitting in the middle of Kinkō Bay, Sakurajima was formerly an island, but when it erupted in 1914, killing thirty-five local residents, it emitted such a large quantity of lava that it is now joined to the mainland by a narrow isthmus. Before the 1914 eruption the volcano had been dormant for more than a century. Since then it has stubbornly refused to go back to sleep, regularly spouting columns of smoke and ash kilometres up into the air, like a mischievous elephant sporting in the waters of the bay. Those that live on the slopes of the volcano, including the farmers who grow the famous football-size white radish *sakuradaikon* in its lava-rich soil, are trained from birth to be ready to leave at a moment's notice. Over 600,000 people live within range of a serious eruption.

The earth's crust is flexible, not rigid; it moves in response to the gravitational pull of both the moon and the sun. Some researchers postulate a correlation between volcanic eruptions and these 'earth tides' that is most marked when the moon is closest to the earth (at its perigee) and when it is full. In the deep space of the internet one can find articles and papers that argue both for and against a direct relationship between the moon's influence and volcanic activity; the balance would appear currently to be against. Yet however dubious the science, the connection between the full moon and volcanic eruptions exists in the popular imagination and is embodied in the parallel world of art.

Kagoshima is not, of course, the only maritime city to sit in the lee of a famously destructive volcano. In the eighteenth century, a resurgently active Vesuvius attracted thousands of early tourists to Naples and gave birth to its own genre image, of an erupting volcano at night, its jets of scalding magma contrasted against the cold light of the moon. I have already decided both to study these works and to visit Naples, which today enjoys twin-city status with Kagoshima. There are strange echoes between the histories of the two cities. Both were southern kingdoms, ruled by colourful dynasties; both were major ports through which contact was made with foreign civilizations;

both had their active volcano; and the power of both was eclipsed by the creation of the modern nation state.

Arriving at Kagoshima Station after a journey of several hours, a passage of time demarcated by a succession of small acts of kindness and breathtaking efficiency, all washed down with cups of green tea, I make my way to an information point to pick up a map. European tourists are not as common a sight in Kagoshima as they are in Kyoto, and the staff behind the counter seem rather startled to see me. They clearly know something important that I don't, but frustratingly they cannot make this obtuse foreigner understand what it is. Eventually an English-speaker is located and pushed forwards. She blinks and bows and opens and closes her mouth soundlessly, before finding the words. 'You know,' she says, gazing anxiously into my face, 'typhoon coming?'

Typhoon? Now that is a word I recognize. When? Now? At what time? Instantly out of my depth linguistically, I resort to gestures, tapping my watch and pointing to the calendar on the wall in what I hope is a questioning way. Do typhoons in Japan stick to schedules as closely as trains? Everyone is too busy nodding and saying the word 'typhoon' to each other to take much notice. Eventually my meaning becomes clear. They look up at the television on a shelf above their heads that I now see is carrying a weather report, complete with complicated high-tech graphics and satellite images of the approaching storm. 'Today-tomorrow,' the woman tells me, and her words again are echoed with much nodding among the other staff. 'Check TV.' I resolve to do so. Any intention I may have had of trawling the city for a perfect, inexpensive and traditional *ryokan* evaporates. I need somewhere with a television, that won't blow down in a high wind. I head for the attractively solid business hotel attached to the station, owned by the Japanese railway network. No paper walls for me.

As the evening draws in I take a tram down to the harbour to see if I can catch a glimpse of Sakurajima. The rain has grown heavier, but the temperature has risen with the humidity, making it too hot to wear a coat. Fortunately, as I leave the hotel, the receptionist bows and holds out an umbrella, one of the transparent kind popular in Japan that allows you to be right underneath its cover and still see out. Despite the fact that I seem to be the only European visible in the crowds thronging the city, nobody pays me any attention, even those forced to take an adjoining seat to mine on the tram. They must, I begin to think, be making an active effort to avoid seeing me, as if my presence is simply too inexplicable to merit acknowledgement. It is a pleasant, heady feeling, like being the Invisible Man. I experiment as I walk towards the sea. If I greet people, with a bow and a 'good afternoon' in Japanese, they respond, with perfect politeness and apparent lack of surprise. If I do not, I retain my invisibility to a remarkable degree. It is part of the character of the place, I realize, as distinct from that of Kyoto as the local cuisine that I am anxious to try.

Tonight is full moon according to the Western, rather than the Japanese, lunar calendar, and I had fantasized about seeing the volcano lit by moonlight across Kinkō Bay. Despite the fact that it is a mere four kilometres away, serviced by ferries that run around the clock, Sakurajima is all but invisible across the water through a veil of rain, a volcano-shaped smudge on the sky. The docks are deserted apart from a man emptying the bins in the small pavilions built on the seafront, and a tortoiseshell cat without a tail that follows him, scampering between the shelter of one pavilion and the next, then lying down on a bench with its back legs stretched straight out, licking a forepaw. They are ignoring each other in a companionable kind of way, but acknowledge my presence politely enough.

There is a sadness associated with the full moon of autumn;

while the moon is eternal, on earth seasons pass and people blaze briefly and then fall, like the leaves of the maple. Perhaps this is why the moon often features in the 'death poems', or *jisei*, traditionally written in the last moments of a poet's life. The haiku poet Ihara Saikaku, who died on the eighth day of the eighth month in 1730, wrote:

> I borrow moonlight
> for this journey of
> a million miles.

At the time of viewing the autumn moon, haiku poets often took up their brushes to describe its beauty. In his death poem, Koha, who died in 1897, wrote

> I cast the brush aside –
> from here on, I'll speak to the moon
> face to face.

The most concise and enigmatic of all death poems must be that of Shisui, who died on the ninth day of the ninth month in 1764, aged only forty-four, of whom it has been written: 'During his last moments, Shisui's followers requested that he write a death poem. He grasped his brush, painted a circle, cast the brush aside, and died.'★

The circle (*enso*) is one of the most important symbols in Zen, meaning both the void and enlightenment, everything and nothing. The full moon of autumn, like Shisui's circle, is a reminder of the transitory nature of all things, as well as a symbol of enlightenment.

★ 'The Sound of the One Hand', trans. Yoel Hoffmann (New York: Bantam, 1977), cited in Yoel Hoffmann, *Japanese Death Poems: Written by Zen Monks and Haiku Poets on the Verge of Death* (Tokyo: Tuttle Publishing, 1986), from which all translations of death poems are taken.

I return to my room after buying a simple meal from a stall in the arcade that connects the station to my hotel. That night I dream the typhoon has arrived but wake to find it is only the air-conditioning switching on in my room.

The next day the rain is heavier and a wind has got up, tugging at my ankles as I make my way to the ferry for Sakurajima. The other passengers on board are clustered around the television, gesticulating and commenting on the weather report. Some appear concerned, others are laughing with excitement. The typhoon is taking its time wandering up the archipelago, stopping off to beat up individual islands on its way towards Kagoshima. Footage from Okinawa shows palm trees bent double, crashing waves and metal vending machines being knocked over and blown along the street. In the satellite pictures that accompany the reports, the storm spins like a Catherine wheel. It does not appear a completely sensible day on which to visit an island, even if it is located just the other side of a sheltered harbour. Will I be able to return? In rudimentary Japanese I manage to ask my fellow travellers when the typhoon will be arriving in Kagoshima. There seems to be general agreement that it won't be with us before nine o'clock tomorrow morning, which is reassuring. I go out on deck, into a fierce wind. Kinkō Bay is famous for its leaping dolphins but today there is no sight of them. Instead, a submarine has surfaced, emerging from one watery world into another, its grey hull dolphin-like in the choppy seas.

Even as the boat nears port the volcano continues to hide behind its veil of rain, present only as a looming shadow, a solidity hanging over us as we prepare to disembark. I think sadly of my plans, dissolving in the rainwater rushing off the deck and into the sea. I had intended to hire a bicycle and circumnavigate the volcano; to walk in its lava fields; to take the sightseeing coach to its summit and peer into its smoking rim. None of these now appear remotely practical. One option remains, however. There is a sacred hot spring, or *rotenburo*, on the island, in which I wish to bathe. To immerse myself in waters heated by the immense furnace that lies just beneath the surface of southern Japan seems a good way to enter into the spirit of the place. A small minibus is parked outside the dock, to take passengers to the hot spring, located within the grounds of a hotel a few miles away. I climb aboard with a small group of other passengers. They, like me, are determined not to let the weather prevent them from having a good time. Today is a public holiday, following the Tsukimi weekend. There is nothing more traditional in Japan than to make a visit to a hot spring as part of a holiday. It seems that a communal soak in hot water, whether an indoor *onsen* of the type that one finds in traditional hotels, or a *rotenburo*, serves to loosen some of the intricate network of formalities and hierarchies that can make Japanese society stifling. I completely empathize with this passion for hot springs, particularly outdoor ones. I have often succumbed to the urge to hop into lakes, streams, ponds, rivers and even fjords in weather conditions others would find unappealing. There's no quicker way to feel completely alive. At the same time I have always enjoyed an extremely hot bath as a way of erasing the day's troubles. In light of these predilections, an outdoor volcanically heated spring sounds good to me.

Arriving at the hotel, my travelling companions make their way to the gift shop, while I look for the entrance to the *rotenburo*. At a booth I hire towels and a white *yukata* robe which bathers here must wear in the water to cover their nakedness (unlike at other *onsen* baths), out of respect for the sacredness of the site. After going down a stairway I cram my oversized European feet into the largest sandals available and enter a lift, eventually emerging into the rain once more. The location is spectacular. Standing at the top of a path leading down past a changing hut I can see the pool at the foot of the cliff, a few yards from the shore. Rain is falling steadily, reminding me of an old poem:*

> Long rain of May
> The whole world is
> A single sheet of paper
> Under the clouds.

Through the steam rising from the surface of the spring I can see a dozen or so white-clad figures in the water, squatting with arms outstretched, holding murmured conversations with other bathers, or sitting on stones, apparently lost in thought. A large camphor tree growing out of the foot of the cliff spreads its branches over the pool. Hanging between two rocks, a twisted, tasselled rope of straw marks this as a sacred place, favoured by the *kami* (spirits). Standing at the top of the path, unnoticed, I feel like I am witnessing a scene from a dream. In the hut I shower, change into my robe and walk down to the pool. None of the bathers shows any surprise at my arrival. It takes a few seconds to adjust to the scalding heat of the water and then I sink up to my neck, the white robe billowing around me. A man, wearing a small towel over his head to protect his bald pate from the rain, is chatting with a woman who sits on a rock like an elderly mermaid, albeit one somewhat incongruously wearing a wet dressing gown. I soak, gradually becoming aware of a sub-sonic, muttered conversation that forms a background to the bathers' languid splashing; the volcano is grumbling to

* A hokku from a series of linked poems by Nishiyama Sōin and Ihara Saikaku.

itself. This is the sound Shelley noted when he visited Pompeii, describing it in his *Ode to Naples*:

> [I] heard
> The Mountain's slumberous voice at intervals
> Thrill through those roofless halls;
> The oracular thunder penetrating shook
> The listening soul in my suspended blood;
> I felt that Earth out of her deep heart spoke –

'[O]racular thunder' seems a good description of the sound-track to this sacred place. The roots of the camphor tree form a cave, large enough to enter. It is full of stone deities, a natural temple at the sea's edge. One or two of the bathers wade across the pool to pay their respects and once they have finished I follow suit. The hollow beneath the tree is only large enough for one person at a time. It is a magical, secret space, with the huge weight and ancient, primal energy of the tree bearing down above one's head, seemingly held in balance only by the trappings of simple, human ritual.

Back on the mainland I walk from the port up through back-streets towards my hotel. I am dog-tired now; it is as if the bath has finally relaxed me, ridding my body of the adrenalin that has kept my brain spinning through sleepless nights. It is early evening and people are flocking noisily into restaurants but I don't feel hungry. An immense weariness seeps up from the pavement through the soles of my feet, but still I keep walking. All I need, I decide, is to find somewhere quiet to sit and drink a cold beer. The enthusiasm with which the people around me are rushing to eat is exhausting even to watch. There is little chance of hearing what haiku poets refer to as 'the voice of autumn' in this bustling street, or of detecting the poignant melancholy of this time of year, such a feature of the art and literature of Japan.

One woodblock print in particular has been on my mind; from Utagawa Kuniyoshi's series *One Hundred Poems, One Hundred Poets*, it is called *Palanquin Bearers on the Road at Night* and illustrates a poem by Ōe no Chisato:

> I am overcome by the sadness
> of a thousand, thousand things
> even though it is not autumn
> for me alone.

Most artists approaching this scene portray the poet himself contemplating the autumn moon, but Kuniyoshi prefers to universalize its message by making the active subject of his design a common man. Two palanquin bearers are proceeding along a lonely country road in the moonlight, passing an ancient pine tree and a wayside shrine. Their litter is empty, its green curtains pulled back so that they are effectively carrying a moving frame for the landscape beyond. The bearer at the front is pushing purposely forwards, but the man at the back has turned his head aside to look up at the full moon, which has not one but two haloes, delicately and skilfully rendered by the printer. Perhaps his attention has been captured by the poignant call of the migrating geese that seem about to form a *kanji* character as they cross its surface. Even as he trots along the road, probably to collect his master from some revelry, he is lost in contemplation, proving that the mood of this season is not just felt by the educated of noble birth, but by all people; including, presumably, the thousands who would have bought such a print as this to adorn their homes.

To be on an isolated road at night is one thing, but there is no place one can feel as lonely as in the middle of a crowd. After continuing for what feels like several miles through the throng, I see an illuminated sign featuring a tilted neon tankard with a foaming head. I bound up the concrete steps two at a time, to find myself entering a dark corridor ending in a heavy wooden door, as if I had blundered on to the set of a David Lynch film. This feeling is heightened when I push open the door to find myself in a silent, dimly lit room panelled in dark wood, entirely empty except for three immaculately clad barmen in white shirts, black waistcoats and black bow ties, standing behind a bar in front of a wall of neatly arrayed bottles. Their faces register surprise at my sudden appearance and within seconds they are clustered around me and we are exchanging bows. Very sorry, they say, very sorry. What's the matter? Are they going to throw me out? I'm not going without a fight. Cover charge, one of them explains and the other two nod, repeating the words. OK, how much? It turns out to be the equivalent of around five dollars, a small price to pay for entrance to this Valhalla. Once we have negotiated our way through this potentially tricky social situation, we all beam with relief and I am led to a stool at the bar, where I receive their undivided attention.

The barmen represent three generations of their craft. The bar manager is around forty years of age, with buzz-cut hair, rimless glasses and a mouth permanently pursed in an expression indicating an all-encompassing discretion. This is someone who could be trusted with the darkest secrets of a drunken salaryman. Every move he makes is with the utmost elegance and poise. Next to him in rank is an older man, in his sixties perhaps, with a pleasant, open face, thinning hair and a cheerful smile. Finally there is a young man in his early twenties, virtually an apprentice, with film-star good looks. Tonight, the barmen's usual roles are reversed: the youngest has to take the lead in caring for their unexpected visitor, as he is the only one who speaks English with any fluency. He asks me what I would like to drink, hiding any trace of disappointment at the sheer foolishness of asking for beer when three highly skilled cocktail technicians are on standby – the equivalent of being granted a wish by a genie and asking for popcorn – and puts everything he can into the task. An apparently clean glass is freshly rinsed and polished dry, the beer pumped into the glass with a hose and the head sculpted to a mathematically correct millimetre above the rim, before it is set before me on a mat. Three men watch me, eyebrows raised, as I lift it to my lips. Very good, I tell them. Ah, very good! My words are repeated and we all relax a little. The young man has learned his English in Houston where he has a cousin. Proudly he shows me a lapel button he is wearing, bought when he visited the NASA space programme site, the memorial to a different, seemingly abandoned quest for the moon. Ah, so you are an astronaut, I joke. They all laugh. This is a word that needs no translation.

We begin to talk about his time in America. The conversation is a collaborative enterprise. Whenever he is lost for a word the young barman turns to his manager, who goes over to the till, beneath which is an ancient Japanese–English dictionary. He finds the word, points to it on the page and then replaces the dictionary on its shelf and waits, hands behind his back, with attentive, furrowed brow. At first he claims that he enjoyed the nine months he spent there. Then he admits that he found things too large – the roads, the food, the people. He comes from a small island, he explains, far south from here, Yoron-jima, one of the Amami Islands. His island is small enough to walk around – its circumference is almost exactly the distance of a marathon and its highest point is less than 100 metres above sea level. 'When I go to sleep there,' he tells me, 'I hear the sea.' The island has its own language, still spoken by the older generation, and its own distinct culture. Three times a year, at the Kotohira Shrine situated at the top of the island's highest hill, the inhabitants perform the Full Moon Night Dance. 'My people,' he says, 'are like Japanese Indians' – by which he means Native Americans – and now I look at him more closely it is obvious that his

skin colour and his features vary from those of his companions, his high cheekbones speaking of seafaring forebears borne
ashore by different currents. He is intensely proud of his birthplace and ancestry. His parents and his grandparents still live on
the island. 'If I worked in a bar there,' he says, 'all the customers
would be my family and I would not be able to charge them!'
His grandmother is ninety-eight and still very strong. He loves
her very much and speaks with her regularly on the phone. He
is visibly moved as he tells me about his home and his life there;
the other two barmen, when not proffering the dictionary, nod
respectfully and sympathetically. It is a story they have heard
before. My empty glass is silently removed and a fresh one put
in its place. Do you have places like this in London, they ask me?
Not as good, I assure them. And I do at that moment believe
that I have stumbled on the best bar in the world.

The next day the rain has eased slightly and the typhoon still
appears to be delayed in the sidings somewhere, running behind
schedule. I decide to visit the famous garden of Sengan-en, the
home of the Shimazu clan, who ruled here for 700 years, from the
late twelfth to the mid-nineteenth century, gradually extending
their sphere of influence, through force of arms, throughout
southern Japan. It is there, rather than in the streets of the city
centre, that I hope to find objects which symbolize the birth of
modern Japan. Whatever the prevailing attitude of the shogunate
of Japan, the Shimazu continued to look outward, as befitted the
rulers of a region of traders, while retaining their own traditions.
By special dispensation during Japan's period of seclusion local
merchants were permitted to trade with the Chinese Ryukyu
Islands and the Amami Islands. It was on Kyushu's shores that the
first European sailors and missionaries landed and in Kyushu that
the incident occurred which brought Japan and the West into
their first direct conflict in the modern era.

In 1862, a British merchant named Charles Lennox Richardson, who had been working in China, decided to visit Japan on his way home. There was only a very limited European presence in the country at the time and a degree of tension between the barely tolerated foreigners and their host nation. Richardson was riding with three friends on the Tōkaidō road when his party met the retinue of Shimazu Hisamitsu, a regent and commander of the Satsuma navy. Rather than dismounting and prostrating themselves, as tradition dictated, Richardson and his companions continued to ride along the side of the road until they were parallel with the Daimyo's litter. Their mistake was to compound their rudeness by approaching closer than decorum allowed; the regent's samurai guards reacted instantly, attacking them with their swords. The two men and a woman who were with Richardson escaped, but Richardson fell from his horse, fatally wounded. Hisamitsu gave the order for his men to deliver the *todome*, or *coup de grâce*.

The war that ensued was short, but its consequences were far-reaching and unexpected. The British navy was dispatched to Kagoshima where they captured some merchant ships belonging to the Shimazu clan at anchor in the bay. To their surprise, they were fired on by the city's forts, one cannon ball beheading two English sailors at once. The British ships stood offshore, beyond the reach of the Japanese round-shot cannon, and trained their vastly superior arsenal on Kagoshima, pounding it in a barrage that destroyed around 500 houses. Fortunately the city had already been evacuated. What is interesting about this incident is the way the Shimazu reacted to it. Not, as you might expect, by retreating from contact with their attackers. If Japan was to avoid being overrun, they decided, they needed not only to know their enemy but also to understand their enemy's technology. A mere two years after the war a party of nineteen young students from Kagoshima were sent by the Satsuma government to Britain, to learn all they could about Western science. Contemporary photographs show them in three-piece suits, sporting canes, hats and bow ties, dandified ambassadors from one civilization who have already affected the trappings of another. A brass statue of these intrepid pioneers stands outside Kagoshima's main railway station.

In the gardens of Sengan-en, I have been told, I will find evidence of an intellectual curiosity that preceded both the arrival of the British fleet in Kagoshima's harbour and the students' historic journey. Commissioned by a Shimazu lord in the sixteenth century, Sengan-en is a classic example of the 'borrowed view' motif, central to Japanese garden design of the period. The volcano across the bay appears to float in the middle of the lawn – the later arrival of a main road and a railway line are deftly hidden by a hedge – and parties of Japanese tourists huddle together taking photographs of each other, wearing its cone like a hat. What I am most interested in are the grey, sculptural stone shapes that punctuate the garden. These are not the artfully placed boulders that characterize so many Japanese gardens; they have been shaped, as well as placed, by man. Yet they are as hard to read as if they were the strokes of an ink brush forming the characters of an unknown language that had been petrified by the glance of some demon long ago. It is only by the helpful wooden information boards beside them that I recognize them as the very thing that attracted me here in the first place. *Lion Stone Lantern; Crane-shaped Stone Lantern.*

Such lanterns are of course commonplace in the grounds of temples and gardens in Japan but one in particular of those at Sengan-en is historically significant, as it was the first light of any kind in the whole of Japan to be connected to a gas supply. The 27th Shimazu Lord Nariakira commissioned scholars to translate all the books they could find on the technology. A gas holder was installed under the bathroom of the villa and lamps in the garden were lit for the first time in the summer of 1857. The Crane Lantern is situated on a small mound near the perimeter hedge; it is said to be the first light of any kind to be connected to a gas supply in Japan. The single piece of stone representing the flying crane is a curved shape about twelve feet long, balanced on top of a circle stone, a composition as simple and elemental as a sculpture by Isamu Noguchi. One can only imagine the impression the lanterns made on those who were invited to stroll in the garden on a hot August night. One thing their light revealed was that, before the challenge presented by the arrival of a foreign fleet, there was a hunger among those ruling this remote province to understand Western technology. Fifteen years after the lanterns were first lit at Sengan-en and nine years after the bombardment of Kagoshima, gas lighting was introduced to the city of Yokohama. This garden, then, was where the rout of Junchiro Tanizaki's 'world of shadows' began and the modern, brightly illuminated Japanese city was born.

There is another example of a distinctly Japanese technology commemorated at Sengan-en that long pre-dates the nineteenth-century industrial revolution. Behind the villa I find the simple wooden *torii* of a shrine, with a noticeboard more than usually bedecked with the wooden plaques that people buy at such places and inscribe with their own prayers. To my surprise, the plaques are all decorated with a picture of a pair of fat and contented-looking cats, one white and one yellow. This is a cat shrine. The 17th Shimazu Lord Yoshihiro led a military expedition into Korea in the late sixteenth century. Among the possessions that accompanied him were seven cats, brought along not as personal pets but as timepieces – he could tell the time of day by looking at the size of the pupils of their eyes. Only two of the cats survived the expedition and returned to Kagoshima, where they were enshrined on their death at Sengan-en. These faithful feline retainers are the focus of a kind of cult here, it seems; the plaques bear messages from countless cat-owners, imploring the *kami* to keep their own much-loved pets safe. On 10 June every year, the watchmakers and jewellers of Kagoshima still come to this shrine to celebrate Toki-no-Kinenbi, the day in the Japanese calendar that commemorates time.

The artist Kuniyoshi was a great lover of cats, as was his collaborator, the author Santō Kyōzan. Something tells me they would have appreciated this cat shrine. Together they created an illustrated novel called *Oborozuki neko no sōshi* (Hazy Moon Cat Tales) that was a best-seller in Japan in the 1840s. For a time during Kuniyoshi's career, the government censors forbade the making of prints portraying popular kabuki actors. To get around the restrictions he and Kyōzan recast the kabuki tales with cats as heroes, dressed in kabuki costumes. The content of the stories changed with humorous effect to reflect the actors' altered state. One print illustrates a scene in which a shower of gold coins falls on the heroine's head when she strikes an enchanted bowl – except the coins are replaced with a different kind of deluge, this time of dried mackerel. The decorations on the kimono of the feline actress, on close inspection, reveal themselves to be not plum blossoms but motifs of cat collars and bells. These playful, animated prints, rather than the more traditional portrayal of the autumn moon in *Palanquin Bearers on the Road at Night*, are characteristic of the works for which Kuniyoshi is best remembered. His depictions of heroes battling outlandish monsters prefigure manga illustrations of a century later, his assimilation of European influences forging a new synthesis of East and West. The full moon plays a role once more in his print *The Loyal Retainers Attack Kira Yoshinaka's Mansion at Night*. The architecture of the buildings that are under attack, with its dramatic, receding perspective, is copied from a contemporary Dutch book illustration. It is a cold night; the pine trees that rise around the courtyard are capped with snow. One of the samurai can be seen giving meat to the guard dogs, to quiet them. Others are scaling the wall with a rope ladder, its delicate shadow accurately rendered in spectral grey. A man who must be the commander of the raiding party is pointing, giving silent directions to another; the moment is pregnant with tension and foreboding. This is modern moonlight, sinister rather than benevolent. The moon, like Kuniyoshi's art, has undergone a cultural shift.

Before I leave Kagoshima I am determined to pay a last visit to the bar and say goodbye to my friends there. Once again it takes a while to find, partly because I make the mistake of entering a shopping mall in the maze-like interior of which I become disorientated, ejected eventually into a neighbourhood I do not recognize. When I finally reach the bar, there is already another customer occupying one of the stools, a man who speaks some English and joins in the effusive greetings I receive.

'Oh,' the youngest barman says, 'I am glad you came back. Last time you were here I told you a lie.'

Really, I say, rather surprised at this confession. What was that?

'I told you my grandmother is ninety-eight,' he said. 'Afterwards I rang her and she told me she is only ninety-four.'

He seems relieved to have unburdened himself and pours me a beer, with the same attention to detail as before. I exchange pleasantries with the young man sitting next to me. He is insisting that as soon as I finish my beer he be allowed to buy me a cocktail. The barmen watch this exchange attentively. The drink he is offering is one devised by the youngest barman. 'He won a competition with this cocktail!' the man tells me, and the older barmen nod their heads vigorously. A photograph album is brought from behind the bar and in it, sure enough, I see our hero onstage at a black-tie event receiving an award, his eyes cast modestly downward, much as they are tonight while his achievement is the subject of animated discussion. 'If you like, I make it for you,' he offers. How can I refuse? The cocktail is called Tuvalu, named for the first island nation facing evacuation as the result of global warming. Tuvalu is a string of islands, none more than five metres above sea level, inhabited for around 3,000 years. The rising salt-water table looks set to change all that. It is already destroying deep-rooted crops like coconut and taro and eroding the coral reef. The cocktail is a poignant tribute from an inhabitant of one archipelago to the people of another. Will his own home be next to be threatened by the encroaching sea? Will the Full Moon Dance, performed on Yoron-jima for who knows how many centuries, cease to exist? We drink with serious faces; the glass in my hand seems weighted with significance.

Typhoon weather is not ideal for moon-viewing. The sky remains stubbornly overcast the whole of the rest of the time I am in Japan. The only moonlight I encounter is in the works of Japanese literature I read in my room at night. On the last evening before I leave I am walking back to my hotel from downtown Kyoto when I notice something in the window of a twenty-four-hour McDonald's. A large poster depicts a cartoon landscape, above which rides a full, golden moon, complete with rabbit. Halfway between earth and moon hangs a hamburger, topped with a fried egg. Another rabbit leaps from among the stands of pampas grass on earth in an attempt to reach it. Why? What is going on in this picture? Then it dawns on me. Even in the world of twenty-first-century fast food, the old traditions take on new forms and, in some sense, survive. McDonald's, while busily engaged in exporting its anodyne, globalized version of American culture, is equally quick to spot a local marketing opportunity. In its own way, it is marking the autumn moon festival. This week it is running a special promotion on Tsukimi-burgers.

PART THREE

Vesuvio

The Alarming Mountain: Naples, Vesuvius and the Moon

On April 19, 1787, 10h 36' sidereal time, Dr Herschel discovered three volcanoes in different places of the dark part of the new moon; two of them seemed to be almost extinct, but the third shewed an actual eruption of fire, or luminous matter, resembling a small piece of burning charcoal, covered by a thin coat of white ashes; it had a degree of brightness about it, as strong as that with which such a coal would be seen to glow in faint daylight.

Falconer's New Universal Dictionary of the Marine, 1815 Edition

I

Naples has always confounded visitors. Enchanting, frustrating, occasionally dangerous, alive with conversation, music and traffic noise, it is a city that never stops communicating. Simultaneously a stage set and a cauldron, it combines beauty and ugliness, elegance and abject poverty, just as it did when artists, writers and Grand Tourists flocked here in centuries past. They came to see the Sibyl's cave, Virgil's tomb and (later) the ruins of Pompeii and Herculaneum. Above all, eighteenth- and nineteenth-century travellers were drawn by the spectacle of a smouldering and occasionally erupting Vesuvius sending up its smoke signals across the bay. The volcano was and is, as Dickens wrote in *Pictures from Italy*, 'the genius of the scene', the city's most enduring symbol, casting the shadow of its presence equally across the lives of beggars and courtesans, scholars, thieves and kings. The ideal way to view it was at night, when moonlight silvered the Bay of Naples; a panorama so beautiful, an old Neopolitan saying had it, that on moonlit nights even the fishes fell in love. Moonlit views of Vesuvius and of the bay, ranging from full-scale oil paintings to cheap local *vedute*, were carried home by visitors in the eighteenth and nineteenth centuries in their hundreds, making moonlight, for a time, one of Campania principal exports.

As an object, Vesuvius concentrated in itself the aesthetic, the literary and the scientific impulses of modern Europe, providing both a destination for intrepid travellers and a focus for inquiring minds. It could not have fulfilled its function better if it had been specifically designed for an age when poets attended scientific lectures and scientists wrote like poets. Through its own destructive dynamism it had extinguished a notable slice of the ancient world at a stroke, only to reveal it perfectly preserved centuries later as if by a sleight of hand. In doing so it provided an example of both the awesome power of nature and the fragility of man's achievements, themes that appealed deeply to the Romantic imagination. The subject of intensive research and correspondence between the learned minds of Europe, Vesuvius held the key to a greater understanding of the formation of the earth itself. It was therefore a mountain of the mind, a cog in the mechanism that affected a massive shift in humankind's understanding of both its own origins and the history of the planet it called home.

There is no moon on the night I arrive and stagger into a cheap hotel on the Piazza Garibaldi, outside the main station. Named after the man who was welcomed into the city after conquering Sicily and who set off from here to unify Italy, the piazza, with its insane traffic, its streetwalkers and street-hawkers plying their trade between the bus stops and building sites, is perhaps a fitting commemoration of the collapse of a kingdom. I would have preferred to arrive by ship from Genoa, like Mark Twain, or overland from Rome like Johann Wolfgang von Goethe, travelling a century before the American writer, rather than hurtling here in the modern manner, but I do not have access to such reserves of time. It was a long way from northern Europe to Naples for those embarking on the Grand Tour, when the journey had to be made by ship or horse-drawn transport. For most it represented the southernmost point of their excursion into Italy, a time of rest and entertainment at the opera house or the royal court, before the long journey northwards.

Naples in the eighteenth century was an independent kingdom with a monarchy as colourful as its citizens, where the ancient world was close enough to touch and a pleasant frisson of danger could be experienced on the slopes of mainland Europe's only active volcano. By the time it became a regular stop on the Grand Tour, it already had a long history as a destination for those seeking both relaxation and immersion in a rich and foreign culture. For the Romans, the Greek settlement of Neapolis represented an escape from their somewhat regimented society, a place in which to experience Greece's much-admired culture and to taste *otium*, the life of refined leisure. The local population worshipped Aphrodite, goddess of love, Dionysus, god of wine, and Demeter, the goddess of the harvest, a potent combination that resulted in orgiastic rites of the kind recorded by the Roman historian Livy. It was an epic city where, legend has it, Virgil wrote the *Aeneid* and Horace composed his aphorisms, the most famous of which, 'Carpe Diem', remains the city's unofficial motto. (It is easy to see how a life philosophy could be built upon these two words in a place that lives constantly under the threat of its own extinction.)

Locals were happy to provide eighteenth-century tourists with a landscape to match the one they carried in their minds as a result of their classical education. As well as being made sacred by the presence of Virgil and Horace, Naples seemed to visitors the portal to another realm; the hot springs and sulphurous emissions of the Phlegraean Fields spoke of the nearness of the entrance to the underworld. Whether they came from America or northern Europe, tourists felt they had arrived in a distinctly alien culture. The trappings of the most exotic forms of Catholicism, which held a powerful illicit fascination for Protestant visitors, were to be seen everywhere in a metropolis that believed its very existence in the shadow of the volcano depended on a biannual miracle, the liquefaction of a saint's blood. Moreover, Naples had a decidedly risqué reputation. Aristocratic ladies were less formal and more flirtatious than their northern counterparts, making the inevitable social engagements of the season infinitely more interesting, and its backstreets boasted a staggering number of whores, the ancestors of those who form a welcoming committee for my arrival.

Naples attracted some of the greatest artists of the eighteenth and nineteenth centuries, from as far away as France, Germany, the Netherlands and the industrial north of England. It set a particular challenge to the painter of nocturnes, with Vesuvius putting on regular and spectacular fireworks displays across the moonlit bay. The effluvia shot up by the volcano came rich with historical resonance for tourists who knew their Pliny. Scurrying to the lip of the crater, between showers of stones, visitors could look into the volcano's boiling, seething interior and feel as if they were literally seeing history in the making. Such moneyed travellers provided a ready market for artists. One of the richest men in France, Fermier Général Bergeret de Grandcourt, arrived in Naples in 1774, accompanied by the painter Fragonard. An excursion to the top of the volcano was high on de Grandcourt's agenda. He records in his journal that on his way there he met 'a painter called Mr Volaire, supremely skilled in rendering the horror of Vesuvius'. Pierre-Jacques Volaire had worked as an assistant to Claude-Joseph Vernet in Marseilles before moving to Italy in 1763. Vernet was internationally famous as a landscape painter and had also spent time in Italy, particularly specializing in scenes of the coastal landscape south of Rome, where he was employed for a time by the royal court. Volaire was determined to emulate his mentor's success and, rather than making his home in Rome, decided to travel further south to Naples, settling there in 1769. He swiftly recognized the potential of Vesuvius, both as a wage-earning subject and a perfect vehicle for the skills he had acquired through his apprenticeship to his master in Marseilles. Vernet's nocturnal maritime scenes often featured a fire on a beach surrounded by silhouetted figures, its leaping flames providing an opportunity for chiaroscuro effects and contrasting with a cold, moonlit sea. In Vesuvius, these themes were writ large. Vernet was a strong advocate of working direct from nature. Like the good pupil he was, Volaire made numerous on-the-spot sketches of the volcano's activity. He missed a major eruption in 1767 by two years, but Vesuvius was far from dormant during his stay in the city.

In 1772 William Hamilton, the British ambassador to the Bourbon kingdom of Naples and an internationally renowned volcanologist, reported that since 1767 'Vesuvius has never been free of smoke nor ever many months without throwing up red-hot SCORIAE – usually followed by a current of liquid Lava'. Hamilton himself famously ascended the volcano over eighty times and recorded its every utterance in his voluminous writings and correspondence. He was not the only regular visitor to the summit. Volaire was part of the industry that evolved to service tourists who ventured near the maw of the cantankerous giant and wanted to bring back a souvenir from what was often described as the mouth of hell. To his observation of flames and rivers of lava beneath the night sky, Volaire added the silhouetted, gesticulating figures favoured by Vernet, either standing and observing the volcano's activity or fleeing in panic before a torrent of molten rock. Any eruption was, after all, a human catastrophe as well as a phenomenon of nature; why should he restrict himself merely to quasi-scientific observation of the volcano's eruptions, when the potential was there to portray a human drama? If his clients wanted the chill of fear, he would give it to them, with moonlight bringing an added note of melancholy and other-worldliness to the composition.

The fact that Volaire met Bergeret de Grandcourt on the volcano itself suggests that Volaire's sketches, as well as acting as studies for larger works, may have played a useful role in obtaining commissions from well-heeled visitors to his open-air studio. De Grandcourt promptly placed an order for a full-scale oil, *Eruption of Vesuvius by Moonlight*, painted for him the same year. However, if Volaire had been able to jump forwards in time he would have realized that his greatest rival in painting moonlit conflagrations, whose light would eclipse his own in art history, would come from England. Joseph Wright arrived in Naples in October 1774. He had come to Italy on his honeymoon. Wright had made a marriage outside his class, to local girl Hannah Swift, the daughter of a lead miner, unlikely material as the wife of an increasingly well-known and fashionable painter. But he was not one to be bound by convention. The couple left for Italy in October 1773, travelling via Nice and Spain. Once settled in Rome, he painted two self-portraits. In the first, with a nod to Rembrandt, he represents himself in exotic Orientalist attire, the romantic uniform of the northern painter who has escaped the confines of society at home. He announces his qualifications by holding a *porte-crayon* in his right hand, the sketching pencil with black and white chalk used for creating the chiaroscuro effects for which he was already famed. In the other self-portrait he is dressed in the garb of a brigand of the type common in the paintings of one of his favourite artists,

Salvator Rosa, a master of romantic night scenes who was rumoured to be a brigand himself. In both portraits, then, he declares himself a man of the night, creator of 'candlelights' and nocturnes. He added a touch of scandal to this romantic self-image by deciding not to baptize his first child, Anna Romana, who was born in Rome. An English priest living in the city wrote to Lord Arundel that Wright was 'here suspected of being a Jew, or Annabaptist, or something else that is not a Xtian', a description that would probably have amused Wright no end.

Back in England, Wright was on the periphery of the group of inventors, industrialists, poets and philosophers known as the Lunar Men, their name derived from the fact that they met on the Monday nearest the full moon each month, in order to have sufficient light by which to ride home. Spinning out from these lively and enjoyable meetings, and from the minds that attended them, came inventions that would revolutionize industrial production and thus change the lives of countless millions around the world. At the same time, the discussions that took place among them of geology, vulcanology and the origins of life challenged the Mosaic account of the origins of the earth itself. The canals and tunnels that were being dug to propel Britain into the future were uncovering its past; turning up fossils and mysterious, ancient bones, as well as clays and stones that had the potential to be used in the potteries – fuel therefore for both industry and philosophical speculation.

It should not be a surprise that Joseph Wright chose to portray some of the industrial developments that were changing the face of Britain in his paintings, as well as the popular scientific experiments that were the talk of the nation. First and foremost, before any private interest he may have had in scientific discoveries, he was in the entertainment business, a purveyor of the spectacular. Such subject matter gave him ample opportunity to

demonstrate the full extent of his skills, particularly in the handling of light. His images of blacksmiths' shops and iron forges,
pockets of industry in the rural heart of Derbyshire, combine
observation of working practice with human figures that verge
on the heroic. Their humble settings in partially collapsed barns
and millhouses recall the nativity scenes of much earlier painters, which were often also set in picturesque ruins, from within
which light emanates from a spiritual rather than a physical
source. In *An Iron Forge Viewed from Without* (1773), the viewer is
placed beyond the warm glow of the interior, beneath a dramatic moonlit cloudscape, its reflected glitter caught in the
surface of the millstream that powers the tilt-hammer. These
paintings, apparently realistic depictions of working life, also
make a connection between modern science and an ancient, hidden tradition reaching back to earlier times. (It is worth noting
that Wright, like several others in his peer group, was both a
freethinker in matters of religion and a Freemason.) One of his
most famous paintings, *An Experiment on a Bird in the Air Pump*
(1768), shows a popular scientific experiment of the period, in
which a bird is placed in a glass jar from which the air is removed
by means of a pump until it expires. However, Wright's version
of the experiment hints at something else. Instead of a cheap
finch or sparrow, his jar contains an exotic white cockatiel, still
weakly fluttering its outspread wings. Comparison with the
white dove that represents the Holy Spirit in Christian iconography is inevitable. Is something occult going on, hinted at in
the full moon that appears in the window (the same moon that
shines through the casement of an alchemist's studio in another
painting*) and the strange, fixed stare of the master of cere-

---

* *The Alchymist, in Search of the Philosopher's Stone, Discovers Phosphorus, and
prays for the successful Conclusion of his operation, as was the custom of the Ancient
Chymical Astrologers*, 1771, reworked 1779.

monies, who gazes straight out of the picture and into the eyes of the viewer? No wonder the small girl to the right of the scene hides her face. In Wright's universe, esoteric knowledge and the latest discoveries overlap and the changes rendered in the landscape by industry can be as much a source of the sublime as hills pushed up by the movement of glaciers. His painting *Arkwright's Cotton Mills by Night* (1782–3) portrays the tycoon's two factories on a moonlit night lit up like ocean liners with hills and tree-topped crags for waves, their scale and severe architectural style something entirely new.

Of the Lunar Men, Wright was closest to John Whitehurst, a childhood neighbour and friend. A clockmaker by training, Whitehurst was a keen amateur geologist, physicist and student of volcanoes, who believed the earth had been formed in a crucible of subterranean fire. He was familiar, as many of the group would have been, with William Hamilton's observations of Vesuvius. An exhaustive cataloguer of the geological strata of his native Derbyshire, Hamilton had demonstrated the presence there of material that was clearly volcanic in origin, including lava and volcanic ash known as 'toadstone'. Wright would therefore have been aware that though all seemed quiet in his own county, its picturesque landscape had been formed by tectonic convulsions every bit as dramatic as those that gave birth to Neapolitan fields of fire. He came to the mountain with a keen sense of its scientific importance as well as of the 'sublime' qualities that made it such suitable material for a painter of his skills. 'When you see Whitehurst,' he wrote in a letter to his brother, 'tell him I wished for his company when on Mount Vesuvius, his thoughts would have centr'd in the bowels of the mountain, mine skimmed over the surface only; there was a considerable eruption at the time, of which I am going to make a picture.' In saying that he only skimmed the surface of the volcano, Wright is being overly modest. Pencil sketches of the mountain's slopes

show an intense interest in its geological structure. These stud-
ies were followed by as many as thirty exhibition-size paintings
of the volcano in eruption, most completed on his return to
England. Several of his paintings of Vesuvius were made to be
paired and sold together with equally dramatic depictions of the
Girandola, the huge Catherine wheel on the roof of the Castel
Sant'Angelo that formed part of the famous firework display in
Rome, uniting two of the most explosive spectacles on the
Grand Tour. As he explained, one was the greatest sight in
nature, the other in art.

One of Wright's volcanoes, *Vesuvius in Eruption, with a View
over the Islands in the Bay of Naples*, completed on his return to
England, is now to be found on display at Tate Britain in London. The viewpoint is from high on the mountain, at the foot of
the volcanic cone, which is entirely red and orange, pouring lava
in a smoking stream down a narrow valley. An interesting art-
historical legend has grown up around the painting. The colour
of its rivers of lava was thought for a long time to be derived
from a compound of sulphur. When I first read this, I enjoyed
imagining Wright pocketing some of the bright yellow rock as
he wandered around the smoking cone of the volcano, or pur-
chasing some on a visit to one of the shops in Naples that sold
geological specimens, perhaps as a gift for his friend John Whitehurst, later including it in the painting in a kind of literal-minded
sympathetic magic. In fact, more recent analysis of the painting
has failed to detect any trace of the substance.

In Wright's depiction of Vesuvius a major eruption is in progress, with a jet of almost white-hot matter shooting straight up
into the air, scattering rock far and wide. In this blast, more vio-
lent than any Wright would have witnessed himself, he finally
achieves the synthesis he has been looking for. All the heat and
power of the new industries he saw around him as he grew up,
the pounding of hammers, leaping flames and white-hot iron

bars, are combined with the phosphorus jet of the alchemist's studio and the firework display he had witnessed in Rome. A long black cloud of smoke unfurls like a banner across the moon that hangs above the bay. On close inspection the moonlight on the water resolves itself into a complex pattern of zigzags, scratched into the still-wet paint with the handle of a brush in a process called *sgraffito*, revealing the bright, reflective surface beneath. In the foreground, two figures make their way across the smoking ground, bearing the elongated body of a young man, his head lolling back and his arm dangling in the languidness of death. Behind them, walking apart, comes a mourning woman, wrapped in a robe. It is possible that these figures represent the death, or burial, of Pliny the Elder, overcome by the fumes from Vesuvius during the eruption of AD 79. If so, Wright is depicting the allegorical Pliny, rather than the real one. According to the records we have, the admiral of the Roman fleet was old and died by the shore. He would have had more than one mourner at his funeral, which is unlikely to have been staged at night at the top of the volcano that caused his death. However, during the Renaissance Pliny became an idealized figure; the true scholar whose curiosity about the natural world made him unable to resist venturing too close to the erupting volcano. For Wright, an honorary Lunar Man, he would have been a potent symbol.

II

It is not always easy to stick to a schedule on a visit to Naples. The problem, which is also one of the city's chief charms, lies with what might be happening in the streets. Inexplicably, for instance, the bus service may collapse, but lifelong friends may be made among those waiting in the queue, as Neapolitans and any strangers present will soon have been enlisted in a general, inclusive conversation. Any event, however small, is an opportunity for animated discussion, and the limitations of linguistic ability are no ultimate barrier. Those finding you slow to understand their point merely treat you as though you are hard of hearing and speak louder, or appeal good-naturedly to the Mother of God and try again.

The day after my arrival I move from Piazza Garibaldi to a room high among the rooftops, ten minutes' walk from the cathedral in one direction and the sea in the other. I have come to Naples in the last days of October, in the run-up to Italy's own Day of the Dead, when people return to their home cities to visit their family graves and spend time with their departed loved ones. My hostess welcomes me with a slice of *tortoni di morte*, the cake of the dead, a confection of chocolate and nuts that you see everywhere in the shop windows of Naples at this time of year.

After jettisoning my bags I walk out on to Piazza Dante. A statue of the poet, dressed in long robes and in his trademark soft hat, looks benignly down on to the main street; behind his back on the square, beyond the reach of his patrician gaze, a drama is unfolding. The graffitied plinth on which the statue stands has been commandeered by a group of demonstrators protesting against the deep cuts planned in higher-education funding and university research. On the other side of the square, a group of a hundred or so fascist supporters have gathered and are shouting slogans, their arms rising rhythmically in unison in the blackshirt salute. More and more people are arriving from every direction. A single policeman on the corner of the square shows as little interest in events as the stone poet on his plinth. Scooters, often carrying three or four precariously balanced passengers, swarm angrily at the periphery of the crowd, then dart across the pedestrian precinct in between the demonstrators, unloading some of their cargo before circling again. Suddenly the two sides clash. Three or four scooters are on the ground, their wheels spinning; the opposing factions surge towards each other, raised fists coming down in a motion halfway between a slap and a punch that is still more theatrical than vicious. After a minute or so it is over; the two sides pull apart reluctantly like the fingers of locked hands, but blood is still high. I can see one man in particular, well built with blond hair, a boxer's nose and a tight-fitting black nylon jacket, struggling to return to the fight, arguing with the friends who attempt to restrain him. He breaks free and runs back into the middle of the crowd. This time the fighting is a little more serious. Scooter riders are deploying their weapons, swinging padlock chains and helmets. I am just deciding that perhaps it is time to leave when the centre of attention shifts. Mobile phones vibrate with battle signals from elsewhere in the city and the square begins to empty as people wheel-spin or simply run out of the square to the next contested field.

With the university occupied, banners hanging from the facades of the various schools and drummers sitting in upper windows playing to the crowds below, seminars move into the streets. Roadblocks are erected and a venerable professor sits on a chair, his back against a parked car, speaking seriously to the students who sit on the pavement at his feet. A younger woman teacher is walking up and down, using one hand to hold a megaphone and the other to emphasize her points and to flick back her long hair as she lectures her students about Oscar Wilde, who came here at the end of the nineteenth century, a refugee from scandal. All teaching is a kind of performance; in this topsy-turvy world it seems to make perfect sense to take it out of the academy and on to an open-air stage. As Goethe, who clearly fell in love with the city while wandering its streets, wrote in *Italian Journey*, 'One could go on for ever describing similar scenes, each crazier than the last, not to mention the infinite variety of costumes or the hordes of people you can see on the Toledo alone.'

Italian Journey is a work with a powerful nocturnal element. Like many good travel books, as well as being the account of a physical trajectory it is also a story of the author's pursuit of redemption; the resolution, through escape, of a personal crisis. In Germany, Goethe was a prisoner twice over; first of his literary fame and second of his civic duties as a Privy Councillor in the Duchy of Weimar. The book begins with the poet's hurried and unannounced departure, described in a single, resonant sentence:

I slipped out of Carlsbad at three in the morning; otherwise, I would not have been allowed to leave.

This is the first of many nocturnal journeys on his way from Germany, across the Alps and southward towards Rome and ultimately Naples and Sicily. Near Innsbruck he pauses, waiting for fresh horses, watching the mountains disappear into darkness until 'all of a sudden I saw the lofty snow peaks again lit up by the moon'. Arriving at Trento a few days later at eight o'clock at night, he has a short sleep but is then urged by the landlord to press on, 'because the moon would soon be rising and the road was excellent. I knew that he wanted his horses back early the next morning to bring in the second hay crop so his advice was not disinterested . . .' He journeys on all night, keeping watch as his companions sleep, arriving in Bolzano in full daylight. His letters to his friends at home throughout his journal are full of lunar and meteorological dispatches, for the overland traveller in his day was as dependent on these conditions as a maritime one. 'As to the weather in this period I have the following to report. The night of the ninth and tenth was clear and cloudy by turns and there was a constant halo around the moon . . .' For Goethe, the moon was a beneficent, friendly planet whose light allowed entrance into another dimension. On first viewing it through a telescope from his back garden he had exclaimed 'at last, closer acquaintance with this beloved and admired neighbour'. His fascination only seems to intensify throughout *Italian Journey*. Even though he supposedly travelled incognito, to escape the attention of the expatriate community, he nevertheless found himself ensnared in social activities in Rome that were little to his liking, distracting him from his purpose of studying art, sketching and working on various literary projects. The night was his refuge from such time-wasting activities.

To my annoyance I wasted the whole day among the fools. When night fell I went for a walk in the Villa Medici to recover. The new moon is just past. Next to its tenuous sickle, I could almost make out the dark portion of the disc with the naked eye, and through a telescope it was clearly visible.

Picasso, visiting Rome in the early years of the twentieth century, described it as a city made of fountains, shadows and moonlight. Goethe would clearly have understood what he meant. 'The moonlit nights are incredibly beautiful,' he writes. 'When the moon first rises and has not yet climbed above the haze, it is a warm yellow like *il sole d'Inghilterra* ['the English sun'], and for the rest of the night is bright and friendly . . . I tried to transfer some of these moonlight effects to paper and then busied myself with other artistic problems.' In Frascati, he visited villas by moonlight, sketching in the open air, and wrote home that 'on my drawing board I also have some moonscapes, and some other ideas which are really too crazy to tell you about'. Such nocturnal walks were something of a fashion among eighteenth-century tourists in Italy, not least because of the tremendous heat of the country's summer months. In a letter home in July 1772 the English traveller Norton Nicholls writes from Naples that 'the nights are so delightful and the days so hot . . . [that] I am become a greater friend of the moon than the sun'.

Arriving in Naples, Goethe was ensnared on two fronts, the cerebral and the sensual. In another German resident in the city, Jacob Philipp Hackert, he found an artist of a stature and an intellectual standing that he could entrust himself to as a teacher and guide. Installed in some style in a wing at the Palazzo Francavilla, Hackert was a favourite of the King and Queen, and also a close friend of William Hamilton, the British ambassador. He was thus privy to both the latest research on Vesuvius and the gossip of the royal court; conversant with geology and botany as well as the finer points of draughtsmanship.

Goethe was determined to understand Bourbon Naples. 'Everything I have been told . . . about the personages and conditions at the court must be checked,' he tells himself in his journal. 'Today the King has gone wolf-hunting. They expect to kill at least five.' Little matter that the monarch, a famous butcher of wild animals, had an army of footmen to drive all manner of living creatures by the hundreds into nets among which he could stride himself, dispensing summary justice. Better a monarch steeped in the gore of deer, hares, boar, foxes and countless songbirds than in that of his own subjects (that was to come later).

Almost immediately, Goethe felt a sense of release from the constraints that had pursued him, even as far as Rome. The incomparable vista of the horseshoe bay, with its smoking volcano and scattering of islands, once the playthings of Roman emperors; the city's teeming streets and the astonishing vitality of its inhabitants, from well-bred ladies to the famous *lazzare*, ragamuffins and urchins who appeared to his somewhat naive eye to accept their lot so cheerfully; all combined to unlock something in Goethe that had remained frozen until this moment. If he, who had declared himself determined to base his observations on the objective nature of things, was unmanned enough by the beauty of Naples to idealize his surroundings, perhaps he can be forgiven.

The feeling of liberation he experienced was clearly genuine. Once again it is within a description of a nocturnal walk that he hints at his new freedom:

I can't begin to tell you the glory of a night by full moon when we strolled through the streets and squares to the endless promenade of the Chiaia, and then walked up and down the sea shore. I was quite overwhelmed by a feeling of infinite space.

W. H. Auden, himself one of the seemingly innumerable foreign poets to have spent time in Naples, suggested in his introduction to the translation he made with Elizabeth Meyer of *Italian Journey* that the thirty-seven-year-old Goethe may have lost his virginity during his time in Italy. At home he had been caught up in an eleven-year platonic relationship with a married woman a decade his senior. Auden claims to be able to tell from the change in Goethe's appearance in the portraits painted of him before and during his trip that he has finally known sexual satisfaction. Whether this intuition is right or not, Goethe certainly makes the most of what Naples has to offer.

Naturally he must visit Sir William Hamilton and be allowed, as an honoured guest, to view his private collection, including those objects of antiquity that perhaps should have remained the property of the Italian state. He is also privileged to see Hamilton's latest and most precious acquisition, sent to him by his nephew, 'an English girl of twenty, with a beautiful face and a perfect figure'. This is Emma, who is to become the old man's bride and make him the gossip of Europe by cuckolding him with a famous, one-armed English admiral. For their visitors on two successive nights she gives the performance that was the talk of Naples; dressed in a Greek costume, she adopts poses from classical and dramatic scenes in bewildering succession, entrancing at least one of her audience. 'The old knight idolizes her and is enthusiastic about everything she does,' Goethe writes. 'In her he has found all the antiquities, all the profiles on Sicilian coins, even the Apollo Belvedere. This much is certain: as a performance it's like nothing you ever saw before in your life.'

The same could be said for Naples itself. The city keeps some of its greatest art treasures high above its humming centre, in museums on the twin peaks of the Vomero and Capodimonte, but for the first few days my capacity for enjoying art is fully satisfied by what appears, for free, in the streets. The alleys and lanes leading from the Centro Storico to the port area are covered in inventive and entertaining graffiti. There is one motif I keep seeing that somehow transcends time and place and sums up the city. A small round sticker in just three colours that regularly appears on walls, lamp posts, no-entry signs and junction boxes, it carries an image of a stylized white volcano in which a red pool of magma is bubbling towards the surface and shooting up into a black sky. It is only the second time I see it that I realize that this volcano is erupting with exclamation marks, a symbol of a city which may explode at any given moment and that always has something to say.

In 1833 a poet arrived in Naples who will always be associated with the moon. Like Goethe, Giacomo Leopardi was on the run; ostensibly he moved to the southern city for his health, but he was also escaping the stifling clutches of his family, particularly his relationship with his father, an eccentric and overbearing intellectual with reactionary views. Despite the unrelenting pessimism expressed in Leopardi's poetry and his philosophical writings about 'this wearisome and agitated sleep which we call life',⋆ he is regarded by many as one of the greatest Italian writers of the nineteenth century. As Italo Calvino has said, 'the miraculous thing about his poetry is that he simply takes the weight out of language, to the point that it resembles moonlight'. Leopardi was scathing about the city in his correspondence, writing to his father that he could 'no longer endure this half-barbarous and half-African place, where I live in complete isolation from everyone'. The isolation he felt was not from humankind, as he lived in Naples with his friend Antonio Ranieri, whose family treated him as one of their own. Most likely he was thinking of the literary milieu to which he felt he belonged but which he was fated never to join. Certainly, the failure of his romantic life was a continuing source of unhappiness. Already disadvantaged by curvature of the spine, asthma and failing eyesight, Leopardi unfailingly fell in love with unobtainable women who were either older than himself, or already married. Along with most of Europe, it would seem, he had read Goethe's *The Sorrows of Young Werther*. The novel's hero commits suicide as a result of his love for a woman who is married to another; entangled in his own hopeless infatuation at the time, Leopardi briefly contemplated suicide himself. However, he took comfort instead in his writing and in unflinchingly examining the futility, as he saw it, of human existence. He was determined that his readers see his 'philosophy of despair' not as a symptom of his illnesses but only as 'what comes from my understanding'.

The moon seems to have played a central role in Leopardi's life, as it often does for those rendered sleepless through youth or age, illness or anxiety. In several poems its light provides a setting for his thoughts and in some he addresses it directly.

⋆ From Giacomo Leopardi, *Canti* XIX, 'To Count Carlo Pepoli', trans. J. G. Nichols (London: Oneworld Classics, 2008), p. 115.

O gracious moon, now that I recollect,
It was a year ago I climbed this hill,
In terrible distress to gaze on you;
And you were hanging then above that wood
As you do now, suffusing it with light.
But misty then and muddled from the weeping
That clouded both my eyes your face appeared
To me at least, because my life was full
Of anguish then – and is, nor has it changed,
O moon of my delight . . .*

One of his greatest lunar poems, 'Night Song of a Wandering Shepherd of Asia', was inspired by a contemporary traveller's account of the ritual chants addressed to the moon by Kirghiz shepherds. The hero of Leopardi's poem seems to be brimming over with existential questions; the moon that hangs above him in the endless night of the central Asian steppes his only possible outlet.

What are you there for, in the sky? What do
You do there, silent moon?
You rise in the evening, and go
Searching the desert places; then you set.
Have you not had your fill
Of travelling these everlasting ways?

At first he is struck by the similarities between his own life and the life of the moon. Each has its eternal rhythms; each, to him, seems equally futile. As the moon remains stubbornly silent, the shepherd expounds on human fate. Born in anguish and to continual toil, deprived of the blissful ignorance of the sheep they tend, men are tortured by their inability to answer the questions that arise in the world around them. The shepherd looks up at

---

* Ibid., from *Canti* XIV, 'To the Moon', p. 87.

the night sky, attempting to read there some evidence of divine purpose, as so many had before. As he informs the moon, he finds none.

> And often, as I see you
> Stand silently above the empty plain
> Whose distant circle borders on the sky,
> Or watch you follow me
> As step by step my flock and I move on,
> Or see in heaven so many a blazing star,
> I have to ask myself:
> What are these torches for?
>
> . . .
>
> These things do not reveal
> To me their fruit or use. But you, I hope,
> Young and immortal, understand it all.

Of course, the shepherd learns nothing from his 'Young and immortal' lunar companion, concluding in the end, much as Leopardi himself did, that, 'It may well be it always is upon a day of great ill-omen we are born.'

To one of Leopardi's temperament, Vesuvius was a fitting symbol of the foolishness of man's aspirations. It was in a villa on the volcano's slopes at Torre del Greco, surrounded by reminders of the mountain's destructive power, that he was to spend his final days. Here, amid the desolate landscape of the lava fields, he composed the poem that perhaps most perfectly combines his philosophical and lyrical qualities, *La Ginestra, o il Fiore del Deserto* (The Broom, or the Flower of the Desert). It is the poem of a dying man, full of scorn and bitterness, yet unflinching in its determination to hold up a mirror to man's fate. 'On the barren back of the alarming mountain, Vesuvius the destroyer' he contemplates the stars, just as Leopardi's fictional shepherd had done.

> Often, on these bare slopes
> Clothed in a kind of mourning
> By stone waves which apparently still ripple,
> I sit by night and see the distant stars
> High in the clear blue sky
> Flame down upon this melancholy waste,
> And see them mirrored by
> The distant sea, till all this universe
> Sparkles throughout its limpid emptiness . . .

Gazing up into a night sky devoid of light pollution, beyond the nearer planets to 'those tangled knots of stars, which look to us like mist', Leopardi mocks humanity's presumption in supposing that the authors of the universe would have come down to 'this obscure mere grain of sand' to hold a conversation. Yet in the end he does not place the blame for humanity's situation on mankind but on nature; for nature, as Vesuvius has demonstrated, will erase men with as little compunction as if they were ants. The poem is full of extraordinarily vivid descriptions of the volcano's destructive power.

> Down the mountainside
> And raging over grass,
> Molten boulders en masse,
> Melting metal, and sand that was alight
> Swept like a river in spate –
> Smashed those cities upon whose furthest shore
> The moving ocean washed,
> Confounded and covered them
> In a few seconds; so that now the goat
> Browses above, and new
> Cities arise which have their very base
> On those long buried whose demolished walls
> The rugged mountain crushes underfoot.

This imagery has particular resonance for those of us who, in recent memory, have watched a remote Icelandic volcano jet orange magma across our television screens, shrouding the upper air in ash and bringing an eerie silence to our skies.

The year after he completed the poem, four years after he arrived in Naples, Leopardi died at the age of thirty-nine. 'Death is not an ill,' he had written, 'because it frees man from all ills, and with the good things takes away the desire for them.'* His death mask, preserved as a black-and-white photograph, with the sunken craters of its eyes and cheeks and the sharp terminator line of the skullcap, itself looks like an image of the moon. One hundred years later his remains were moved to the park at Piedigrotta in Naples, to lie near the tomb of Virgil, evidence that he had finally achieved the recognition he craved.

III

Leopardi was not the only one to wander the slopes of Vesuvius at night. Local guides were well aware of the inability of visitors to cope with the heat of midday; they also understood the dramatic potential of a full moon for increasing their charges' appreciation and, presumably, the likelihood of receiving a good tip. Charles Dickens took the nocturnal tour, in the very early spring of 1846, on the night of the full moon, describing it in his book *Pictures from Italy*. The considerable party reach the lava fields, 'a bleak bare region where the lava lies confusedly . . . as if the earth had been ploughed up by burning thunderbolts', just as the sun sets. The author is impressed by the 'unutterable solemnity and dreariness' of the place, a sentiment echoed by Mark Twain, who on a visit thirteen years later

* Ibid., 'Thoughts', *Opere* 218.

was struck by the sensation that 'this stormy, far-stretching waste of blackness, with its thrilling suggestion of life, of action, of boiling, surging, furious motion, [is] petrified! – all stricken dead and cold at the instant of its maddest rioting! – fettered, paralyzed, and left to glower at heaven in impotent rage for ever more!'

In delivering Dickens to the scene at sunset, his guides have demonstrated the stage-management skills that seem to come as a birthright with citizenship in the Neapolitan theatre. It is dark by the time his party arrives at the foot of the cone of the active volcano. 'The only light is reflected from the snow, deep, hard, and white, with which the cone is covered. It is now intensely cold, and the air is piercing. The thirty-one have brought no torches, knowing that the moon will rise before we have reached the top.' Rise it does, once again right on cue, as if hauled up into the sky by a system of pulleys worked by the guides, who, unbeknown to Dickens, have transformed from genre comic characters to manipulators of celestial events. Before experiencing the final *coup de théâtre*, the party must make the ascent of the final steep volcanic outcrop. Two ladies and 'a rather heavy gentleman from Naples' must be carried up in litters; the ladies are each carried by six men, the obese Neapolitan by fifteen. Once everyone has been pushed and shoved into position, the curtain can come up. The moonlit scene Dickens encounters as he reaches a small plateau near the summit is every bit as dramatic as those depicted by painters who made portraits of the irascible mountain. 'From tingeing the top of the snow above us, with a band of light, and pouring it in a stream through the valley below, while we have been ascending in the dark, the moon soon lights the whole white mountain-side, and the broad sea below, and tiny Naples in the distance, and every village in the country round . . .' This vision of moonlit serenity is in marked contrast to the scene at the top of the volcano:

From every chink and crevice . . . hot, sulphurous smoke is pouring out; while from another, conical-shaped hill, the present crater, rising abruptly from this platform at the end, great sheets of fire are streaming forth: reddening the night with flame, blackening it with smoke, and spotting it with red-hot stones and cinders, that fly up into the air like feathers, and fall down like lead. What words can paint the gloom and grandeur of this scene!

Indeed, for the twenty-first-century reader, rather than paint images, Dickens's words conjure up images of paintings; when he describes waiting for stragglers in the darkness because 'dense cloud now obscures the moon', he summons up a sky by Wright; when he describes climbing to the edge of the crater with his companions and looking down 'for a moment, into the Hell of boiling fire below', then running back to the main group, 'blackened and singed, and scorched, and hot, and giddy; and each with his dress alight in half-a-dozen places', we think of the silhouetted, gesturing sightseers in a Volaire painting.

Reflecting what is so often the traveller's experience, Dickens's account mingles moments of the sublime with moonlit farce. On descending Vesuvius, his party encounter treacherous sheets of ice and one of their number, whom Dickens has christened Mr Pickle of Portici, loses his footing and rolls down the steep sides of the cone. 'Sickening as it is to look, and be so powerless to help him,' Dickens writes, struggling to suppress his laughter, 'I see him there, in the moonlight – I have had such a dream often – skimming over the white ice, like a cannon-ball.'

Perhaps I should have taken warning from Dickens's account, but I too wish to ascend Vesuvius. So late in the year weather conditions are difficult to predict but the sun is shining as I set off on the Circumvesuviana train line, essentially the same one that Dickens took on his excursions around the bay. Approaching the volcano, things do not look so hopeful. Its lower slopes are brightly lit, highlighting the thin veil of vegetation that looks from this distance like moss growing on a rock, or the

velvet on a deer's antler. However, halfway to its full height the
mountain simply vaporizes behind a solid bank of cloud, as
impenetrable as a burka. In the office of the Vesuvio Express,
the man behind the desk, sensing my hesitation, tells me that a
minibus is leaving in fifteen minutes. It looks very cloudy, I say
doubtfully. Will we be able to see anything? 'Is OK at the summit,' he assures me, without meeting my eye. I look at him
carefully. He is either misleading me or he knows more about
the strange climatic conditions that pertain at the summits of
volcanoes situated next to the sea than I do. It must be that, I tell
myself. None of the other passengers appear to have any qualms
and are already boarding a somewhat battered Ford Transit van
that has pulled up outside. In fact I take the last remaining seat,
which doesn't prevent an extra passenger being crammed in on
a folding chair placed in the stairwell of the sliding door. The
man who sold us our tickets comes out of the office and, after
some discussion, hands a wad of notes to the driver, who starts
the engine. We weave our way through the usual traffic chaos to
the flea-blown outskirts of town, where the streets are decorated with scattered, brightly coloured rubbish. Channels have
been cut into the mountainside to accommodate the winter
rains but these too have been filled, as though the mountain
wept garbage. Gradually we leave the town behind. The lower
slopes of the volcano are famously fertile, producing the small
tomatoes prized for pasta sauces and the grapes from which the
local Lacrima Christi wine is produced. However, there is no
feeling of prosperity along the road to the volcano's summit.
The town's detritus follows us, combining with the litter tossed
from the tourist coaches of summer. Every bush is festooned
with plastic, every passing-place with flattened paper cups and
food wrappers. Beneath us Naples is laid out in all its sprawling
majesty, a tumble of ochre dice thrown down the valley towards
the brilliant blue of the bay.

We continue to climb, the passenger on the folding chair rocking from side to side on the hairpin bends. But already the view is becoming brittle, as if seen through scratched glass. In less than a minute we are plunged into dense cloud, swirling across the road in ribbons, cutting our visibility to a few yards. Unlike any other form of public transport in Naples, which would be humming with excited conversation, the minibus, packed tight with foreigners, is already hushed. Now it falls silent, as though we were songbirds and the mist a blanket thrown over our cage. Ghostly structures, seemingly abandoned, emerge momentarily by the roadside and then vanish again. We have entered, I can just make out, the lava fields that so impressed previous travellers. The higher we climb, the worse the visibility gets.

We disembark in a gentle drizzle in a car park where the ascent on foot begins. There is no chance of slipping on the excellently maintained paths. And they are about all there is to look at, apart from the dripping figures of other tourists in the mist. I avoid looking into the faces of those descending, in case I read disappointment there. I am still holding on to the idea that the very top of the volcano might be above the cloud. After about twenty minutes I stop at a wooden hut selling souvenirs and coffee and ask the woman behind the till how far we are from the summit. 'You are standing at the lip of the crater,' she explains, picking up a postcard and pointing to our position. I turn and look out into the whiteness, straining to see, but it is as blank as this

Vesuvius, the ever-present threat that has shaped the psychology of the city of Naples, that one day inevitably will explode again with cataclysmic force, is hidden, like a murderer behind a curtain. I think briefly of all the descriptions I have read of this scene that the weather has painted out of my own experience. I will have to continue to see the caldera of the volcano only in my mind's eye, relying on travellers' accounts and artists' renderings, just as Joseph Wright of Derby did when he painted Mount Etna in Sicily, a place he never visited. I turn back to the stall and the helpful, apologetic woman who runs it. She offers to stamp a postcard for me, to prove that I have made the ascent. I have noticed others doing this, as if the primary purpose of coming to the summit was to tick it off a list – something that perhaps hasn't changed a great deal from the earliest days of tourism in the region. *Allora*, how much would it be if I took two postcards and this small box of volcanic stones, I ask her. And, trying a joke, how much to make this fog go away? She laughs and makes one hand into the shape of a telephone by her ear and with the other points upwards. 'For that,' she says, 'you must ring God.'

IV

In my last days in Naples I search out more art inspired by this extraordinary city, its setting and the quality of its moonlight. Beneath the metal roof of the contemporary gallery added to the top of the museum at Capidomonte, which creaks and sings as it expands in the unseasonably hot early November sun, I find the painting Andy Warhol did of Vesuvius on his visit to the city in 1985. Of course the master of Pop recognized it as the icon of the city and appropriated it, showing it in a full-scale eruption, which of course he had never seen. But his volcano,

with its cute, bubblegum colours, its red cone jetting out yellow, green and purple lava, is more soda fountain than time
bomb. I am completely alone apart from the painting, the only
sounds the gentle roar of air-conditioning, the occasional note
from the musical roof and distant sirens from the city, far below.

The museum is huge; it was a palace, after all. Descending from
the heights, I walk (it seems) past wall after wall of *Natura morta
con pesci*, still lifes of the day's catch, hauled, wet and glistening,
from the sea. In dramatic chiaroscuro, these seventeenth-century
artists painted portraits of all manner of fish, as well as lobsters,
cuttlefish, squid and sad-faced turtles, each garnished with seaweed and gaping in death. Elsewhere there are Titians and a
Botticelli, but the gallery I am most interested in is roped off and
guarded by a young woman attendant who is leaning back lan-
guidly in a chair. I ask if I can enter. I'm sorry, it's closed, she tells
me, with a shrug. But these are the paintings I came to see, I tell
her. She gives in immediately with an exhausted wave of the
hand, as if too tired to argue. I step over the rope. On the wall are
two paintings by Volaire: *Eruzione del Vesuvio dal ponte della Mad-
dalena*, from 1782; and *Notterno Napoletano con Tarantella in Riva del
Mare*, from 1784. The first picture shows Vesuvius from the seashore. A river of lava pours down from the volcano's summit
towards the ocean. People are fleeing in terror over the bridge,
horses are rearing and at the shore a group pray frantically to San
Gennaro. In the foreground a comely, long-haired woman faints
in the picturesque manner; the whole scene is lit by a full moon,
reflected in the mirror-still sea.

Some critics have suggested that Volaire was influenced by
Wright in choosing to depict eruptions by night, but a quick
glance at the second painting reminds us that he had his own
sources of moonshine. This is a genre maritime scene that
derives much of its subject matter from the stock of effects
deployed by Volaire's teacher, Claude-Joseph Vernet. In 1750

Vernet was commissioned to create four oval coastal scenes depicting the times of day, to be set in a stately home in Ireland. His painting *Night* features a city in the distance reminiscent of Naples, with a party of fishermen and women on the shore, the light of their fire contrasting with the brilliantly handled, silvery moonshine on the bay. In Volaire's painting the sea is also lit by a full moon; the oars of the boats that cross the bay are reflected in the water, the sense of theatricality added to by the fact that they make no ripples in its glassy surface. On the shore a woman is in the act of pulling a fish from the sea, watched by an admiring male companion, who is smoking a pipe while lying on his stomach. Further along the beach a crowd is dancing around a blazing cask accompanied by a small group of musicians, their frenzied shapes dramatically lit by the flames, which cast their leaping shadows behind them.

This is the local touch Volaire has added to make the picture marketable: the tarantella dance, specific to the south of Italy, which was said to be derived from the bite of the tarantula spider. Those affected believed themselves possessed, entering a trance state, the only release from which came through dancing to the repetitive beat of the *tamburello* (tambourine). The dancers, known as *taranti*, abandoned all restraint, male and female alike throwing up their heels – a seductive idea in an age governed by clearly defined codes of behaviour. The spider's bite is therefore a kind of licence, allowing its victim to step outside society's bounds of decorum, a mark of those set apart; the fact that the dance is occurring at full moon making a link in viewers' minds with the perennial legends of the witches' orgiastic Sabbath. While Volaire's painting has considerably more human drama than his teacher's, its principal selling point is still its masterful handling of moonlight.

I turn back towards the door to find that the attendant has been watching me vigilantly, in case I am inspired to begin acting in a similarly wild manner. I thank her and step back across the rope. Outside, in the grounds of the royal palace, ragamuffins play soccer beneath the palm trees and a pack of dogs sniff each other and frolic, breaking off to chase a remote-controlled car that is racing across the scorched grass, its high-octane whine puncturing the air.

On my last afternoon, in sweltering heat, I ride the funicular railway up to Vomero, its station a few streets from the unremarkable Via Kagoshima, a physical reminder of the strange resonances that link Naples with its Japanese cousin. Not the least of these is the bond each city has with a famous naval commander. During his time in Naples, Horatio Nelson took grave risks with his good name. Bewitched by another man's wife, he made himself the gossip of Europe, and partly under her influence ruthlessly suppressed a democratic uprising in her adopted city, sending poets and revolutionaries to their deaths and hanging an admiral on board his ship. However, his life story, like that of so many modern celebrities, was one of a journey from fame to disgrace and then back to sainthood. He was redeemed by his heroic death at Trafalgar, from which scene of battle his pickled body was carried home, a holy relic of the saint that saved a nation.

Tōgō Heihachirō, that loyal son of Kashogima, was almost as renowned as Nelson in his own lifetime, particularly for the destruction of the Russian Baltic Fleet in the Russo-Japanese War, a victory often credited with triggering the first Russian Revolution of 1905. In recognition of his naval prowess, Western journalists christened him 'The Nelson of the Orient'. This was the pinnacle of a career that began when he took part in the defence of Kagoshima as a fifteen-year-old when the naval descendants of Nelson sailed into Kinkō Bay. Like Nelson, when Tōgō died he was given a state funeral; the navies of the great powers paraded in his honour in Tokyo Bay. After his death and against his stated wishes, he received one final promotion, to the status of Shinto *kami*; a temple was built in his honour in Tokyo, which is still in use today.

Two Nelsons; two volcanoes; one moon. From a café opposite the castle I watch the shadow of the hill lengthen across the city below. At last, on this golden Sunday afternoon, the cars and scooters have come to rest and all is still. The treacherous cloud that had confounded me at the summit of Vesuvius has vanished. From where I sit, every indentation in the slopes of the volcano is etched in the evening sun. I can see its crater clearly with the naked eye. I linger as long as I can until the waiters make it plain that they want to close; it is Sunday, after all. Walking back to the funicular station I turn to see the new moon, its comma making a pause in the evening sky.

Two weeks later, back in England, I get off the train and see the full moon riding high above the bicycle racks outside the station. On the spur of the moment I decide to ride home along the river rather than by road. The air is absolutely still. Wood smoke rises straight up into the moonlight from the funnels of the houseboats moored near the bridge. The towpath is striped with deep shadows where the moon is caught in the tangle of the winter trees. My eyes are drawn to the far bank of the river, where orange flames leap from a pile of scavenged wooden pallets, their glow contrasting with the sheen of the moonlit water. A gesticulating group of rough sleepers are gathered round the fire, lurching in ramshackle fashion to the music of a transistor radio, raising their voices above its tinny din. It is a scene, of course, straight out of Volaire. Landscapes and centuries shift, but human behaviour does not. I have stepped through the frame and into the world of his *taranti*, still recognizable after their migration from another place and time.

PART FOUR

Lunada

From Vegas to Vega: American Moon

I

If there is one place above any other that represents mankind's conquest of darkness it is Las Vegas, Nevada. Planted at the western edge of the great deserts of the south-western states of America, the city has no natural resources to sustain it. Running entirely on imported power and water it is a twenty-first-century gold-rush town, fuelled by the same quest that drove nineteenth-century fortune-seekers westward in search of instant, unimaginable riches, a search still accompanied by its attendant hungers for booze, whoring and old-fashioned entertainment. Since the 1950s it has been known as the world's neon capital, the brightest place on the planet once darkness falls; in Glitter Gulch, the city's old downtown area (now roofed over and turned into an 'experience'), it has long been possible to read a newspaper on the street at midnight. Now the historic neon lights on Fremont Street are turned off once an hour to make way for a digital 'light spectacular', featuring two million incandescent light bulbs orchestrated by 121 computers.

The control of light is essential to this city's operations. While on its streets Las Vegas turns night into day, inside the hotels and casinos that line its boulevards, it turns day into a perpetual, intoxicating twilight where dreams and desires coil and float like cigar smoke. In what remains the classic study of the architectural psychology of the city, *Learning from Las Vegas*, this control of natural light is seen as essential to its function. 'The combination of darkness and enclosure of the gambling room and its subspaces makes for privacy, protection, concentration and control,' the authors write. 'The intricate maze under the low ceiling never connects with outside light or outside space. This disorientates the occupant in space and time. One loses track of where one is and when it is. Time is limitless because the light of noon and midnight are exactly the same.'* In the twenty-first century, improvements in technology give even more scope for manipulation of the senses. In some casinos it is rumoured that in the small hours the lights are imperceptibly and gradually dimmed, increasing gamblers' feelings of exhaustion, and then brought up again as oxygen is pumped into the air, producing feelings of euphoria and renewed energy, giving players a 'second wind', encouraging them to carrying on gaming through the night.

While moonlight is banished from the streets of Las Vegas, the great deserts that wash up at its concrete fringes are home to some of the world's largest telescopes. Arizona boasts more of them than any other state, its high altitudes and dry climate making vast tracts of it a huge, natural observatory. My aim is to travel from Vegas, the city where night does not exist, through Nevada and on through Arizona, arriving near the Mexican border in time for the full moon. Outside Tucson, not far from Kitt Peak Observatory, a couple have sunk their life savings into building what they call an Interstellar Light Collector, a five-storey-high array of parabolic mirrors that they use to collect and 'amplify' the light of the full moon. Its inventors suggest that the light spectrum of moonbeams, concentrated by the mirrors many hundreds of times, could offer cures for any number of ailments. Whatever the truth of their claims, I am interested in travelling to a place with little or no light pollution and being exposed there to what I can only think of as distilled moonlight.

* Robert Venturi, Denise Scott Brown, Steven Izenour, *Learning from Las Vegas* (Cambridge, MA: MIT Press, 1972, revised edition, 1977).

I have another reason for wanting to visit Tucson. In my email correspondence with the helpful woman running the office at the Interstellar Light Collector, she suggests that I might want to meet a scientist, Dr Corinne Davies, who has done some research on plant seeds exposed to the concentrated beams of moonlight provided by the Collector. Davies is writing a book about moonlight, I am told. A book about moonlight? Naturally this interests me very much. When two people who are working in a similar field encounter each other it is natural for there to be some wariness between them, some defensiveness about the subject matter they have chosen to study. On the other hand, both will be keen to establish whether their potential rival really has wandered on to their territory, and what implications this might have for their own project. I am fairly sure that my uniquely unscientific approach will pose no threat to her research. I just hope I can convince her of this, as I am keen to meet her. I email her to introduce myself and tell her a little about my book. A reply arrives, saying that she would be happy to speak with me, and so one evening I ring her from England. Davies is a geneticist, specializing in plants. Some years ago she became interested in the role of moonlight in plant and animal reproductive cycles, including human ones. Exactly as I hoped she quickly agrees that my book is entirely different to her own; perhaps there is a note of wistfulness in her voice that I can spend my time searching the art and literature of the world while she has to back up her propositions with hard data. She is friendly with the people at the Interstellar Light Collector, tolerant of the fact that they mention her name frequently as one of the only scientists who has done any research into the efficacy of their invention. She agrees to meet up when I am in Tucson and suggests we can go out to the Collector together.

★

It is early June and Vegas is in the high nineties, with points further south towards the Mexican border reporting temperatures nearer 110 degrees Fahrenheit. As I approach the city by plane from New York my neighbour points out Lake Mead, the vast reservoir formed by the damming of the Colorado River as a source of water for Las Vegas and several other urban conurbations in this dry latitude. The lake is turquoise in the endless ochre of the land-scape; even from the air, its startling white rim is clearly visible, showing where levels have fallen by 100 feet or so since its creation. 'I don't think people are supposed to live in the desert,' the man sighs, even though he himself moved to Vegas three years ago. 'The amount of water we waste in Vegas, it's not sustainable. I don't know whether the city will survive another fifteen years.'

I am staying at the Sahara, one of the remaining 1950s 'Rat Pack' hotels and casinos whose architecture was such a feature of the post-war city. Standing at the north end of the Strip, it retains its iconic sign, complete with twin, neon-lit camels and Moorish dome, to which the nearby Stratosphere Tower pro-vides an outsize minaret. Its interior even merits a sentence in *Learning from Las Vegas* – 'Illuminated *baldacchini*, more than in all Rome, hover over tables in the limitless shadowy restaurant at the Sahara Hotel' – so I feel connected both to 'old' Vegas and to the Vegas on the desks and shelves of several generations of architecture students and urban theorists. In an effort to beat the recession, the hotel is offering rooms at twenty-six dollars a night – anything to get the punters into the building, where their money can be extracted in a myriad other ways.

Stepping through the front doors of the Sahara you are in the entrance to a Byzantine cathedral, complete with stained-glass windows of yellow, blue and green. Beyond them you plunge into the dimly lit world that lies inside every such building in Las Vegas and which you must journey through before you even reach reception. Hundreds of slot machines wink and blink, lights

flashing beneath their intricately decorated glass facades. Their
names alone are a kind of poem to playing the slots: Money
Storm, King Kong Cash, Spin and Win, and Dollars, Dollars,
Dollars. Some evoke an exotic, alternative reality, where anything could happen: Frog Princess, Enchanted Unicorn, Wild
Magic, Mata Hari, Houdini, Temple of Treasure. Still others
summon up aspects of American culture, from its deathless celebrities to its multi-ethnic streets: Great Eagle, Cops and Donuts,
Marilyn Monroe, Chez Tabasco, Dean Martin's Wild Party. As I
wheel my suticase down the narrow aisles a machine pays out,
coughing up counterfeit coins into a tray which a middle-aged
lady with bright red lipstick and dyed black hair scoops into an
empty coffee cup. 'Having a lucky day?' I ask her. 'Put it like this,'
she says, 'I wish these machines were chickens – I'd sure like to
know 'em'. Leaving me to ponder the meaning of this remark she
takes a long pull on her drink and goes back to her scooping. Here
too are tables of the games for which the city is famous: blackjack,
craps, roulette, poker; and their variants, with ever-more exotic
names – Texas Hold 'Em, Emperor's Challenge, Triple Up.

Arriving at the desk, having threaded my way through this
beguiling and treacherous landscape and already feeling discon-
nected from the world outside, I realize I am a couple of hours
early to book in. The ancient clerk gives me a wink. 'Don't
worry, sir – it's three o'clock somewhere.' I dump my bags in
my room and emerge with camera and notebook, eager to begin
a reconnaissance of this strange terrain. Something tells me that
people here are not necessarily keen to have their presence
recorded; perhaps some of them are ostensibly on business trips
in Philly, or visiting their mothers, rather than perched at a
gambling table next to a lady of recent acquaintance or slumped
on a stool before a slot. Surreptitiously I manage to take a
photograph of a game of poker taking place at a red baize table.
A burly croupier, white-haired and red-faced with pendulous

ears and deep lines etched each side of his large, fleshy nose, is dealing to a full table of players, their ages and ethnicities a wide-ranging sample of American manhood. They wait, shuffling and stacking their chips compulsively; some unconsciously have their hands clasped in an attitude of prayer. I try a shot at another table but an angry-faced croupier gestures for me to put the camera away. In fact, I learn later, photography is forbidden inside the casinos, officially for security reasons (to prevent grifters studying ways to beat the house) but also to protect the anonymity of their clients. Meanwhile every inch of the gambling floors is surveyed by the management through hidden cameras, crawling over the territory inch by inch, on the lookout for anybody trying to shorten the odds.

A friend once told me the story of how they had found themselves sitting next to a well-known American writer and critic at dinner and asked him why he had written so much and so approvingly about Las Vegas. 'Because it's the only place left where a man can live free,' he said, tersely. As I walk down the Strip, half dazed in the mid-afternoon sun, I think I see what he means. Vegas is a very secular idea of paradise, created by the Mob and enthusiastically endorsed by entrepreneurs of all stripes. Every carnal desire is immediately and profusely catered for, with sensory derangement encouraged, for obvious reasons. The usual American restrictions on alcohol in public places seem to have been relaxed; people stroll the streets happily grasping alcoholic beverages at all hours of the day. An advertising truck passes repeatedly, on its side a hoarding emblazoned with the words HOT BABES DIRECT TO YOU! GIRLS THAT WANT TO MEET YOU. Three topless girls pose in G-strings, gyrating coquettishly, their nipples obscured by the message CALL 24 HOURS. Groups of men stand at the edge of the sidewalk handing out prostitutes' phone numbers; they flick and snap the cards repeatedly in between thrusting them

towards passers-by; the sound, along with the click of chips at
the tables, swiftly comes to characterize the city for me, replacing
the crickets that would once have chirped at the oasis this once
was, set in the desert landscape.

The exteriors of recent buildings in Vegas are reflective, protecting the cool interiors where waterfalls, fountains and
aquariums complete with schools of playing dolphins are fed by
pipelines across the desert. The Wynne Hotel is chocolate brown
and ripples like rumpled silk. The Trump Tower is gold and its
surface shimmers in the heat. In this showgirl town it seems to be
shimmying and sashaying across a vast, sandy parking lot, punctuated by shipped-in ponderosa pines growing in wooden tubs,
tethered to the ground by wire. I wander in and out of these vast
edifices, through acres of their low-ceilinged gambling halls
where the slot machines flash their endless coded messages and
shouts go up when someone throws successfully on the crap
tables or turns up a lucky hand. I stop at an outdoor café at a
mall. The sound system is playing an endless loop of a pop song
very loud; it is just the chorus that plays, never the verse, the
pay-off, never the build-up, so that we are kept continually at
the climax point, as though all of us sitting here, rehydrating on
iced lattes and frappucinos, are plugged in to a perpetual gratifi-
cation machine, which in Vegas I suppose we are.

The moon is rising over the Paris Las Vegas Eiffel Tower, pale
against the desert sky. By eight o'clock, it seems that every building on the Strip is pulsating with light, either old-fashioned
neon or glittering LEDs. It drips, flows, sparkles, flashes and
runs in circles, chasing its tail across the front of casinos and bars,
illuminating the giant screens stalked by pop stars and showgirls,
the gods and goddesses of Las Vegas. As the darkness deepens
the real city emerges; the tawdry, vulgar Strip of the daylight
hours becomes sublime. At its north end the Stratosphere Tower,
which looked like nothing so much as a stretched concrete water

tower in the day, has slipped into a silver ball gown sheer enough to grace any red carpet, accessorized with blue neon earrings and a red headdress. The Flamingo spreads its electric tail feathers and the facade of the Riviera is a sheer cliff of exploding stars. Cultural historian Dave Hickey has called neon 'the only indigenous visual culture on the North American continent'. In Vegas, you see what he means. However indefensible, unsustainable and ultimately pathological the city undoubtedly is, at night it is one of the wonders of the world.

I join the promenade up and down the Strip for hours, enjoying the show. It is while I am refuelling on burritos in a cheap eatery that I hear a clap of thunder and rush outside. Las Vegas's own volcano, at the Mirage Hotel, is getting ready to perform, as it does every hour on the hour once darkness falls. Gouts of flame shoot upwards from the fifty-foot pile of rocks at the hotel's entrance, accompanied by puffs of smoke, and more amplified sound effects are unleashed before the volcano erupts promptly on the hour with jets of water in place of lava coloured red by hidden lights. How much more reliable this mechanized version of nature is than the real volcanoes I have encountered on my travels.

Tonight, although a three-quarter moon hangs overhead, as though I had stepped into a twenty-first-century version of a Neopolitan *veduta*, the city is too bright for any moonlight to illuminate the eruption on the Sunset Strip; the man-made mountain concludes its performance swiftly, and the crowds disperse. By midnight I am feeling as though I am trapped inside a giant pinball machine, richocheted here and there between walls of illumination. It is time to leave the city and strike out for places where the moon still has a territory and my eyes can experience light unchanged by human intervention.

The next morning I hire a car and head out on Highway 93 over the Hoover Dam, picking up the remaining section of the old

Route 66 through the toe of the Havasupai Reservation and up on to a plateau bounded by the Aubrey Cliffs. The sun is going down in the rear-view mirror when I pull over to watch the landscape change colour. The cliffs are really a steep escarpment, eroded in deep grooves and striped with scrub. They catch the sinking sun, changing colour through the spectrum from pink, through mauve to blue. Caught in the low angle of the last sunbeams, the tufts of desert grass glow white. The moon is now high overhead, still pale. I am tempted to stay here and watch the plain descend into darkness, but first I need to find a bed for the night. I follow the road round the edge of the cliffs and down into Seligman and check into a motel.

There is an autographed photo of Bill Haley and the Comets in reception from one of their endless roadhouse tours back in the 1960s and the door of my cabin bears a plaque saying that a more recent visitor, *National Geographic* photographer Vince Musi, has stayed here. I feel honoured to be in the company of such intrepid travellers. A portrait of a Navajo chief painted by a certain A. Rodriguez is mounted above the bed in a rough-hewn frame nailed together from bits of board; the place used to be called the Navaho Motel, in the days before the interstate took the traffic away from Route 66, leaving just this section of the road as a kind of stage set for Harley-riding nostalgia-seekers. Against a kitsch backdrop of pines and snowy peaks, dressed in his buckskins with two tremendous plaits running down his chest and two feathers in his hair, the brave's expression is one of fierce dignity. It reminds me of a sentence from a leaflet released by the Navaho to give guidance to visitors to their land which is reproduced in my guidebook, warning against back-slapping, hand-shaking, intrusive eye contact and other crass, white-man behaviour. It is a sentence of such concise power as to be worth quoting: 'The general exuberance many cultures define as friendliness,' it reads, 'is not considered such by American Indians.' Time has proved the cultural instincts of the Diné right. But outside it is growing dark, the moon is bright and even the lights of this tiny strip development with its self-consciously eccentric stores and diners celebrating the history of 'the mother road' are irksome.

I reject the inviting neon of the Road Kill Café although I haven't eaten for eight hours or so and head back up on to the high plateau. I continue until I cannot see a single artificial light anywhere in the distance, pull over once more and shut off the engine. It is silent apart from the trilling of crickets and the ticking and crackling of the car as it begins to cool down. I walk away to lose its sound and scent, down a red dirt trail towards the railroad track. As my vision begins to adjust I have no trouble seeing where I am going. My shadow is long and dark in the moonlight and the sky is huge and full of stars and I cannot take my eyes from it. This is the canopy mankind dwelled beneath before we elected to live in a permanent Vegas strip of our own creation. Among the fixed stars are one or two drifting, flashing ones; aeroplanes, their invasive presence put into perspective by the vastness of space. They look no bigger than the fireflies that are making their appearance in North America at this time of year and that were the subject of a phone-in I listened to on Rebel Radio as I drove down here: 'Their asses made a green smear where they hit my windshield,' a trucker reported with a chuckle. And of course our furthest-flung projectiles are infinitely smaller than fireflies in the context of what I am looking at. And then I notice the vapour trails created by two of the planes caught in the moonlight, weightless and delicate as gossamer, and it's a beautiful thing. I'm reminded that in the tradition of the Hopi Indians, the moon is a spider-woman who taught the people of earth to weave. I have never made a connection between moonlight and spiders' webs until this moment. Perhaps many thousands of years ago a Hopi noticed the way the moonlight caught the smoke of a fire and had the same thought, the human brain responding to the hardwired impulse evolution has bestowed upon us, an impulse that lies at the root of poetry and legend, to see one thing as like another.

I've been thinking about snakes a little. Before leaving on my trip I told a friend that I was considering sleeping out in the desert one night during my stay and she forwarded some photos she had been sent by a friend in Tucson, captioned 'Spring is Here!' Taken on a stroll in the Sonora Desert outside the city, they show two large rattlesnakes as thick as a man's wrist approaching each other across a trail, rearing up and then entwining necks in an elaborate mating dance. I am not nervous about such things – in fact I like snakes – but I believe in showing respect to the inhabitants of whatever country I visit. Arizona boasts an impressive array of venomous reptiles: the strange, semi-albino hypomelanistic West Diamondback Rattlesnake, its pale colouring the result of a lack of melanin, which causes the most deaths of any snake in North America; the Black and Mohave rattlesnakes; and the poisonous Gila lizard, which can grow up to two feet long. I am conscious of where I am placing my feet, especially as I am not wearing boots in the desert heat. Suddenly, almost at the tip of my sandals, I see a long slender snake gliding across the path. The moonlight glistens on its scales as it moves. It doesn't have the diamond markings of a rattler. Could it be the mainly nocturnal Glossy Snake, a non-venomous, slender creature that can reach six feet in length? I stop and watch a foot or two away, fascinated. Then I notice something strange. Although it appears to be continuously in motion, it isn't going anywhere – its head never seems to get any further forward. I pick up a stick and approach closer, but what I am seeing still doesn't make sense. I bend down and prod the mysterious reptile. As soon as I do so, my sense of touch tells me that this is no snake, but a piece of wire, lying discarded in the dirt. I lift it with the stick and let it fall again and it lands stiffly, completely un-snakelike in every way. Yet when I squat and focus all my attention on it, despite what I know to be the case, my eyes still tell a different story. The moonlight appears to flow along the surface of the wire, the only reflective object on the dry and dusty track, creating the impression of sinuous, rippling movement. I pick it up in my hand, jubilantly, like a Louisiana snake-handling Holy Roller – it cannot harm me. What I have seen is a perfect demonstration of the way in which pure, undiluted moonlight plays with our vision and has the power to render the mundane uncanny.

A month or so after this incident, back in London, I attend a lecture at the Royal Society by a neurologist called R. Beau Lotto, entitled 'Seeing Ourselves See'. The ancient lecture theatre in John Adam Street is packed; in the twenty-first century, neurology obviously creates nearly as much excitement as demonstrations of electricity or working models of volcanoes did in the eighteenth. Lotto's subject is visual perception and the part the brain plays in it. He explains that the light patterns which fall on our retina, and which provide us with our only direct access to the world, are essentially meaningless; or, rather, they could mean one of an infinite number of things, as light reflected off very different objects will create essentially the same signal. The 'liquid architecture' of the brain, he tells a rapt audience, did not evolve to see the world as it is. We see what it has proved useful to see in the past. Vision is like a text with missing letters that the brain makes guesses at, informed by accumulated experience. Studying human perception by asking people what they see is deeply flawed as no one is an independent observer of nature – their perception, and therefore their answers, can only be from within their own ecology of knowledge and learned experience. Lotto instead studies what we do. He also studies bees, and the common aspects between the perception of human beings and these well-organized insects. He is clearly a great admirer of bees; he has brought some with him in a plastic box, a queen bumblebee along with some of her daughters and eggs. With a brain around the size of the head of a pin, comprising only a million cells – fewer cells than are in the human retina – they can count to five and navigate better than the most advanced robot yet created. His talk is interspersed with a number of startling optical illusions that demonstrate not so much the fallibility of our perception as the brain's facility at making assumptions about the nature of objects, based on their context. An audience member asks if, having worked with these illusions for a number of years, Lotto is able to 'see through' them – whether his brain, knowing that they are illusory, is able to make adjustments and 'correct' his vision. No, he replies. They are cognitively impenetrable. It is his belief that an understanding of the way perception works can increase our tolerance for, and empathy with, others. They have no choice but to see things differently to the way we do. Their entire databank of learned behaviour tells them to do so.

After the lecture I manage to catch him for a moment and tell him my story of meeting a snake in the desert and of the way I couldn't shake the illusion, even when my other senses were giving me a different message. Yes, he says. You prepared your brain to think there might be snakes in the desert and it was doing what it was supposed to do. Even when I didn't feel in any way nervous or jumpy about snakes? Exactly. The brain received a signal and decoded it as 'snake', and that signal was cognitively impenetrable, even when your other senses were telling you differently. Speaking with Lotto makes me feel immensely grateful to the complex and mysterious organ I carry around inside my skull, my hidden guardian and the constructor of my reality.

The day after my night walk in the desert, according to my original itinerary, I should be heading south towards Tucson,

but every person I have spoken with in New York is so scandal-
ized that I would even think of visiting the south-west without
going to see the Grand Canyon that I realize that to do so would
be plain bad manners, rather like not calling on a family member
if you are in their area when visiting from overseas. The canyon
is, after all, the sole geographical feature in North America that
is unique in the world (with the possible exception of Las Vegas).
So I add nearly 200 miles to my trip, queue in a trail of cars to
get into the park and peer over the edge with a group of Japanese tourists and gasp. Then I drive away from the crowds and
hike along an unmarked trail through ponderosa pines, meet an
elk, his antlers so impressive that in a Macbeth moment I think
the forest itself is moving, and come to the rim on my own,
where I sit for an hour completely alone, without fences or gift
shops or senior tour parties, with the crickets clicking their cas-
tanets in the trees and the colours of the canyon shifting before
my eyes. Fortunately I am disturbed by a family who have also
hiked the trail. I am able to hear their approach some distance
away. 'We're invading your solitude,' the mother says to me
cheerfully, when they spot me with my back to a rock in the
shadow of a tree. 'Sir, you're our only hope for a family photograph,' the father says, holding his camera out towards me.
'Would you mind?' I happily comply. I am very glad to see
them; if they hadn't appeared I might be there still.

After a desperately long drive that crosses deserts and climbs
and descends thousands of feet, passing forests and snow-topped
extinct volcanoes, and during which the staggering beauty of
the landscape repeatedly forces me to stop the car and stare, just
when I seem to be making some progress, I am around thirty
miles outside Flagstaff when I catch sight of the volcanic domes
of the San Francisco Peaks. An inviting dirt road leads off the
highway and I can't resist bumping along it. The place feels
ancient; once the home of the Anasazi people, the ground is

littered with cinders, a reminder of its volcanic past. Cloud shadows chase each other across the yellow grassland and up the smooth sides of the craters themselves. I am, I realize, close to Roden Crater, the volcano owned by artist James Turrell that he is sculpting into something between a vast artwork and an observatory. Light is Turrell's raw material, the medium he works in, both artificial light in the gallery space and natural light outside. As an artist he is keenly aware of the ways the mechanisms within the human eye interact with stimuli to create our perception of the world. I have seen him make light in a controlled environment appear like a solid block of colour, and experienced his 'skyspaces', architectural features that direct and mould our view of the sky, turning it into a living artwork. Turrell has written about how the dark nights at the crater enable him to blend moonlight, reflected from the sun and only a matter of minutes old, with ancient light from the stars that is at least four and a half billion years old, older than our solar system itself. Like a celestial cocktail waiter, he has spoken of how these different lights can make us feel, comparing moonlight with Beaujolais Nouveau and starlight with an older, more mature wine. Using large-scale construction equipment he is sculpting spaces in the volcano's crater in which it will be possible to experience these different lights and creating tunnels beneath it in celestial alignment with the moon. Those fortunate enough to be granted a visit – usually those who have contributed towards the millions of dollars that have been required to realize the project – have spoken of a brass staircase leading upwards into the empty sky. I have arrived a couple of years too early to gain admittance and I have no desire to wander on to his territory unannounced. The high altitude and dry desert air make the San Francisco Peaks a perfect place for astronomical observation as well as for an artist wishing to work with the light of the moon and stars. The night sky here is protected by Flagstaff's 'Dark Skies' ordinance, which strictly controls upward-directed light at night. Arizona seems to sprout almost as many telescopes as cactii; limiting light pollution is therefore good business as well as life-enhancing for local residents. I hope that when Roden Crater finally opens to the public the crowds it draws won't compromise the sense of solitude that is such a special feature of this part of the desert. It is one of the ironies of being human that we seem fated to destroy the things we love.

It is already sunset by the time I arrive at Arcosanti, the utopian architectural community in the high desert north of Phoenix where I intend to spend the night. Arcosanti was set up by the Italian-born architect Paolo Soleri as an experiment in Arcology – a term he coined to describe a combination of architecture and ecology that he suggests offers a sustainable model for urban development. His original plan was that the high-density development, with mixed-use business and residential units and shared communal areas, would house 5,000 people in an area of only 25 acres, surrounded by the natural environment. Much of the settlement's food would be produced in solar greenhouses and the buildings' orientation and shape would utilize natural cooling processes to minimize power use. After nearly forty years, only a handful of structures are clustered on a series of terraces above a dry river canyon, among mature cypress trees, their domed roofs reminiscent of a cluster of beehives. When I arrive I am greeted by a couple of students, here to study, work and help build the place, who are climbing the steps to enjoy a cigarette and the sunset. 'Hey, you're James, right?' the girl says, in what sounds like an Italian accent. 'Don't ask me how I know. I think they left your key in the café.' I find my way to the communal cafeteria and there's my key, sitting on the counter. The café, also run by volunteers, is closing up for the night. Could I get a little food, I ask? No, we've put most of it away already, I'm told with a smile. Couldn't they get it out again, I wonder?

I haven't eaten much since breakfast and I have been driving for hours. Apparently not. If I want to eat, there's nothing for it but to drive back to the highway. This wouldn't be so bad, but the same thing had happened to me the night before. After my encounter with the imaginary snake in the desert, I had returned to Seligman to find that all the diners closed their doors at nine o'clock at night. I had ended up eating at a Shell station where the only two items left in the hot-food display were a corn dog and a burrito, both of which forlorn items I washed down with a Sprite. I had been looking forward to sampling something more wholesome at Arcosanti.

Sometimes it is only through things going wrong that we experience the best moments of the day. As I hurry back along the dirt road, resigned to another gas station supper, moonlight begins to take over from the fading sun. The sky is a powder blue and the landscape takes on a similar tinge. An animal lopes across the road in front of me. For a second in the uncertain light I think it must be a desert fox – it looks large enough – but then it pauses in the brush and I see it is a hare; around two foot long, larger than any I have seen in Europe and with black tips to its long ears and a black tail. It must have emerged from its shelter in the shadow of a cactus or rock to begin its nocturnal search for food. It pauses and looks back over its shoulder at me, its weight hunched forward over its front legs and its haunches raised like a racing cyclist, confident in its own ability to turn its nonchalant gait into a burst of speed should I decide to follow. (Desert hares, or black-tailed jackrabbits as they are better known, can reach speeds of forty-five miles per hour). In cultures around the world, from China to Zambia to the Great Lakes, hares are associated with the moon, so it is hard not to take its presence as some sort of encouragement on my journey. In Native American legends Michabo, or the Great Manitou, is the best known of mythical heroes. He acquired the distinctive black-tipped ears that I am looking at now when he was singed attempting to steal fire from man, narrowly escaping ending up in the cooking pot himself.

Cordes Junction is an average American fast-food hell. I sit at a plastic table in a forecourt with trucks rushing past on the highway amid the smell of gasoline. A couple of tables down a dangerously overweight family are eating next to the trash bin that has long since overflowed on to the asphalt. There is little to detain me and after a few minutes I am bumping back down the track to Arcosanti. Guest accommodation is a line of cabins on a dirt road below the main development, their front walls mainly glass, looking over a small, dry river wash. The moon is fully up and shining directly into my room. I seem to be the only guest; no other lights spill into the canyon and I am loath to turn one on. At the same time, I need to write up some of my notes. I try sitting on a chair outside the door in the moonlight with my laptop, but quickly realize this is a stupid idea. The screen robs me of my night vision; when I look up, the moon rides in a black sky devoid of stars. In addition, every moth, bug and flying creature in the vicinity is attracted by the computer's white-blue glow, and is soon crawling all over it, giving my notes a close, insect edit. My words have never found such an attentive audience. The text looks as if it is fragmenting, the letters detaching themselves from the lines, walking about and then taking off, back into the ether, watched by their companions who remain glued to the light.

II

The next morning I wake early to the sound of construction work on a new building, right behind my accommodation, which starts shortly after six o'clock, to avoid the midday heat.

I eat breakfast in the communal café and take an unaccompanied walk around the complex. My grumpiness at being refused food the night before hasn't completely left me, but there is something cheering in the banter among the multilingual co-workers going about their tasks. You can catch a whiff, if you pay attention, of something in the air, almost as if one had been transported to one of the future cities dreamed up by members of the Situationist International, a utopian New Babylon. I cross the river canyon and climb a hillside, where lizards flash among the rocks. From here the settlement looks even more like the set from a 1960s science-fiction movie, a retro-futurist oasis in the parched scrubland of the present. Close up, some of Soleri's architecture hasn't fared particularly well in its passage through time; there is something about cast concrete that has begun to look very ancient, redolent of the high modernism he intended to question. In the cafeteria, a member of the permanent staff is talking with workmen, tasked to paint the interior of part of the dining hall. There is much discussion as to how successfully the surface will take the paint and the problems they have had in other areas of the complex. 'It's a mess, basically,' someone says. And you have to agree that it is. The clutter collected outside the living quarters is reminiscent of a hippy commune; improvised hangings are pinned up in the building's trademark circular windows, undermining its minimalist aesthetic. And then there are the bells, forged to Soleri's over-ornate, fantastical designs to raise money for the project, on sale in the gallery. We are urged to purchase different designs of bells and ring them for specific 'causes': peace, friendship and so on. Quite apart from my innate scepticism, I have to declare a particular hatred for wind chimes, hanging bells and all such paraphernalia. Despite remaining a fan of extremely loud music, I object to pointless jangling. Perfectly appropriate a few thousand feet up in the Himalayas at a Buddhist shrine, a wind chime is the last thing needed at a window or in an urban garden, already a fragile refuge from omnipresent noise. Here they merely serve to further insulate us from a direct relationship with the natural world. (What is it with human beings and sound? Why aren't we ever content to *just shut the fuck up*?) Bells aside, there is a sense that Arcosanti is somewhat stalled through reverence for its founder, now less than a decade short of his own centenary, some of whose ideas are inevitably in need of an overhaul. Yet for all this quibbling, Arcosanti is a noble experiment, as much in living as in architecture, its international volunteer-workers no doubt empowered to return home and update its vision in line with the requirements of their own environment.

But it is not a desire to look at experimental architecture that has brought me to the Arizona desert. Tonight will be the first of the two Full Moon Events held in the run-up to the full moon at the Interstellar Light Collector in Tucson. After my experiences in Japan and Naples my anxiety about cloud cover began before I left home. When I nervously emailed from England asking about the likely weather conditions, I was assured that cloudy skies in early June in Tucson are almost unknown. The monsoons arrive in July and August; this is when flash floods roar down canyons, tossing trees and boulders before them so that the danger for those out in the desert comes not from thirst but drowning. Yet as I have driven southward the airwaves are full of reports of a freakish weather front that is bringing unseasonable rain and cloud to a wide swathe of states in the south. It is, dishearteningly, as if I travel with atmospheric low pressure gathered around my shoulders like a cloak. Nervously, I ring Corinne Davies from Arcosanti for a weather report. Yes, she confirms that the skies in Tucson are clouding over; the cover might burn off in the afternoon but it might not. She advises me to drive down today, so that I have two opportunities to experience the full moon at the Collector, tonight and tomorrow night. I am reluctant to get back in my car so early. I would rather book another night, stay in my hermit's cell and write up some of my impressions of the trip so far. However, I cannot risk missing my appointment with the moon. As I drink another coffee in the café, I look at the documentation I have down-loaded from the Interstellar Light Applications site about visiting the Collector. First, as we are approaching midsummer, the angle of the moon requires those wishing to bask in its light to go some of the way to meet it.

IMPORTANT NOTE: For both evenings, in order for our interstellar telescope to get the best use of moonlight, it is necessary to elevate attendees (in a secure boom lift) up to 23 feet in the air. If you are uncom-fortable with heights, you may want to plan to attend again in September, when we're back at ground level. Participants are elevated, two at a time, for an agreed upon amount of time.

Second, and inevitably, there is a charge for using the facility.

Our fee structure is as follows: The charge for being in the focused and concentrated moonlight is $25 per person for three (3) minutes, $50 per person for seven (7) minutes, $100 per person for fifteen (15) minutes and $200 per person for thirty (30) minutes. You may decide, after you are in the moonlight, that you would like to extend your time – we can accom-modate you at that time. If you would like to pay in advance, we will accept debit and credit cards; otherwise, you may pay by cash, credit card, or check on the evening you attend.

While it seems a little surreal to charge for moonlight, these fees do not look extortionate when you realize that the Collector can operate only for a few hours on two days out of every month, weather permitting. The Chapins, a prosperous couple who run a successful swap meet in Tucson, have put everything they have into building the Collector and into founding their company, ILA. Already, in my email correspondence with their office, I have been struck both by their kindness and their sincerity; they clearly believe there are sound scientific principles underlying the efficacy of their invention, for which they have already registered a US patent. This sincerity, naturally, is not allowed to stand in the way of the American entrepreneurial spirit. What drug company, after all, would not cash in if they had found a cure for cancer; what inventor would not want recompense for harnessing the energy of the stars?

The people at ILA have suggested a few places I can stay in Tucson, mostly of the kind that come complete with Guardian Angel sculptures in the garden and hosts of 'exceptional spiritual discernment', but I have other plans. The Congress is Tucson's rock 'n' roll hotel, with a vibrant bar and live music venue inhouse, and I am trusting it will be the perfect antidote, if one is needed, to an overdose of the mystical. The reception desk in the lobby, its 1930s ambience still intact, does not disappoint. A goldfish swims in a bowl on a shelf, bearing the inscription 'My name is Jules Bastien-Lepage'. I never do ascertain why the Congress mascot should be named after a nineteenth-century French painter. The hotel's main claim to fame is that it was here that the Dillinger gang was discovered. They had come to Tucson to take a break from their busy schedule of robberies but had been unable to resist boasting of their exploits while living it up around town. When the top floor of the Congress caught fire they tipped some firemen twelve dollars each to run up and bring down their bags. This might not have been as generous as it sounds; the bags were exceptionally weighty because they were full of guns and ammunition. The firemen were suspicious and later identified the heavy tippers with equally heavy bags from a picture in *True Detective* magazine. Lured into a trap, Dillinger himself was confronted by a policeman who told him, 'Reach for the moon, or I'll cut you in half!' (Even policemen in this town use a lunar idiom, it seems.)

To which the notorious criminal merely replied, 'I'll be damned!'

I'm here to reach for the moon myself, or at least I'm hoping the moon will reach me. As night falls I take Ajo Way out of Tucson, keeping an eye out for the milestone that will warn me of the dirt road I must take towards the Interstellar Light Collector. Gradually I leave the city behind and enter the desert. Tucson, like Flagstaff, has legal restrictions on the amount of light that is allowed to spill up into the night sky; with Kitt Peak Observatory a few miles further on down the highway, darkness is good business here. This far south, night draws in early to my northern eyes, even though it is approaching midsummer. The sky is still overcast, congested with solid-looking clouds, like dirty grey ice floes in a river. Through the left-hand window of my car I can see the spot where the sky is brightest and the clouds are edged in silver. Briefly, the moon itself makes an appearance, like a pop star on a balcony tantalizing the crowds below. I am hoping against hope that this isn't a wasted trip. I have, after all, read and signed the release form, with its slightly alarming warnings and comprehensive disclaimers.

In consideration of the acceptance of my request to enter into Interstellar Light Applications' Designated Moonlit Area And Any Surrounding Areas That May Be Illuminated By Moon Light Reflector, I hereby waive, release and discharge any and all claims for damages for death, personal injury or property damage which I may have, or which may subsequently accrue to me, as a result of my viewing the moonlight. This release is intended to discharge in advance the owners and their respective officers, agents and employees from and against any and all liability arising out of or connected in any way with my participation in viewing the moonlight, even though any liability may arise out of negligence or carelessness on the part of the persons or entities mentioned above.

I further understand that it is unknown what effects, if any, the moonlight may cause. Knowing that there may be unknown risks, I hereby agree to assume those risks and to release and hold harmless all of the persons or entities mentioned above who (through negligence or carelessness) might otherwise be liable to me or my heirs or assigns for damages.

I further understand and agree that this waiver, release and assumption of risk is binding upon my heirs and assigns.

I acknowledge that no physical or medical benefits are claimed or have been demonstrated by viewing the moonlight.

This last assertion appears to undermine all the other information on the site, but in a litigious country I guess it is better to contradict yourself than go bankrupt. I follow another car a mile or so down a dirt track into the desert, keeping far enough behind to escape at least some of the cloud of orange dust kicked up by its wheels. It is approaching eight o'clock as we arrive at a gateway where a notice proclaims 'ILA Moon Viewing Event This Evening: YES'. As I get out of my car I fear this assertion may prove over-optimistic. The sky is backlit, the moon itself curtained by grey cloud. At the entrance to the site, where I have to hand in my signed disclaimer at a desk, I meet the driver of the other car, who turns out to be Corinne Davies. Even if the moon does not make an appearance, at least we will have had the opportunity to meet. We join a small gathering of around a dozen people. A handful of mobile homes and gazebos face the Collector itself, a vast construction a couple of storeys high, sunk into a large, circular pit in the ground. In front of it stands a gantry, in which those wishing to enter the focused moonlight are raised to the correct angle of elevation.

Corinne introduces me to Monica Chapin. Dressed in a pale trouser suit, Chapin is bustling around acting like something between a society hostess and a minister at a revival meeting. She acknowledges apologetically that the chances of access to moonlight unimpeded by cloud are not looking good. She is particularly concerned about one visitor who is suffering from colon cancer and has travelled from Spain in the hope of a session in the concentrated moonlight. Such occurrences must be an occupational hazard for those offering therapies based on changeable natural phenomena. My presence, in my role as a writer from Europe, in addition to that of an astrophysicist and a naturopath, both of whom have arrived despite the weather conditions and are expressing curiosity about the Collector, must be adding to the pressure. I am introduced to Mike, one of the team operating the Collector; he works the gantry, taking people two by two up into the moonlight. I might as well give you the dollar tour, he says wryly. We go down into the artificial crater in which the Chapins' fifty-foot-wide invention is sited and walk round to its business end to look up at its reflective face. Mike explains that each of the eighty-four eight-foot-long parabolic mirrors of which it is built can be angled individually, but the whole makes up a single geometric shape, an off-axis paraboloid, with a focal distance of around 100 feet. Anyone getting in range during the day when sunlight was falling on the reflector would be in trouble. 'This thing would strip the paint off a car in seconds,' he tells me. 'We just point it downwards and let it fry that wall of earth there.' Scientists and technicians from Kitt Peak Observatory and the University of Arizona optics department helped in the construction of the Collector. To the Chapins' bemusement, none of them now want to have their names attached to the project.

In the hope that the skies will clear, Mrs Chapin proceeds with the evening talk she always gives before a viewing. We take our seats in a tent where refreshments have been laid out on a table. At the back of the tent, Monica Chapin's daughter is manning a stall selling crystals for the family business, Moonlight Infusions. Monica begins with the story, familiar to many of

those present, of how she and her husband embarked on building the Moonlight Collector. She is a practised speaker; as she
talks, she walks back and forth, gesturing with her hands in the
manner of an evangelical lay preacher. She explains that the
project began when a good friend, who wasn't yet fifty years
old, contracted pancreatic cancer. She came to the Chapins having tried every treatment available, both mainstream medicine
and alternative remedies. 'There's nothing on this planet that
can save me,' she said. 'Richard, you're a man who thinks outside the box; can't you think of something to help?' Richard
disappeared into the reference library at the University of Arizona; according to Monica, she barely saw him for months.
Gradually his attention was drawn to papers related to research
on light frequencies, some of them similar to the frequencies
found in moonlight. It is rich in the same penetrating, red spectrums that are present in sunlight and which give people vital
vitamin D, but moonlight doesn't burn in the way sunlight does.
NASA scientists, he believed, would turn the Space Shuttle
around if an astronaut was sick so that moonlight could shine
into the craft's only window. However, here on earth the light
of the moon is very weak. Why not create something capable of
amplifying that light hundreds of times? And so the process of
building the Collector began, a process that cost the Chapins
more than a million dollars; as Monica explains, 'We mortgaged
everything we had to try and make a change on the planet.'
Pointing out of the tent to where their invention looms in the
dusk, she says, with a rueful smile, 'I got this instead of a retirement home in Hawaii!' Sadly, their friend did not survive long
enough to try out the therapeutic effects of moonlight. 'But I
feel her presence with us out here in the desert,' Monica says
enthusiastically. The atmosphere is gradually changing, becoming nearer to that of a Pentecostal meeting. Can she get a
witness? Yes she can. A man in his early twenties, a regular vis-

itor and helper at the site, explains that his asthma has been cured by sessions in the Collector. Another man attempts to describe the experience: 'You feel the rays of this light on your being,' he tells us. 'It is almost like a wind that is not blowing. It feels good.' A man with a shaved head and a small, neatly trimmed beard that is dyed a dark black is holding a toy dog, some sort of long-haired terrier, in his arms. They are clearly devoted to each other. His dog is asthmatic also, he explains, and has been treated successfully at the Collector. No one comments on the fact that, despite the sweltering heat in the tent, the animal is wearing a tight tartan coat. It is panting continually. Take its coat off, I feel like saying, and you won't be forced to bring it out here at full moon to help it breathe. Better still, don't force a long-haired dog to live in a place where daytime temperatures in summer regularly reach 107 degrees Fahrenheit. But I keep my advice to myself.

There is no lack of anecdotal evidence of the benefits of exposure to the concentrated moonlight. Asthma seems to respond best, followed by skin diseases and heavy scarring, precancerous conditions and first-stage cancer – 'We haven't cured anyone of cancer yet but we have extended lives,' Monica tells us. And who is to say this is not so? Hope itself, as elusive as moonlight, is a powerful panacea. Many subjects report pain relief and release from depression. Others have thrown their glasses away. A severely overweight fireman returned from a session at the Collector filled with new energy and went for a four-mile run at midnight. Over the next five months he lost 100 lbs and gained promotion at work.

At the conclusion of her talk, Chapin reveals a new direction for the research they are undertaking. For the first time they have operated the Collector during the dark, moonless nights of the month, pointing it at the brightest stars in the sky, gathering and concentrating their light. A limited number of trusted

friends have been exposed to this magnified starlight, as a trial
before the public are allowed access to the sessions. So far they
have focused their efforts on gathering the light of the stars
Sirius, Vega and Arcturus. This light is very different to moonlight. While the moon is a passive reflector, Chapin points out,
stars are positive and have their own energy source. Sirius, part
of the Canis Major constellation, is over nine light years from
earth and gives off a blue light. Vega is the brightest star in the
summer sky in Arizona, part of the constellation Lyra, and looks
blue-white, while Arcturus, the most distant of the three stars at
thirty-six light years away in the constellation Boötes, looks
orange in the sky. 'We are bringing in spectrums of light not
experienced before on the planet,' Chapin tells us proudly. As
they have never been experienced before, I can't resist asking,
what makes you think it will be beneficial to amplify their light
and expose human beings to it in this way? But apparently the
effects have already proved profound. The light from Sirius and
Vega produced a sense of euphoria and peace in those who
experienced it. Arcturus, in contrast, 'felt creepy and weird'.

As the night wears on and the moon itself, the power-source
fuelling this small enclave of sky watchers in the desert, still
refuses to cooperate, the formal talk breaks down into a loose
network of conversations. Several people, including Corinne
Davies, have decided to go home, as it looks increasingly
unlikely that the skies will clear. Before she leaves, we agree to
be in touch the next day, either to come out to the Collector
again if she has time, or to meet up and talk about our common
interest in the moon. Those remaining are enthusiasts, who do
not need to be convinced of the benefits of the Chapins' invention. Some of their unguarded talk makes it clear why the
Collector has so far not succeeded in attracting serious investigation from the scientific community. There are reports of
figures appearing on the array during the time it is pointed

towards the stars, of a sense of a 'light portal' opening and some form of communication going on. Monica tells of visitors to her star evening who claimed that they actually came from Vega. Gradually it emerges that during one session several of those who were exposed to the light of a particular star independently reported seeing the letters L-O-V-E appear in the mirrors. I half expect the theme music from *E.T.* to start coming through the loudspeakers. Suddenly I am tired and wishing I was back in my hotel room, or at least in the hotel bar. It is time to leave.

The next morning I decide to shake off my sense of disappointment at the way things are working out by going for a walk. There is construction carrying on round the clock on the freeway coming into Tucson and the night before, trying to avoid it on my return from the Collector, I had managed to get lost in the eerily empty streets to the south of the city. As a European used to compact, densely populated cities, what I find disorientating is the endless sprawl of low-rise buildings, the long roads apparently devoid of landmarks that seem to be heading nowhere. It is well after midnight when I see two patrol cars pulled up at the side of the road, lights flashing, having a late-night consultation. I pull over as one draws away and get out of the car. Adopting my best English accent, I tell the man watching me warily from the front seat, no doubt with a hand on his gun as I approach, that I am a tourist, that I'm lost and that I've been driving round the area for some time. 'Oh-oh,' he says. I tell him where I am trying to get to and he replies slowly, as if to a child, 'This is the bad part of town. You don't want to stay around here. Keep driving that-away and you'll get to downtown.' And he is gone, with a screech of tyres. So I do keep going, despite the visual evidence suggesting I am heading out of, rather than into, the city, until eventually the buildings get bigger, there are people on the streets and miraculously I find my hotel. So this morning it is a relief to leave my car in the lot and walk to the Tucson Museum of Art.

In the Latin American collection I see a Mexican crucifixion with the same sun and moon motif that I saw in the Perugino painting in Siena, the theme brought across the Atlantic by Spanish missionaries and passed on to Mexican artists employed by the Jesuits to embody their religion in a visual language the local population will recognize. In the contemporary section of the museum I get talking to one of the gallery attendants, who we'll call Dan, a barrel-chested man in his sixties with slicked-back white hair, who personalizes his uniform with distinctive rings and jewellery at his throat. We begin by discussing the heat outside, but I soon learn I know nothing about the subject of 'hot'. Dan tells me that he worked for many years as a black-smith in the Arizona copper mines at an underground forge where temperatures must have been almost unbearable. He used to use a 200 lb double-sided jackhammer to beat the metal, he tells me, but with the handle sawn off, so that he could wield it with one massively powerful arm. Then one day his boss asked him to carry something, a large container, a distance of a couple of blocks along the underground corridors of the mine. Dan was proud of his strength and picked the load up easily even though his boss had told him to carry it with another man. He set it down in the appointed place and at that moment his right arm and hand ceased to work. He could hardly make a fist. He hurried back to the office where his boss was in a meeting and told him that he needed to get to hospital. His boss told him to wait as he was busy, but Dan grasped him around the throat with his good hand and explained that the matter was urgent, in a manner the man could not ignore. At the hospital they opened up his arm, only to tell him there was nothing they could do. His grip in his right hand had gone from 225 lb down to 3 lb, and that was what he would be left with for the rest of his life.

Dan wasn't having any. 'I never give up,' he told them. 'It's mine. I'm getting it back.' Confined to his house on sick leave for month after month he ordered up crates of used tennis balls and crushed them until they popped, one by one. He did weights. After a year he went back to see the same doctor and squeezed his hand, hard. The doctor was forced to admit that perhaps he had been wrong. (I imagine, having shaken hands with Dan myself, the admission came sooner rather than later.) Now, as well as working at the museum, Dan is an artist and jeweller, making the distinctive rings and necklaces he wears with his uniform, influenced by the crafts of the Native American cultures of the south-west. His story is the tonic I need to lift me out of my momentary depression and loss of momentum. If he could come back from such a calamitous event, I have no right to let a few clouds throw me off course.

As evening draws in, Corinne rings to say the skies are clearing and that she intends to travel out to the Collector again tonight. When I arrive, she asks whether I notice a difference in the atmosphere. It's true there is an air of expectancy among the twenty or so people gathered in the tent as they chatter and browse the snacks that have been put out for them. I can hear the motor of the gantry running, ready to lift people into the air to meet the moon, which is appearing sporadically between tattered streamers of cloud. Somewhere, a loudspeaker is emitting a stream of generic, new-age music. Richard Chapin has arrived and is talking to Corinne and I walk over and join them. While we speak he is constantly taking nervous peeks at the sky – he clearly finds the uncertain weather conditions torturous as he hates to turn people away. 'Three thousand people have been through the Collector,' he says, 'but why not thirty thousand? We should be building lots of these things. But the scientists just want proof after proof . . .' He is a bundle of nerves, his body twisting this way and that as he speaks. He explains more about the technical capabilities of the Collector as Monica begins her talk. 'Given the optimum conditions, if the earth was flat and there was nothing in the way, you know this thing has the ability to see a striking match at three thousand miles? Yes, if you got within its focal range during the day, your clothes would just catch fire . . . We're pointing it at the stars now, did Monica tell you that?' Yes, I say, she was speaking about it last night. 'Did she mention the L-word?' The L-word? 'Yes, the L-word. She's not telling everyone, she's worried how it will sound.' I realize he is referring to the L-O-V-E incident. He shifts from foot to foot uncomfortably, darting a look at me to try to gauge my reaction. 'We're trying to be very scientific here . . .'

He asks me why I think scientists are so slow to come out and run tests on the Collector. 'When we built it we thought they'd come rushing out here, but no,' he says, his disappointment obvious. Perhaps it is a matter of language, I say. If you want scientific approval, you have to speak scientific language and run tests based on scientific methods. It's almost as though you need an interpreter. 'Maybe,' he says. 'But it takes so long . . .'

I tune in to some of Monica's talk in the tent and try to make some notes as she speaks, while keeping an eye on the sky outside. She is speaking of how the structure of crystals can be changed by exposure to concentrated moonlight. A geo-scientist in the University of Arizona studies the different 'signatures' of various types of rock using a laser spectrometer that can measure the light emitted by their atoms. A second signature for each specimen is created by the imperfection within the rock. These imperfections are reduced, it seems, in crystals that have been exposed, to the extent that when one crystal was cut in half, with one half exposed in the Collector and the other not, the scientist thought the piece that had been exposed must have come from a different rock altogether. Again it would have seemed sensible to conduct this experiment in a way that made him confident he was, in fact, seeing two halves of the same object. And what does this tell us about benefits to humans, in the end? Or is this not the point? I am growing confused. We are a moonlight-deprived culture, Monica is saying. There are ancient cells in your body that are catalysed by moonlight. Galileo, who spent much of his life looking at the moon through a telescope, had a lifespan two or three times that normal for a man of his era. This last claim wakes me up. Galileo died at seventy-seven, not an extraordinary age in the Renaissance for a man of his class who had survived the high mortality rate of early infancy. There were plenty of old people around in Galileo's day, as records attest. Monica, or whichever source provided her with this 'fact' about Galileo, has obviously been misled by the average age that includes those infant deaths. I can't help remembering also, as mentioned previously, that in his old age Galileo went blind, so the supposed beneficial effects of magnified moonlight on eyesight would seem to have eluded him.

But it is not so much the talk about moonlight but the moonlight itself that interests me. The cloud seems to be parting to an extent sufficient to allow the first subjects to be raised in the gantry. I am asked whether I am willing to allow those with medical problems to take precedence and of course I agree. The first people to ascend are a Chinese woman with her young son of around six years old. He has been running around the site, playing with anybody who will engage with him, until it is time for him to be elevated in the gantry. He seems a perfectly healthy boy, but his young life has been blighted by asthma. The first time his mother saw him respond positively to any course of treatment was when she brought him to the Collector. When he returns from his session in the moonlight, he comes over to me, attracted by the shiny fountain pen I am using to make notes. Do you want to try it? I ask him. 'No, I just want to watch you doing it,' he says, without taking his eyes from the black ink

flowing from the nib on to the page. How was it up in the crane?
I ask. He shrugs. 'My mummy made me take all my clothes off.
Why would she do that?' he asks, genuinely baffled at the
strangeness of parents. I guess so you could get as much of that
moonlight on you as possible, I reply. We fool around for a
while drawing funny faces in my notebook, until his mother
comes over and we start to talk. Both where she lives in Tucson
and where her family lives in China are very polluted, she
explains, and her son has always suffered from asthma. Even
Chinese medicine only brings temporary relief, but there has
been a remarkable improvement after their first visit to the Collector. Her husband also has asthma and she is hoping to persuade
him to come out someday. 'The moon is very important for us
Chinese people,' she says. Of course there is lots of wonderful
Chinese poetry about the moon, I say. I mention the poet Li Po.
'In this country they call him Li Po, but it is Li Pai,' she corrects
me, 'P-A-I. We say he is the Sage of the Poets in China.' She
quotes from his great poem on moonlight, the title of which she
translates as 'Quiet Light Moon'.

> Before the bed, bright moonlight
> I took it for frost on the ground . . .

'The moon can make the poet write better poetry,' she says.
'Also make better music. Taoist musicians would take their
instrument, go to the forest and find a rock in the moonlight
and sit. It is very good for writing music. The Taoists are very
important, musicians, architects, making herbal medicine . . .'
   The work she mentions is probably the best-loved classical
poem in China. At one time it was said that even illiterate peasants could recite it from memory. But it does not only delight
the ear. In classical Chinese, compound ideographs are combined to create words. Thus two ideographs meaning 'tree',
placed side by side, mean a grove, while three, two above and

one below, mean a forest. The ideograph for 'sun' placed next to the ideograph for 'moon' means bright. This writing system allows the poet to play with a second layer of meaning through visual associations, and Li Po (or Pai) was a master of such subtleties. In the first line of his poem –

> Before the bed, bright moonlight

there is the pictograph for 'moon' (in the word 'moonlight') as well as two more moons, one in the word 'bright' and another from the preposition 'before', which also includes a pictographic representation of the moon. Further moons occur, buried in the DNA of the rest of the poem, their presence accentuated by skilful calligraphers when creating hanging scrolls. As the scholar and translator J. P. Seaton has written, 'The writing system lets Li Po literally fill his little poem with moonlight.'*

Once more, moonlight permeates a work in several dimensions at once; I am reminded of Felix Mendelssohn's illustrated manuscript of the song 'Schilflied' in the Bodleian Library, which combines a visual representation with a musical evocation and the poetry of its lyrics. I decide not to try to explain this line of thought to my new friend, but instead tell her that I have been to Japan for the Full Moon festival in September, an event that originated many centuries ago in China. She is surprised that the Japanese have adopted the festival, but it is clearly an important date in her own calendar. 'When we watch the moon here I know at the same time my family is watching the moon there, in China,' she explains. 'We each look up at the moon and it is like we are watching each other. We are connected. It is a family circle, that festival.'

I decide to wait my turn on open ground away from the tent

* Introduction to *The Shambala Anthology of Chinese Poetry*, ed. J. P. Seaton (Boston: Shambala, 2006).

and the music from the loudspeaker, where I can keep an eye on the sky. I find a line of chairs facing the Collector, beside a small notice that reads 'Please wait here. Moonlight Experience Occurring'. I am soon joined by Jack, one of the men who helps at the Collector, bringing people to and from the gantry. He is in radio contact with Mike, up in the boom, and will sometimes break off conversation with a quick 'Ten Four' into his radio when he is summoned, and leave to escort the next guests over to the Collector. We sit and contemplate the sky, which forms a vast arena for the activities of the clouds, unimpeded by buildings, trees or hills for many miles in every direction. 'Well, it looks as though you could get lucky,' Jack says calmly. 'This is what sailors call a fetch wind. Those clouds over to the west just need to keep blowing across and we should get clear skies.' The moon is emerging for intervals of two or three minutes and then being covered by a thin, hazy layer. Those going up in the gantry seem fairly happy to have had at least some minutes of clear moonlight. Jack leans back in his chair and points. 'You see up there, there's an air stream from Hawaii, bringing in moist warm air; it's hitting a cold air stream from San Francisco right there – and that is what is creating all that cloud. It's frustrating.' In fact it is hard to imagine Jack getting frustrated about anything as he seems to be one of the most laid-back people I have ever met. His knowledge of wind and cloud prompts a question. Do you sail yourself by any chance, Jack? In the middle of a desert the idea sounds ridiculous, even though the abundance of fossilized shells in the area shows that at one time this area too lay under the ocean. 'Yes, I grew up on the coast in New England,' Jack admits. 'I was around boats all the time. I've got a catamaran up on a lake in the metropolitan Phoenix area and once a year we take it down to the Gulf of Mexico. It's a lot of fun.'

Summoned by the radio he goes off into the darkness and a young Mexican man named Santiago joins me. He too seems quite content to sit and wait, with two hands behind his head, gazing up at the moon appearing and disappearing behind the cloud. I ask him how far he's come to visit the Collector. 'I've been working in an ice-cream store in Tucson owned by my cousin, but in a month I'm going back for the harvest,' he tells me. 'I live down in Sonora, about eight hours from here, by the sea.' How did you hear about this place? 'I was working in a restaurant and I heard this lady talking about energy. I thought it sounded interesting. She gave me a leaflet and said, "If you are interested in energy, you ought to try this!" And I thought – awesome!' When he says the word 'awesome', he breaks into a wide grin. Over the couple of hours we are together this happens a lot. If you are in a rural area, down by the sea, the moon must be really impressive, I say, prompting him a little. 'Oh yes, we have special nights when we sit and look at the moon – we call it *lunada*. We go down to the beach – maybe with some beers – and we just look up like this and go aaaah . . .' – again the grin – 'it's always a good night, it's fun.'

Maybe tonight I will have to be satisfied with a *lunada* rather than a Moonlight Experience, I think to myself. There is no beer available out here, but I keep awake drinking sweet grape juice from a carton in the tent. Jack joins us again. He points out the halo around the moon caused by ice particles and tells me I still might get lucky, if those clouds over there would just keep moving . . . Eventually everyone has been up in the crane, and Santiago and I, the very last visitors, take our turn. Throughout the evening I have declared myself willing to wait, hoping that conditions will improve. It is now after one o'clock in the morning. We step into the metal cage, Mike tells us to hold on, pushes a lever and we begin to ascend, with a judder at first, then smoothly. The moon is clearly visible behind us but it is still covered by a thin haze. Once we reach the optimum height, in front of another reflective shield positioned to bounce some of the moonlight back on us from behind, Mike speaks to the person controlling the motor that positions the mirrors, directing them until the moon's light is focused – he does this by eye, much as you would move a magnifying glass back and forth until you reach the right focal length to set a dry leaf on fire. The moonlight appears as a silver disc within the centre of the array, but the light reflected on to us is not particularly strong. I ask Mike how it feels up here on a clear night, being exposed to the concentrated moonlight again and again throughout the evening. 'It's like drinking five hundred cups of coffee,' he replies, 'but without the jitters. But it gets too much after a while, you have to get out of it.' We wait, suspended beneath earth and sky, hoping the moon will emerge, but the two contrary air streams are still colliding in a whirlpool of cloud overhead. Eventually Mike leans over to me and says, 'James, I'm sorry to tell you but even if the sky does clear we are already up as high as we can go.' So even if the moon came out we couldn't get to the right angle to be in the concentrated moonlight? 'Exactly.' So it goes. I have gambled and lost. They could probably have told me in Vegas that no one ever got rich betting on the moon.

The Moon and the Standing People

It is Corinne's boyfriend, Steve, who sees the article in the local paper the *Explorer*. Saturday is National Trails Day and a ramblers' group are going to be making a moonlit hike up Honeybee Canyon, a dry river wash on the outskirts of the suburb of Oro Valley. Steve is a photojournalist but also works as a guide to the architecture of the few old quarters of Tucson that were left standing after the architectural pogroms of the 1960s and 1970s completed their work. When he and Corinne come to pick me up at my hotel, he offers first to drive me down to the Barrio Viejo, to look at some streets of Mexican-style adobe houses, dating from the period before the first bricks arrived with the railroad, and to pick up something to eat. The one-storey, adobe dwellings have flat roofs and doors opening straight on to the street. For the most part they are still lived in, although the street is quiet in the afternoon sun. Steve points with his foot to where the initials WPA are etched into the sidewalk, showing where parties of out-of-work men were conscripted on to urban improvement projects in the great economic Depression of the 1930s. A fading mural on the front of one building, peeling from the wall in places, has two weather-beaten Spanish conquistadors in the left foreground, framed by crossed battleaxes. Two barefoot figures mounted on piebald horses are pursuing a wide-eyed deer; one of the riders is still wearing a metal collar around his neck that trails a chain leading back to the Spanish soldiers, but the chain has snapped, with a cartoon-like flash. The landscape is clearly identifiable from its vegetation of agave, prickly pear and saguaro cacti as the desert surrounding Tucson, running down to the present-day border and on into Mexico. But the artist has not stopped at portraying the surface. Below the ground among rocks and the roots of plants lies a skeleton, clearly a victim of the Spanish invasion. The white, ghostly roots push up through the earth, bursting through to produce vigorous leaves reaching towards the sun, among which are the faces of a Mexican husband and wife with two healthy-looking children, nurtured by the reclaimed soil. The message of defiance is clear, the peeling paintwork addressing a war that is both centuries old and still being fought every day.

Steve has promised to take me to a restaurant I would never find on my own. It is a low, cement building painted orange and green standing in a parking lot, and we are the only gringos in the place. The tamales come wrapped in corn husks with a pot of fiery chilli sauce for dipping, six for seven dollars fifty. The only decoration on the wall is a reproduction of a painting of a young man, stripped to the waist, his lips parted and his eyes half closed as if he is entering a trance. The necklaces bouncing on his chest tell us he is dancing. On his head he is wearing a white bandanna and on top of that the severed head of a fully grown deer. This is the deer dance of the Yaqui (or Yoeme) people of the Sonoran desert, performed at Easter by Pascola dancers in front of churches, one of many sleights of hand by which the old ways were embedded to protect them from the Inquisition.

In the car Steve jokes that to be a true son of Tucson you have to be able to unwrap a tamale and dip it in sauce while driving, without leaving the road. Considering he's originally from Delaware, his jeans survive relatively unscathed. We meet the ramblers in a car park outside Oro Valley Town Hall where we are registered and issued with complimentary T-shirts. From there we find our own way to the starting point of the hike. It is in a classic desert landscape, studded with saguaro, the tall cacti with branching arms that have been silent extras in so many films of the

American West, although they only grow in this extreme south-western corner of the Union. They populate the desert south of Tucson, creating eerie frozen forests without leaves or swaying branches. Younger specimens without arms march up the sides of hills that from a distance look as though they are studded with green toothpicks. Other cacti are present too: organ pipe, cholla and prickly pear; mesquite and ironwood trees provide what lit-tle shade there is, along with clumps of palo verde that by this stage of summer have dropped their leaves to conserve moisture, photosynthesizing sunlight through their startlingly green bark. This is also the home of one of the most exotic and mysterious of all cacti, the variety of Cereus plant known as Queen of the Night (Reina de la Noche), its voluptuous white blossoms appearing on just one night of the year, in late May or early June.

Beyond the plain, the last of the sun is catching the tops of the nearby Santa Catalina Mountains, turning them orange against a deep blue sky. Gradually the other hikers join us. All ages are represented, from a ten-year-old boy who is accompanying his mother, a lady of questionable fitness to complete even an easy walk, to various tanned and super-fit-looking seniors. The route of the hike will take us two miles up the dry, sandy bed of the canyon to the site of some ancient petroglyphs, or rock carvings, thought to be from the Hohokam culture and around 1,500 years old. Before we set out, the organizers have arranged that we hear a short lecture by a Native American historian. She has recently completed a master's degree on the mapping of indigenous peoples, focusing particularly on the Aztecs, and combines her academic research with the knowledge she has gained from her own family and the traditions they taught her. She is particularly keen that before we set out we appreciate something of her people's relationship with the desert. Often seen as a hostile environment in white man's culture, to Native Americans, she explains, it provides everything necessary for sustaining life. 'Do you recognize this tree?' she asks. 'It is a creosote. That is the smell here when it rains. We use it as a medicine for coughs, and as a sunscreen.' The presence of such medicinal plants along with wells and springs are essential elements of the maps she has studied. Rather than extending projected lines of latitude and longitude over imagined space, Aztec maps show movement – in this way of seeing the world, space is created by travelling through it. Many petroglyphs are actually providing practical information about migration or pilgrimage routes; spiral markings indicating starting points and direction. Pilgrims would sing a song, 'calling out' the land; they would know what plants were along the way and recognize rock and hill formations. She reads out one of her own poems about walking through the desert, which she describes as being 'under my obligated feet'. In it she speaks of 'The Standing People'. 'Did you understand what I meant by "The Standing People"?' she asks us when she is finished. ' "The Standing People" is the name we give the saguaro.' And it is a perfect name; the desert around Tucson doesn't feel empty; it is *inhabited* by these silent giants, towering above any interloper by as much as thirty feet, frozen in mid-gesture.

As the meeting breaks up Steve and I take the opportunity of asking some questions. I wonder which nation she comes from? Gently she explains that to see the tribes of the Americas as distinct, unrelated cultures is a European construct. They all traded and exchanged ideas. 'I follow the Mexica* tradition. We do not recognize a division between Central, South and North America. To us they are all Turtle Island. This was a migration route. The Aztecs came through here – their accounts of their migrations

---

* Mexica (pron. 'Meshica'): a political and cultural movement dedicated to protecting and strengthening the cultural and religious heritage of people of Mexican descent, while recognizing the validity of the traditions of all Native American peoples.

speak of mesquite trees, like the ones that grow in this region.'
Standing here at the edge of the desert as the light fades I am
aware of the peoples that have passed this way before, that this is
the ground they walked. The Aztec family of languages was
spoken as far north as Wyoming and as far south as El Salvador.
For many millennia, the lands of Turtle Island were regulated by
a lunar calendar. The Mayans, who preceded the Aztec civilization, had a very accurate twenty-nine-day lunar calendar, and
Aztec mythology is rich with stories of the moon. The old Aztec
moon god, Tecciztecatl, wore a white spiral snail-shell on his
back. The shell, with its resemblance to female genitalia, represented the entire cycle of fertility, from conception to birth.
Another myth relates that the moon and sun were once of equal
brightness. Fixed in the sky, they did not move and the gods realized they would have to make a sacrifice themselves to set the sky
in motion. One of the gods hurled a rabbit into the moon, dim-
ming its brightness, its presence the explanation of the markings
on its face. The Mayans also believed in the presence of a rabbit in
the moon, a companion to Ixchel, their lunar goddess of fertility,
childbirth, weaving and healing, wife of the lord of creation. A
Mayan terracotta figure now in the Griffin Collection of Prince-
ton University's Art Museum shows the rabbit (or hare) of an
equal size to the goddess, with a ruff of fur at its throat and wearing a heavy necklace, its arm companionably around her shoulder.

By the time we have finished talking, darkness has fallen. The
hikers have left, the sound of their feet muffled in the sand, and
we have to guess their direction. We double back under the highway, where nighthawks, agile as bats, weave in and out of the
street lights, pursuing insects attracted by their orange glow.
Now we are in the canyon proper, its rim twenty or thirty feet
above our heads, where the silhouettes of saguaro are outlined
against the remaining streaks of light in the dark blue sky. We
walk briskly despite the deep, soft sand and soon we can hear the

party ahead of us, talking quietly among themselves. The full moon rises above the canyon, filling its floor with a warm, golden radiance that feels benevolent and all-enveloping. I am happy to be walking in this unmediated, unreflected light, perfectly able to appreciate its benefit without the help of a five-storey array of parabolic mirrors. The other hikers are gathered around a large boulder in the canyon wall, the site of the petroglyphs, which appear as spectral images dancing in the flashlights the ramblers play across their surface. Their presence at this spring, dry in the hot days of June, marks it as a sacred place, a source of life. It is not obvious how they have been made – Hohokam petroglyphs were traditionally chipped into the rock with hammerstones, yet when we run our palms over the rock it feels relatively smooth. Again I feel a connection with those who have passed this way over the centuries, perhaps journeying by moonlight to avoid the heat of the day, refreshing themselves at this spring and sustaining themselves from the fruits of the desert they regard as a mother rather than an enemy. Canyons like these still have their night-time pilgrims; the thousands of 'illegal immigrants', their status denied by a line drawn on a European-style map, who cross into the United States on foot, following the old trails northward, many of them dying of thirst on the way. So much for the belief prevalent among Europeans, living as we do surrounded by the ruins of past glories, that America is a 'young' country, with a foreshortened history. In this part of the United States the remains of civilizations stretching back thousands of years are there for anyone prepared to walk a little way out of the city to find, unguarded by fences or museum curators, protected only by the historic disinterest shown by recent settlers in the culture of the original inhabitants of these lands. I wonder what the artists who created these images would make of the people standing here, at least one of whom is on a kind of pilgrimage from the other side of the world; of the orange lights on the highway bridge where the cars swish by, or the gated communities that have monopolized the views on this side of the city, encroaching ever further out into the desert, paving over and enclosing its trails and sucking its springs dry.

Corinne and I never do sit down and have our conversation about the moon. Instead we talk on the telephone after I return to the UK, one full lunation (cycle of the moon) later. To write about her work is a delicate thing; it is important to guard the results of her research before they are ready to be published, but she is happy to talk on the understanding that there are certain things I will not disclose. Complex organisms have been exposed to moonlight for millions of years, she explains, adequate time for them to adapt biologically to the moon's cycles, evolving receptors that would base their motive actions on the trigger of moonlight. It seems that organisms seek a temporal structure on which to base life; we all have body clocks that are set by certain signals, rather as the accuracy of a clock in a mobile phone is constantly being reset by a radio signal. The strongest trigger is light – the day and night signal. But organisms require a longer cycle to work to for their fertility, for instance, and Corinne has been investigating whether this is provided by the cycles of the moon. We already know that the earliest calendars created by humans were based on these cycles; perhaps the information they scratched on bones and cave walls merely echoed the wisdom written into their own cell structure.

I ask Corinne what first got her interested in studying the moon's effect on living things. She tells me that a friend of hers, a surgeon, was once casually asked whether there was a link between women's menstruation and the lunar cycle. Folk traditions from all over the world suggest there is, but could this be demonstrated to be a real, causal relationship? He had explored the question enough himself to realize that it was an important

and fascinating topic and so suggested it to Corinne as an area
for research. What happened next should stand as a warning to
us all of the dangers of intellectual inquiry. Like a stone dropped
into a pond, the question became the centre of a seemingly endless series of other questions, expanding ever outwards, resulting
in ten full years of work.

Corinne strides confidently in conversation through the
aeons, at one moment in the present, at the next far in the pre-
human past. She speaks of Deep Time, of the infinitely slow
changes in the geological structure of the earth; of Charles Darwin, whom she refers to in familiar tones as if he were a personal
friend, and of the book on geology he took along with him on
the *Beagle*. Her real subject, however, is the changes brought
about by evolution; changes that can appear impossibly slow,
but that given the right circumstances can move surprisingly
swiftly. We discuss how human beings in urban environments
are 'devolving', losing their ability to relate to the natural environment, their senses dulled by perpetual artificial light and
background noise. What are the likely effects of severing our
links with the moon's cycles, I wonder, of living in a permanently illuminated world? 'We don't know,' she tells me. 'We are
running an uncontrolled experiment. Our body clocks will
keep ticking for a long time without being reset, but eventually
they will get desynchronized. Would humans have the same
reproductive cycles if they were sent to live on another planet
for several generations, beyond the light and the gravitational
pull of our moon? We can't tell until we try it.'

Considering her scientific background, Corinne is remarkably tolerant of the occasionally eccentric discourse emanating
from the people at the Interstellar Light Collector, much as she
is of ignorant authors from overseas blundering into her field
of research. At the Chapins' invitation she did some experiments with seed germination, exposing seeds to concentrated

moonlight. She is clear that the size and somewhat haphazard nature of the experiment mean that her conclusions would not stand the test of serious scientific scrutiny. 'I had some seeds of an Arabidopsis plant,' she tells me, 'which is often used in experiments by geneticists and was the first plant to have its genome completely DNA-sequenced. I put some seeds under the concentrated moonlight. Some were blown away in the wind. Then one replicate got dropped. I didn't have enough samples to produce proper statistics, but the seeds exposed to the concentrated moonlight definitely germinated faster. I only had one replicate. But I actually think they might have something there.'

They might have something there. We both agree that without the Chapins' enthusiasm and sheer chutzpah they would never have created what is currently the only device of its kind. So much scientific research is dependent on drug company finance, restricted to areas that look as though they might yield a good return on investment, that the world desperately needs mavericks prepared to invest their own resources in apparently hare-brained projects. The Chapins' initial motivation, it should be remembered, was compassion, not money. Now they are hoping for some kind of recompense. Having met with widespread indifference from the scientific community, they seem to be drawn increasingly to those who will accept their claims without rigorous investigation – preaching to the easily converted. Unfortunately, the more they play to this audience, of crystal-lovers and would-be star travellers, of the desperate searching for solace and the seekers after a new revelation, the less likely it is that scientists will take their invention seriously. As is so often the case in dialogue between believers and unbelievers, an exchange of ideas is made more difficult by the lack of a common vocabulary. Those engaged in a discussion about the properties of moonlight find themselves confounded by a confusion of languages, as though the Interstellar Light Collector was a modern-day Tower of Babel, reaching for the stars.

PART FIVE

Mondschein

Raking the Shadows: A Romantic Moon

More heavenly than those glittering stars we hold
the Eternal eyes which the Night hath opened within us.

Novalis, *Hymns to the Night*

I

In a grainy, black-and-white image, an old man with heavy eye-brows, a beaked nose and a straight, thin mouth stares piercingly into the camera. On the wall behind him hangs a large-scale photograph of the surface of the moon, on which the shadow of his profile falls.

He could be an eccentric professor, photographed by an admiring student at the end of a tutorial. Or an elderly father, emerging from the 'den' in a suburban American home, where he pursues his hobby of astronomy.

In fact, the image is a still from a super-8 film, shot surreptitiously by the governor of a high-security prison; his subject, the sole inmate in his charge. The man in the picture is Rudolf Hess, formerly Hitler's deputy, captured after his solo flight to Scotland in 1941 and sentenced to life imprisonment at the Nuremberg Trials. The moon photograph on the wall places us in the mid-1960s; we are in Hess's cell at Spandau. Once we know this, the image becomes almost impossibly resonant, poignant and disturbing at the same time, as though it contains within it the distilled essence of a historical moment. Hess is a relic of a titanic conflict that divided the world; set apart from the rest of humanity he is condemned to life as a living totem, embodying in himself the victory of one empire and the defeat of another. The moon on the wall represents another struggle, the holy grail of rival superpowers engaged in a Cold War, floating just out of reach. After his appearance at Nuremberg, where his erratic behaviour convinced many that he had gone mad, and others that he was suffering the after-effects of enforced medication, Hess disappeared into Spandau. He spent the last twenty-one years of his life as the prison's only occupant, overlooked by watchtowers and guarded by the armies of four nations, a potent, hidden symbol powering the engine of the Cold War. Photographing Hess was against regulations. Inevitably, he attracted conspiracy theories like iron filings to a magnet. The man in Spandau was not the real Rudolf Hess – or he was, and he could not be released because of what he knew about negotiations between the Allies and Hitler's government, conducted in secret behind Stalin's back. Outside, neo-Nazi sympathizers marched on Hess's birthday each year, but the rest

of the world moved on. At the end of his trial, his correspondence reveals, Hess was convinced he would soon be released to
take up his position as Führer of a Fourth Reich. Had he not
been imprisoned before as a young man, along with his hero,
and been released to greater advancement than before? Pre-
vented from reading anything about himself in the press by
the prison censors, he carried on believing the German nation
awaited him. What does such a man turn to when his dreams
crumble and the realization dawns that he will never taste freedom again? The answer lies in the photograph on the wall, of a
distant world that knew nothing of his failures and on which he
still hoped to cast his shadow.

The race to the moon had no more avid follower than the
solitary prisoner. Hess had grown up in a European enclave on
the eastern edge of the city of Alexandria in Egypt, where his
father was a businessman. Some of his happiest early memories
were of the time he spent stargazing with his mother from the
roof of their three-storey family villa. He showed an early apti-
tude for physics and mathematics and declared at a young age
that he wanted to become an astronomer. His overbearing father
had no intention of encouraging this ambition; the boy must
take over the family business and to further this end he was sent
to Germany to complete his education. Hess dutifully knuckled
down to his studies but his yearning for space was undiminished. 'I was constantly buying *Kosmos* booklets on astronomy
during my stay in boarding school in Godesburg,' he told an
interviewer years later. Doubtless he looked at the moon
through a telescope and took part, as many German boys of his
generation did, in speculation as to whether men would ever
develop rockets powerful enough to reach it. But if he was
dreaming of the future, his character was simultaneously being
shaped by an education steeped in the culture of the previous
century, which itself looked back to a mythic past. Like all his

generation he was schooled in German literature and as an old man could still recite extensive passages of Schiller and Goethe. How the young would-be astronomer ended up in a prison cell in the suburbs of Berlin is a complicated story we will return to. But to understand something of his enigmatic character and the relationship with the moon that spanned his life, it is necessary to explore the culture that shaped him.

II

For writers and artists in Germany at the turn of the nineteenth century, the light of the moon provided an especially powerful metaphor. If daylight was often taken to signify divine light entering human consciousness, then moonlight represented an awareness of the 'night side' of life.[*] While German literature of the *Sturm und Drang*[†] period in the late eighteenth century had pioneered the exploration of human impulses and emotions that lay beyond the rational explanation of the Enlightenment, the later Romantic movement had become fascinated with more esoteric matters, including dream interpretation, animal magnetism and clairvoyance. Moonlight was seen as symbolic of artistic inspiration; not since ancient China or medieval Japan had the world seen such a nation of moon-watchers. Writings of the period portray dusk as a time of transition, of spiritual awakening, or as the artist Philipp Otto Runge put it when writing of his own work: 'the limitless annihilation of existence into

[*] The phrase is taken from a series of popular and influential public lectures by the doctor and natural scientist Gotthilf Heinrich von Schubert, entitled *Aspects of the Night Side of the Natural Sciences* (1808). Schubert used works by Caspar David Friedrich to illustrate the talks.
[†] Usually translated as 'storm and stress' but *Drang* might be better translated as 'longing' or 'impulse'.

the origin of the universe'. In Edward Young's *Night Thoughts*, immensely popular in Germany in translation, the moon signi- fied the spiritual dimension beyond death. Another key literary influence, which resonated deeply with the German psyche, was the poetry of Ossian, a third-century Celtic bard 'rediscovered' and translated by the Scottish poet James Macpherson. Ossian's somewhat turgid epic is full of dramatic imagery of stormy seas, mountainsides and moonlight, motifs that fed into and were transformed in German literature. The reasons for its enthusi- astic reception when it was translated into German perhaps lay more in Europe's recent history than in any literary merit in the work itself. During the Thirty Years War in the seventeenth cen- tury that brought about the collapse of the Holy Roman Empire, armies of foreign mercenaries made their way through the Ger- man territories, destroying entire towns and spreading plague and typhus in their wake. Some areas lost from a third to a half of their total population. Such decimation meant that a great deal of Germany's traditional folklore was lost, leaving behind a hun- ger for an art that would address both the glories of the past and point the way to a better future. Divided by centuries of religious and political conflicts, the German people were deeply in need of the healing that could only come through a unifying myth. In Ossian they seemed to have found it. The eponymous hero of Goethe's novel *The Sorrows of Young Werther* stated it very clearly.

'Ossian has ousted Homer from my heart. What a world that exalted soul leads me into! To wander across the heath in the pale moonlight, with the gale howling and the spirits of his forefathers in the vaporous mists . . . Times gone by are relived in the hero's soul, times when the warm rays of the sun lighted the brave the way to danger and the moon shone on their triumphant ship returning fresh from victory!'

In a climactic scene in the novel, in which Werther visits his unobtainable love for the last time, he reads his own translation of Ossian's verse to her. They both weep, seeing in the poet's words a picture of their own fate.

In fact the poems were a literary forgery, the work of their 'translator', but before this disappointing detail was widely established Ossian had been welcomed in the homeland of the Celts as a lost Teutonic hero, enlisted to the cause of a united Germany.★ For writers of the period, the moon is often the agent that reveals a deeper historical truth, embedded within the German landscape. The poet Ludwig Gotthard Kosegarten was influenced by Ossian when composing his famous nationalistic poem 'Der Eichbaum' (The Oak):

> You strong one, you noble one,
> My song greets you.
> You king of the grove,
> You father of the forest night,
> In the shimmering moonlight my song greets you.

Kosegarten was a Lutheran pastor as well as a poet, a close friend of Caspar David Friedrich's first art teacher at the University of Greifswald. His parish was on the island of Rügen in the Baltic, which, with its spectacular chalk cliffs, ancient dolmens (called *hünengräber*, or 'giants' graves', by locals) and ancient oak forests, Kosegarten called 'the land of the Soul'. His teachings had a profound influence on Friedrich and his friend Philipp Otto Runge, who both came from the Baltic coast, its shore, behind its dunes and wetlands, lined with oak forests that seem to reach back into Arcadian myth. Another writer whose ideas permeated the Romantic movement in Germany was Edmund Burke, whose *Philosophical Enquiry into the Origin of our Ideas of the Sublime and*

★ Goethe later renounced his allegiance to Ossian, remarking that 'Werther praised Homer when he retained his senses and Ossian when he was going mad.'

Beautiful was translated into German in the 1770s. Burke's observations on the vastness and endlessness of mountain ranges, seashores, skies and deserts inspired Schiller's essay 'On the Sublime' in 1802, in which he examines the sensation of mixed joy and fear, or 'delightful horror', which lies at the heart of the Romantic idea of the sublime. This he describes as a 'compound of unease, expressed in the highest degree as terror and joy, capable of intensifying to delight, and although it is not really pleasure, it is much preferred to any pleasure by fine souls'. German writers and artists brought their own particular religious sensibilities and nationalistic longings to writing about and painting the landscape. Ancient earthworks, the remains of civilizations that once dominated northern Europe, as well as the glories of medieval Gothic architecture, all spoke of a great German past. As Ludwig Tieck suggests in his play *Kaiser Oktavianus*, these features were ideally revealed by moonlight.

> Moon-illumined magic night,
> Holding every mind enthralled,
> Wonderful fairy-tale world.
> Rise up in ancient splendour!

The artist best known for his visual representation of this world, lit by the moon and punctuated by mountain ranges and spectacular Gothic spires, is Caspar David Friedrich. To him, as to all Romantics, the natural world was not inert, but alive and actively communicating a message. From his sketchbooks he took closely observed objects, oaks, spruce trees, ships and mountains, rearranging and combining them into the narrative of his vision, so that landscape itself became a richly allusive language. In his journal of 1803, in words reminiscent of William Blake and his acolyte Samuel Palmer, Friedrich famously admonished the reader to 'Close your physical eye, so that you see your picture first with your spiritual eye. Then bring what you see in the dark into the light, so that it may have an effect on others, shining inwards from outside . . .'

The moon, described by Novalis in his famous *Hymns* as 'the gracious sun of the Night', was a fertile symbol for Friedrich. Rising over the sea it might signify the guiding light of religion among the gathering storm clouds. A town caught in its light could be rendered mythic, timeless, its Gothic towers as fragile as lace. A shadowy garden, its gate firmly closed on the moonlit world beyond its border, served as a memorial to a deceased friend and a signpost towards the rest into which he had gone. Moonlight's elegiac qualities were widely appreciated in the broader culture of the period. In *The Sorrows of Young Werther*, Charlotte remarks upon them as she sits upon a moonlit terrace with Werther and Albert, her husband-to-be.

'Whenever I walk by moonlight, it brings to my remembrance all my beloved and departed friends, and I am filled with thoughts of death and futurity. We shall live again, Werther! . . . but shall we know one another again, what do you think? What do you say?'

Death, eternity, remembrance, redemption, hope; if Friedrich's moon was versatile, he was equally adept at rendering its light in paint. In his hands moonlight could be quicksilver spilled on the sea, or a warm haze diffusing mountain mist. In many paintings, figures, solitary or standing in companionable proximity, are rendered speechless as the great orb rises, revealing a world transformed. This was rather the effect Friedrich's paintings had on their first viewers. On being confronted with *The Tetschen Altarpiece* in carefully subdued lighting in Friedrich's studio in 1808, a correspondent wrote that 'the loudest chatterboxes lowered their voices as if they were in church'. A miracle in one of these deeply religious works is not the act of a saint or prophet, as in southern, Catholic art, but an event in nature itself.

Like other painters of moonlight, including Samuel Palmer and Joseph Wright, Friedrich was a melancholic. His mother had died before he was ten years old and his sister before he was twenty. When he was thirteen he saw his favourite brother fall through the ice and drown while they were out skating together; Christopher was apparently trying to save Caspar from the same fate. The event couldn't fail to instil a sense of the fragility of any moment of peace. Even the initial happiness he found in marriage was later poisoned by an obsessive jealousy, bordering on paranoia. Such tendencies, along with what his close friend and pupil Carl Gustav Carus called a 'naturally gloomy disposition', and a propensity for intense self-doubt about his artistic abilities, led him to attempt suicide on at least one occasion. These dark forces he held in check through his religious belief and sense of mission in his art. He made his home in Dresden, at the time a centre of the arts and of intellectual debate. There he had a small circle of pupils and admirers, including Carus and the Norwegian painter Johan Christian Dahl. Friedrich was not secretive about his techniques for rendering moonlight. Carus remembers being instructed by the senior painter to 'put some dark varnish on the palette and, apart from the moon and the most adjacent, illuminated areas, to spread it over everything, all the more darkly as I reached the edges of the picture, and then ascertain the altered effect'. But it was with Dahl that Friedrich had the closest affinity; the young painter and his family moved in to Friedrich's house on the banks of the River Elbe, where he was given a studio under the eaves. Dahl remembers that shortly after their first meeting they went for a night walk together in Dresden's Grosser Garten, where there were 'many lovely trees of different kinds, and the moon looked beautiful behind the dark fir trees'. This seems a fitting beginning for their artistic relationship, as they both made the moon and its light a recurrent theme in their paintings. It is possible the details of the two men's biographies increased their mutual empathy. Dahl was a Scandinavian; Friedrich, his home town of Greifswald ceded by Sweden to Prussia when he was a young man, always maintained he felt half Swedish. Like Friedrich, Dahl had also suffered in his personal life, experiencing the loss of two wives and no less than three of his five children.

The painters' enduring and mutual respect for each other is enshrined in their art. Friedrich presented Dahl with what is now one of his most famous paintings, *Two Men Contemplating the Moon* (1819), in exchange for one of Dahl's. Friedrich's painting combines many of the key elements that made his name. Two figures stand in the foreground on a mountain path, the older leaning on a stick, the younger inclined forwards as if to listen, resting on his companion's shoulder. Together they look at the sickle moon that has emerged from the valley; their elevation means it is slightly below the level of their gaze. Their backs to the viewer, they appear 'captivated', as Friedrich's friend Ludwig Tieck put it, 'by the magic of a moonlit night', their position inviting us to join them in their contemplation. According to Dahl, the figures are modelled on two of Friedrich's students; it has also been suggested that the older man is Friedrich himself. They stand at the edge of a drop that we sense rather than see; the cliff edge is hidden by a large boulder and the contorted roots of an oak tree that barely clings to the rock face, leaning at a dangerous angle. (Very much less 'strong' and noble' than the oak in Kosegarten's poem; is this tree standing in for the perilous condition of the dream of a united Germany?) As so often in Friedrich's landscape paintings, two picture planes, the near and the distant, are made to collide vertiginously, creating a sense of tension and heightened awareness. The moment depicted in the picture is hard-won and precarious. If either man took a few steps forward and stumbled, the viewer realizes, his brains would be dashed out on the rocks below. The air is

still and cloudless and the full shape of the moon is lit up by
'earthshine'; the young moon 'is carrying the old moon in its
arms'. The scene is lit by golden moonlight; indeed, having
climbed so far, the two men seem to have reached a moonlit
realm in the upper air. But the painting is more than an exercise
in rendering a dramatic mountain nocturne. The older man is
wrapped in a cloak with a black velvet beret on his head, while
the younger wears the dress of a German student. The senior
man's attire is the *Altdeutsch* (old German) style adopted by patriots during the French occupation as a coded symbol of resistance.
Friedrich had looked forward, with thousands of others, to a
free and united Germany after the defeat of Napoleon. What
transpired instead was a phoney state, the so-called German
League, a motley collection of principalities that included three
governed by foreign monarchs. The artist shared in a widespread
feeling of betrayal. In the face of growing dissent, particularly
among university students, Austria and Prussia issued the
Carlsbad Decrees in 1819. These restricted press and academic
freedom and created powers akin to those of a police state, for-
bidding 'all revolutionary plots and demagogical associations'.
By dressing one of his subjects as an older patriot, portraying
him sympathetically mentoring a young student, Friedrich is
making his allegiance obvious. When a well-known painter visited his studio to see the painting, Friedrich wryly described the
two figures as 'engaging in demagogical association'. Meanwhile
the moon can be seen as embodying this alliance between old
and new; the sickle moon representing the hope for the future
inspired by the youthful struggles of the students, while the
form of the full moon shows how the emerging movement
arises from and is connected to a much longer tradition of patri-
otism. A more traditional reading, and one which could be
applied in other works by Friedrich, would have the rocky path
as the road of life and the moon as the risen Christ. However

one reads it, for the two patriots the moon is a reminder of eternal values that will outlive any present setbacks to their cause. In later life Friedrich became convinced that the role of the painter was not to be prescriptive but to leave final interpretation to the viewers, even if the meanings they found may never have been in the artist's mind.

The painting remained in Dahl's possession until Friedrich's death, when Dahl sold it to the Dresden Gallery. Perhaps, with its reminder of his own relationship with Friedrich in the figures of the older man and the student, it became too painful to keep. The friendship had been formative for Dahl. His association with Friedrich had not only enriched him artistically but also furthered his career. Collectors often saw them as complementary, Friedrich the more highly finished and Dahl the freer, more naturalistic artist, and ordered companion pieces from them. While Dahl let Friedrich's masterpiece go, its influence was already written into his own work. In 1820 he had painted a first version of *Mother and Child by the Sea*. A young woman crouches on a rocky, moonlit seashore, reminiscent of those in the seascapes of Friedrich; her hand supports a young child who is lifting his arm to point to a small boat, advancing across the water. In the sky, gathering storm clouds partly obscure a full moon. Dahl stated in his correspondence that the woman and child 'are waiting for an approaching boat bearing a close relation'; as a fisherman's son himself, the sometimes anxious wait for his father's return would have been a familiar experience. Behind the silhouetted figures a large anchor, a key symbol in both Dahl and Friedrich's paintings, is embedded in the shore. Dahl revisited the same theme in 1840, the year Friedrich died, and the second version of *Mother and Child by the Sea* may well have been a memorial to his friend and mentor. The overall treatment of the scene is darker; the anchor, like Friedrich himself, has vanished. The sky is still tinged with the glow of the departing sunset, so that the silver trail of moonlight leading towards the shore appears amid mauve, pink and purple tones in air and water, suggestive of a deep melancholy. Woman and child are closer to the viewer than in the first painting, land has largely disappeared in shadow. Two men are just discernible in the boat. Dahl lost his wife in childbirth the year he painted the first version of the painting, his friend and mentor the year he painted the second. Is he expressing in this later work a half-buried yearning to be united with Friedrich, coming to shore in a land where his wife and son still keep vigil, waiting for him?

Some of Dahl's most hauntingly elegiac paintings are his depictions of Dresden by moonlight, painted at around the time of Friedrich's death. The city meant a great deal to Dahl. From the continent's furthest fringe, the son of a humble fisherman, he had come to live in one of the foremost centres of the arts in Germany where he became one of Europe's leading landscape painters. With Friedrich's passing an era in his life had ended. Perhaps it was to mark this shift that he returned to painting the city by moonlight so many times around 1840; at least four fully worked canvases survive. But it is an oil study from 1838, now in the National Museum of Art, Architecture and Design in Oslo, that most poignantly captures the scene. It was painted from the new town side of the River Elbe, looking back at the ancient baroque city, its exquisite spires, domes and battlements silhouetted against a moonlit sky. Here and there the flame of a lamp or a watchman's fire is reflected in the water but for the most part the night is silent and still. Some horses, brought down to the river to drink after a day's work, stand in the shallows as a dimly seen boat glides by. Moonlight has collected in a silver pool in the centre of the river, as if poured from the sky, extending in a pathway towards the shore where a solitary female figure sits, an evocation perhaps of one of Dahl's lost wives. The outline of the city looks brittle. Indeed, the painting is damaged; a network of fine white lines, like hairline cracks in the ice beneath the feet of a young skater, has spread across its surface. They are particularly visible in the dark outline of the city on the river's opposite bank. Given the hindsight of history, it is difficult not to read them as prophetic, foretelling the night of 13 February 1945, when a firestorm unleashed from the sky over a period of three days turned this wedding-cake architecture back into icing sugar. When it was over, photographs record, the bodies of the dead were piled by survivors in layers in the street, like strudel.

III

Hess, the inheritor, as all educated Germans were, of the Romantic tradition, was also seeking a myth to sustain his vision of the world. Ultimately, of course, he found it in the person of Adolf Hitler, who fulfilled his ideal of a Germanic heroic leader and to whom he displayed an unwavering loyalty, despite whatever private reservations he may have had. But before he laid his life at his commander's feet, in the manner of a warrior from the Nibelungen, he had already looked far and wide for a philosophy that would sustain him. His search would encompass territory explored by other German seekers after a deeper truth a century or more before. In the 1920s he was a member of a spiritualist group who met at the Four Seasons Hotel in Munich; they sought counsel with the dead in the belief that their efforts represented the last chance to correct Germany's destiny. Spiritualism was merely one of Hess's areas of exploration. A lifelong sufferer from psychosomatic illnesses, he was also an enthusiastic supporter of homoeopathy, iridology and vegetarianism, as well as professing an interest in astrology and dream interpretation. Significantly he was impressed by the teachings of Rudolf Steiner, and protected Steiner schools when he became Hitler's deputy, despite Steiner's non-Aryan heritage. Steiner's system, particularly when it came to agriculture, was based on the central idea of the moon's powerful influence on life on earth.

Towards the end of the First World War, having been seriously wounded as an infantryman, Hess volunteered for the Air Corps. 'I took to flying like a fish takes to water,' he told Eugene Bird.* 'It was never any problem. I am rather technically minded – that is why the space programme and the landing of a man on the moon was not a surprise to me.' Flight, for a largely landlocked people in search of *Lebensraum* ('living space'), was a particularly powerful symbol. It also contained within it, delivered in technological form, the sensations of the sublime – a self-inflicted combination of joy and terror, beauty and fear. Hess's decision in 1941 to make a solo flight to Britain to offer terms of peace epitomized the deep Romantic streak within his character, as well as his capacity to misread the situation. Despite the fact that he was still nominally vice-Führer, his authority was diminishing and his eccentricities were increasingly the subject of scornful gossip within Hitler's inner circle. Did he see his self-appointed mission as the chance to perform an act that would win back the respect of his hero? Or was his flight made, as some believe, with the full knowledge of his leader, permitted on the condition that if it succeeded Hess would be lauded as one of the great Germans and if he failed he would be denounced as a madman? His misapprehensions were several: that a member of the British aristocracy (the Duke of Hamilton) would have the ear of the British King; that the King held sway over Great Britain's foreign policy; and that

* Eugene Bird, *The Loneliest Man in the World: The Inside Story of the Thirty-Year Imprisonment of Rudolf Hess* (London: Sphere, 1980).

a Nazi politician of his rank would be received with fawning respect by Churchill's government. Setting off on his long journey through the lonely immensity of skies rendered perilous by the forces amassed against the Fatherland, he was as solitary as the figure on the shore in Caspar David Friedrich's *Monk by the Sea*, contemplating the vastness of the ocean. The fact that the night was moonlit made his journey more dangerous; he narrowly evaded being intercepted by a British plane when he reached the Scottish coast, but managed to complete his journey flying inside cloud cover that rendered him invisible from the ground. It is telling that, in the account he later made of the flight for his wife, at this climactic moment he paused to survey the scene:

At about twenty minutes to eleven I found myself over Dungavel, the estate of the Duke of Hamilton, my unsuspecting host-to-be. But in order to rule out any error, I flew a few minutes farther to the West coast. The mirror-smooth surface of the water glistened in the rising light of the full moon; an island mountain rose without a beachline, about 500 metres high, out of the sea, rising in a reddish light – the beauty and peace of the scenery was in stark contrast to my daring and exciting undertaking.*

The presence of the moon would have reminded Hess of home; it was the same moon, after all, that would be shining on his wife's house and on whichever building his leader was in at that moment, perhaps pacing the floor thinking of his faithful deputy's perilous mission, perhaps peacefully asleep. Hess was already a prisoner of history. As long as he remained airborne, circling like a skater above the mirror of the moonlit sea, his dreams could remain intact. Surely the British would see the

---

* Cited in Wulf Schwarzwäller, *Rudolf Hess: The Deputy* (London: Quartet Books, 1988), p. 162.

sense of reaching an accommodation similar to the one proposed by the Chamberlain government before the outbreak of
war? This would leave Germany free to rid the world of Communism; the very task for which the international industrialists
who invested in the country in the 1930s had selected it. Had
secret communications led him to expect a welcoming committee? In a few moments he must jump from his Messerschmitt,
allowing that masterpiece of German technology, the designer
of which he knew personally, to fly on without him and crash at
an unknown destination. He was carrying no form of identification; not even a change of clothes. All that he did have with
him, apart from the ready-prepared speech spinning round
inside his head, was a medical kit full of alternative remedies to
strengthen him in his impending task, including a gall-bladder
tonic he believed to have been prepared by a Tibetan lama. He
had never made a parachute jump before. The temptation to just
keep flying into the moon, or into the moon's reflection, must
have been very strong.

In the end, of course, he jumped – descending through the
moonlit air to land awkwardly, injuring his ankle. He was taken
prisoner by a startled Scottish farmer named David McLean,
who recounts the story of the arrival of his uninvited guest in a
Pathé newsreel of 11 May 1941 while grasping an impressive-
looking pitchfork. While they waited for the authorities,
McLean's elderly mother made Hess a cup of tea. In his fur-lined
leather flying suit and with his haughty demeanour Hess must
have cut an incongruous figure in the Scottish kitchen; as if the
man in the moon had come down out of curiosity to wander
among humankind, and been captured.

So began Hess's second life, spent behind bars; the expert
pilot would never fly again. All the more reason to follow the
moon-shot, to fly as it were remotely, inside his cell. The space
race was, in essence, the continuation of the argument he had

never been able to put to Churchill. Although the Western powers had allowed Communism to grow and form its own empire in the vacuum after the fall of the Reich, the Americans now seemed willing to challenge the Soviet conquest of space. At least the moon should not be allowed to become a satellite state of Russia! Rocket technology had been a central part of the Nazi war effort towards the end of the war, the source of considerable pride in the Nazi regime, especially to a man like Hess, fascinated by all aspects of flight.

The mastermind of the German rocket programme was a brilliant scientist named Wernher von Braun, who had been obsessed with the idea of putting a man into space since boyhood; a film in the Imperial War Museum in London shows the young von Braun on a beach, surrounded by school friends, at the launch of one of his home-made projectiles. His university dissertation, on rocket technology, was immediately classified by the German military. After taking a job with the Ordnance Department, he was made Technical Director of the Peenemünde Rocket Centre on the Baltic coast; the same mythic shore evoked in the poetry of Kosegarten and the paintings of Friedrich. There the little boy finally had all the backing and equipment he needed to make his rockets fly. The factory was hidden from Allied bombers below ground in a former gypsum mine. The workforce consisted of 60,000 slave-labourers drafted in from concentration camps who worked on subterranean assembly lines, subject to torture, beatings and summary execution. As many as a third of them were worked to death, their bodies gathered in piles at the First Aid stations at the end of each day, as little remarked upon, according to survivors, as broken tools or discarded overalls. The facility produced 600 V-2 rockets a month, powered by liquid jet engines fuelled with alcohol and oxygen, silently delivering a ton of high explosive: missiles dipped in death before they flew. This was the warfare of the future, but it came too late to secure victory for the Nazi regime. As Soviet troops invaded Germany from the east, von Braun fled westward with more than 100 of his team of scientists and technicians, carrying plans and equipment, so that he could surrender to advancing American forces rather than to Soviet troops. After a brief period of imprisonment in Europe the Americans moved him, along with his staff, to America and eventually to the headquarters of the US Army's Ballistic Missile Agency at Huntsville, Alabama. The influx earned the town the nickname 'Hunsville' with locals. The next time we hear of Wernher von Braun, he has left Alabama and joined NASA, to become the mastermind of the Apollo Space Programme.

Thus the scientist sidestepped the consequences of collaboration with the Nazi regime because of his eminent usefulness to the victors in the conflict. By contrast, the only possible role for Hess in the new world order was to carry the burden of the Nazis' defeat. Yet he too wanted to be part of this race to the moon, this symbolic defeat of Communism. He took the task entirely seriously and seems to have been allowed to enter into detailed correspondence with NASA from his prison cell. He spent hours each day reading complicated details of the moon landings and probes; dozens of scientific books were bought from prison funds, including a dictionary of space terms. He became convinced that lunar astronauts would experience dangerous heart strain on their return to the earth's atmosphere and wrote to NASA, recommending they made use of a rotating exercise table of his own invention. If only his writings on space could be published, he assured the prison governor, they would be an immediate success, simply because he was Rudolf Hess. Someone at NASA either took him seriously or had reason to feel sympathy for him; he was sent a minute-by-minute timetable for the Apollo 15 mission, along with photographs of the lunar surface, brochures and other materials. Why did these contacts at NASA take time to correspond with an elderly Nazi prisoner? Could they have been former colleagues from the Party, now working under a different flag? 'You know they have been most kind to me,' Hess told Eugene Bird. 'Would it not be a good idea to send off a signed photograph of me? I would autograph and date it and they could have it as a token of my thanks.' At this moment, then, in Bird's account, the would-be scientist appears a vainglorious and deluded old man. At the next, as the two men stroll in the garden, he is once again the boy who watched the moon from the roof of his home in Egypt, or the lonely kid in boarding school taking comfort in his astronomy magazines. 'As we walked in the mid-afternoon sunshine,' Bird recalls, 'he suddenly stopped in his tracks to point up at the full moon shining over the steeple of the church opposite. He pointed out the various seas that were identifiable to the naked eye. "Isn't it beautiful? I cannot get over it. That man has walked on the surface of that moon . . ."'

IV

One question remains for the alert reader: how did I manage to acquire an image of Hess from the period when he was held in Berlin, a hidden pawn to be passed back and forth each month in a secret ritual so elaborate that it seemed as if the whole of the Cold War depended on it? The official story has always been that no one managed to photograph Hess until much later, in the 1980s. My discovery came through a chance meeting. Some books begin as a random accumulation of ideas, spinning like the debris of rock fragments, ice and gases that follow an impact in space. Gradually, as more material is added, they attain mass and attract more objects to themselves, eventually, as their inner cores cool, achieving solidity. It is thought that this is how the moon was formed. At a stage in the development of this project, when the shape of a book had begun to emerge from among the fragments, I happened to attend a function where I ran into an old friend. He asked me what I was working on. We spoke for a couple of minutes before another man approached whom I had not met before. 'You must meet James,' my friend said to him, 'he's writing a book about the moon.' Without missing a beat, the man turned to me and said, 'In that case I might have something that would interest you.' He had in his possession, he explained, footage of Rudolf Hess taken clandestinely at Spandau; it included a sequence taken in his cell of Hess standing in front of a photograph of the moon, then shakily climbing up on a stool to point out the exact position of the Apollo 15 lunar landing. 'Perhaps you would like to take a still from it for your book?' he suggested gently, as if there might be any doubt about the matter. My new acquaintance turned out to be the German-born art historian and film-maker Lutz Becker, who had made a documentary about Hess for German television in the 1980s. He had been given the film by Eugene Bird, Hess's jailer and biographer, and had included it in his documentary, but it had not been shown outside Germany.

A week or so after my meeting with Becker, with a copy of the documentary on its way to me and already playing in my imagination, I found myself telling the story of its imminent arrival to a veteran newspaper journalist, John Knight. 'I've got a Hess story myself,' he said (like many Fleet Street journalists of his generation he appears to have been everywhere, met everyone). In the early 1980s, he explained, he had gone to Berlin for the *Sunday Mirror* on the trail of a story about a suspected chemical weapons unit situated just the other side of the Berlin Wall. He and another writer, Rupert Hart-Davis, were taken up in a four-man helicopter along with two military personnel. They flew up to the wall and hovered so that Hart-Davis, who had a powerful camera, could get a shot of the suspicious installation; he generously offered to let Knight have a photograph for his article. Once they were finished, the helicopter swung back across the city, crossing the suburb of Spandau with its scenic lakes, and the military liaison officer they were flying with, acting as an unofficial tour guide, pointed out the walls of the famous prison. 'My God,' his passengers exclaimed, 'who is that man walking alone in the garden? Can you take this thing down any closer?' It has to be remembered that as far as the news media were concerned, Hess had disappeared in the centre of Berlin as completely as if he had fled to the depths of the jungle. The pilot brought the helicopter down to the minimum height allowed by army regulations and they hovered over the prison. The man below them looked up idly, without apparent interest; helicopters were commonplace in these heavily patrolled skies. It was Rudolf Hess. Hart-Davis got the shot, the first known image of Hess since his trial at Nuremberg. 'He said something like "I think that one's mine, don't you, old boy?"' Knight told me; there would be no sharing this photographic property. It went on to be syndicated around the world.

For an experienced journalist, finding yourself alongside history in the making must all be part of a day's work. I, however, was struck by a coincidence. Two chance conversations within a fortnight and the troubling figure of Rudolf Hess, previously a historical footnote buried somewhere deep within my consciousness, had moved centre stage. He landed on my book like an eccentric astronaut, laden with the most dubious baggage, casting his shadow across its lunar surface.

Was I right to see traces in Hess's strangely conflicted character of the Romantics' enthusiasm for the 'night side' of life? Many have run the equation the other way. Just as the cracks in the surface of a nineteenth-century painting can catapult us a century forward in time to a shameful episode in our collective history, so the work of artists like Friedrich has somehow been infected retrospectively in people's minds by the virus of fascism. This pollution has extended beyond the realm of art and into nature itself. It is as if the poison of the revelations of what went on in the death camps has leached into the groundwater of the German landscape, rendering it suspect, hostile. Gerhard Richter, one of Germany's greatest post-war painters, describes nature in words as distinct as it is possible to imagine from those of the Romantics; it is, he has written, 'against us in all its forms because it knows . . . nothing, is absolutely without mind or spirit, is the total opposite of ourselves . . . Its stupidity is absolute.'* In contrast, suspicious as he is of the landscape, painting it (as if to protect himself) only from photographic sources, he is relatively warm about Caspar David Friedrich. A painting by Friedrich, he explains, is not 'a thing of the past'; only the ideologies that prompted its creation are of the past, the painting itself, if it is good, affects us as art. Thus the artist, unburdened by ideology, 'can paint like C. D. "today"'.†

The Nazis, prone from their leader down to making judgements on the art both of history and their contemporaries, divided the Romantic painters into those who were effeminate and degenerate and those who were patriots. Friedrich was assigned to the latter camp, approved by the Führer. In reality, of course, a man of Friedrich's sensitivity would have been horrified by the grotesque savagery that was unleashed in the name of the united Germany he longed for. Any demons that lurk in his paintings are the product of his own sadly morbid soul. We should repel any attempt to overrun the art of the past with the

---

* Gerhard Richter, 18 February 1986, from *Notes 1986–1990*, in Sean Rainbird (ed.), *Gerhard Richter* (London: Tate Publishing, 1991), p. 117.
† From a letter to Jean-Christophe Ammann, 24 February 1973, ibid., p. 110.

same vigour that previous generations employed to resist invasion, otherwise their battle was in vain.

V

If one twentieth-century painting embodies the struggle over
the right to employ Romantic imagery, it is a work by the British painter Paul Nash entitled *Totes Meer* (Dead Sea). Nash,
commissioned by the War Artists Advisory Committee, came to
Oxford in 1940 to look at the place where the remnants of shot-
down planes were gathered to be recycled for the war effort.
The Metal and Produce Recovery Unit was a gigantic scrapyard
in a field behind the Morris Car Factory in Cowley on the city's
eastern fringe, a few minutes from where I am writing these
words. (A car factory still dominates the site, now owned by the
German company BMW.) Nash arrived in Cowley shortly after
the Battle of Britain; the other-worldly landscape he found there
had a powerful effect on his imagination. He made a number of
drawings and took photographs of the Recovery Unit, recreat-
ing his impressions in this remarkable painting. Very consciously,
he borrowed the language of German Romantic art, choosing to
set the scene at night, beneath a waning moon. His depiction of
the desolate expanse clearly references Caspar David Friedrich's
evocation of another landscape, *The Sea of Ice*; the shifting planes
of moonlit metal, with here a wheel, there a Luftwaffe insignia,
echo the broken ice floes that in Friedrich's painting form a tomb
for the ship of a doomed Polar expedition. 'The thing looked to
me, suddenly, like a great inundating sea,' Nash wrote.

You might feel, under certain circumstances – a moonlit night, for
instance – this is a vast tide moving across the fields, the breakers rearing
up and crashing on the plain. And then, no, nothing moves, it is not water
or even ice, it is something static and dead. It is metal piled up, wreckage.

It is hundreds and hundreds of flying creatures which invaded these shores (how many Nazi planes have been shot down or otherwise wrecked in this country since they first invaded?). Well, here they are, or some of them. By moonlight, the waning moon, one could swear they began to move and twist and turn as they did in the air. A sort of rigor mortis? No, they are quite dead and still. The only moving creature is the white owl flying low over the bodies of the other predatory creatures, raking the shadows for rats and voles.

The moon appeared early in Nash's work. His first exhibition, at the Carfax Gallery, featured a drawing called *The Falling Stars*, which was bought by William Rothenstein, later the director of the Tate Gallery. It featured, Herbert Read wrote, 'two contorted pine-trees moulded in ghostly moonlight against a night sky, across which two falling stars trace their burning way', displaying the influence of William Blake.* Nash had already made a connection between flight and the moon in his watercolour *Moonlight Voyage: Flying against Germany* of 1940, in which a British bomber, its propellers a Futurist blur, climbs above moonlit clouds and seemingly above the moon itself, which hangs, a football-sized planet, above the landscape below. In the works he made during the 1930s, in which he sought to discover through 'imaginative research' the *genius loci* of the English countryside, the moon often featured, connecting the present-day wanderer with the remote past hinted at by megaliths and tumuli. *Pillar and Moon* is such a work, painted in 1932 and reworked in the war years, with its full moon in a clear sky above a line of beech trees, the solitary pillar by a drystone wall as strange an architectural feature as any in a de Chirico painting, yet typical of the remnants of the large estates that litter the Chilterns.

For Read, even Nash's warplanes are part of his portrayal of

---

* Herbert Read, *Penguin Modern Painters: Paul Nash* (Harmondsworth: Penguin Books, 3rd revised edition, 1948), pp. 7, 8.

the natural world, monolithic objects 'fallen unexpectedly from the sky but endowed with an additional mystery, ominous and deathly'.* Here, then, is the end of Hess's dreams of flight, and of a nation's dreams of conquest; a painted 'Ozymandias' fore-telling the collapse of an empire against a background not of desert sands but moonlit suburban fields. It is moonlight that allows Nash to see this landlocked scene in central England as a sea, and moonlight that perhaps made him think of Friedrich – there must have been some satisfaction in co-opting the visual vocabulary of such a great German icon. With a somewhat naive belief in the efficacy of art to change history, Nash saw his paint-ing not just as propaganda but also as a weapon; he designed a postcard version, intended to be dropped from planes over Ger-many, in which the face of Hitler is superimposed upon the shattered remnants of the German air force. In reality of course the vision offered by Nash's painting is transparently selective, its message far more complex and contradictory than its creator intended. Moonlight would have glinted on as many British 'predatory creatures' in the scrapyard as German, the owl, busy 'raking the shadows' for its prey, flying indifferently over both. In the end, wrecked planes speak more of the futility of war than the victory of one side over the other. The ideologies that created the vast poem in twisted metal that Nash discovered behind the Cowley Works have passed away, at least for the moment; yet his painting survives, not as 'a thing of the past' so much as a warning that such forces should never shape our future again.

---

* Ibid., p. 16.

PART SIX

Thamesis

Through Midnight Streets: The Thames and a London Moon

I did not intend to paint a portrait of the bridge, but only a painting of a moonlight scene. As to what the picture represents, that depends upon who looks at it. To some persons it may represent all that I intended; to others it may represent nothing . . . The thing is intended simply as a representation of moonlight.

James McNeill Whistler, *Whistler vs Ruskin*,
The Old Law Courts, 25, 26 November 1878

I

London is a city with a river running through it. Or rather it is a city *because* it has a river running through it. The Thames is the liquid autobahn upon which the building blocks of the metropolis have been moved into position over the centuries: wood, stone, iron, sand, straw, brick, concrete; a chameleon tongue, extended from the capital's mouth to pluck the fruits of the fecund country far inland in one direction and unrolled to deliver its booty to the sea in the other. The city's position marks the broadest point at which Roman engineers were able to span the Thames with a bridge, pinching its width like a woman's coarse, mud-coloured braid. Like any urban river, this one is also a mirror, reflecting London's mood as much as the sky above it. In one period thicketed with masts and funnels, churned by oars, paddles and turbines into a sewage soup as filthy and busy as the most solid street; in another a metaphorical highway only,

populated by tourists gliding past the scenes of national comed-
ies and tragedies, from Parliament via the slowly spinning Eye
to Shakespeare's Globe, a promenade through history.

Water, as we have learned, is the medium that best grounds
moonlight, plugging us into its subtle voltage and providing a
multitude of miniature skies for the moon to swim in. At various times, people have even believed that they could ingest the
moon in water, or if not the moon itself then its virtue. Hence
the humorous classical story of the peasant and his donkey, collected and retold by Robert Burton in his *Anatomy of Melancholy*,
a tale of 'a silly country fellow, that killed his ass for drinking up
the moon, *ut lunam mundo redderet* [that he might restore the
moon to the world]'. So also the Irish tradition that saw women
who wished to bear children making a pilgrimage at full moon
to the shores of a certain lake and drinking down the moonlight
it had captured; a different kind of immaculate conception,
with a hovering dove replaced by a silver disc floating in the
lake's dark waters.

For the past few years I have had the good luck to work by
the river, its presence a constant outside the window. In spare
moments at low tide I have descended to its shore, picking up
treasures: a rusted ship's rivet, clay-pipe stems, oyster shells,
bricks and tiles, their corners worn smooth by the action of the
tides, and the workings of a clock undone by time. (Who would
throw a clock into the Thames, prompted by what symbolic
impulse? Perhaps the same one that propelled a mobile phone
into its depths decades later, washed up now at my feet, its voice
equally silent, its memory licked clean.) There is a moment that
I like, on winter afternoons, when the sun sinks low enough in
the west to shine beneath the arches of Vauxhall Bridge, uplight-
ing their vaulted metalwork while the rest of the scene sinks
into dusk. And then the moon, on summer nights, seen from
Millennium Bridge, swollen by the distortion of the earth's

atmosphere, rising like a blood orange into the sky above St Paul's. However, my luck has never extended to living by the river (although I have always felt a powerful envy for those that do). There is a flat in Hammersmith with a small patio garden a few steps across, bounded by a brick wall in which there is a wooden gate. Open the gate and you meet the Thames. I have stood on the footpath as the sun went down with a group of Italian and Portuguese visitors as joggers pounded past, and listened to their astonishment as they leaned over the railings, looking down at the stony, bird-stalked mudbanks between which the olive water sluices. Is the river always this empty? they ask, worried perhaps that London is afflicted by drought. I explain, to their surprise, that the Thames that they have heard so much about is tidal. But yes, an Italian woman cries with the excitement of discovery, it must be right – I can smell the sea! And it is true, at this moment as the tide turns, a salt smell is broadcast upriver, like a message of hope and renewal to the city's beleaguered inhabitants. This twice-daily refreshment London owes, of course, to the moon's powerful attraction.

At low tide it is hard to believe the central role the Thames has played in the life of the city. *London Night and Day*, a guidebook published by The Architectural Press in 1951, explains it succinctly.

A map of London shows one thing clearly: London has no High Street. The Thames has no name-plate but High Street it was until about 1820 . . . That year over 3,000 wherries plied the river. The call was 'Oars', not 'Taxi', at the top of any of the 17 public stairs between Lambeth and Limehouse. But in 1829 came the omnibus and in 1836 the railway, and the river lost favour with travellers.

Emile Zola put it even more forcefully. 'The Thames from London Bridge to Greenwich,' he told the *Manchester Guardian* newspaper in October 1893, 'I can only compare to an immense, moving street of ships, large and small, something suggestive to the European mind of an aquatic Rue de Rivoli . . . The Thames is, in fact, the heart or stomach, if you like, of London, as the West End is the head of its wonderful organism.'

London Night and Day advertised itself as 'A Guide to Places the Other Books Don't Take You'. One of the principal of these was the deserted streets of the city at night. The guide is divided up hour by hour, around the clock. The section for one o'clock in the morning proposes a moonlit walk through London's financial district, empty in those days outside office hours and known, in recognition of its status as the site of the original Roman settlement, as the City. The author begins with an explanation of the word 'townscape', lately coined by *The Architectural Review*.

Don't get the idea from what's gone before that townscape is just another exhibition game. Now that the moon is out and the traffic thinning out, what about an exercise in the real thing? Easier to concentrate when one can stand in the roadway without wounding the feelings of a bus driver. But what roadway? In this full moon? The City? The City, of course.

The moonlit guided tour begins at St Paul's Cathedral, the site of the temple that dominated one of the two hills in the original Roman city of Londinium, which is described in a passage reminiscent of Goethe's descriptions of moonlit Rome in his *Italian Journey*.

Start at the altar steps of Bow Church from which, through the West Window and door, can be seen, unbelievably beautiful in the full moon, the dome and east end of St Paul's. There isn't another view in London to compare with this product of the blitz . . . Don't overlook, as you stand there, the weird effects (purely fortuitous, the results of the blitz) of the waste land around the Cathedral suggesting cliff and sea-scape, out of which rise single church towers and strange ruins, tantalizingly beautiful in the moonlight.

One of the things that made London in the 1950s a different world from the city of today, apart from the deserts of scattered brick and pulverized masonry opened up by German bombardment, was that the river was still alive, crawling with traffic, right at its heart. After leading his readers up and down and through the alleyways and streets that survive from the old medieval city plan (or lack of it) – Fish Street Hill, Love Lane, St Dunstan's Alley, Idol Lane, Monument Street, Pudding Lane, George Lane, Botolph Alley ('pitch-black, very romantic'), the Alley to St-Mary-at-Hill, and so on, the author of *London Night and Day* returns them to the river.

Now comes a great hooting of steamers (which means the tide is high), a strange homeless sound in the deserted, dark street, and then the booming chime of cathedral clocks, the two sounds which tell one sharper than words that one is on the water-front of the world's port. Authentic London . . .

We will leave you overlooking the moonlit Pool of London, guarded to the east by the twin gothic towers of Tower Bridge, a magnificent dream of half a century ago. Across the river, acting as a backdrop to this scene, the modern wharves. And in between the river, the working space for watermen, rivermen, pilots, tugmen, bargemen, policemen, firemen, customs officers, river rats and dock rats and the temporary resting place for deep-sea sailors from every port in the world.

In a congested city, a river provides more than just sustenance for an entire alternate universe of trades and occupations. It also offers visual escape from narrow streets; an uncluttered horizon; a breathing space. Perhaps this is partly why rivers attract artists.

One who spent much of his life within a few minutes' walk of the Thames was William Blake. In the winter of 1790–91 he moved from Westminster to a terraced house at no. 13 Hercules Buildings in Lambeth, where he could be observed through the front window, at work at his press. These were heady times; London had lived through the Gordon Riots and watched the King go mad, a living demonstration for a man of Blake's radical leanings of the absurdity of the structures of earthly power. The aftershocks of the French Revolution were more than a distant rumble in Britain; for a moment it must have felt as if everything might change. Blake wore a red cap in the street in sympathy. In the bloody aftermath of the Revolution, many previously sympathetic English observers changed their views. It is possible that Westminster grew too hot for someone of Blake's political persuasion. Yet it is clear that Blake also longed for a calm, sequestered space in which to pursue his dreams. However, while the house at Lambeth, with its garden, at first seemed to offer respite from what Mrs Blake described to a correspondent as 'the terrible desart of London', the area was changing fast. A radical poet and his wife were not the only problems that Westminster expelled across the water: new legislation meant that noxious industries were forced to relocate south of the river, adding to the stench and misery of the crowded lanes that backed on to the Thames. Blake describes them in his poem 'London':

> I wander thro' each dirty* street,
> Near where the dirty Thames does flow,
> And mark in every face I meet
> Marks of weakness, marks of woe.

For Blake, escape from the oppression of the present came through the powerful tool of the imagination. It was while living in Hercules Buildings that he created the book of engravings

---

* In the version of the poem included in the *Songs of Innocence and of Experience*, Blake substituted the word 'charter'd' for 'dirty', reflecting contemporary discussions of the Magna Carta.

For Children: The Gates of Paradise. One image particularly reson-
ates as a depiction of his own sense of yearning for another state
of being. Entitled *I Want! I Want!*, it shows a child, watched by
its parents, propping a long and slender ladder against the crescent moon, placing its foot on the second step and preparing to
climb. The surface of the earth is shown merely with a few
cross-hatched lines and could itself be that of another planet, or
an asteroid. The figures, too, are barely described, the child, in
its one-piece suit and with its oversized oval head, looking
uncannily like a modern space-traveller. Stars burn in the dark
night sky and the moon hangs conveniently close, a paring from
a large cheese perhaps, or a rowing boat in which the child can
set off on a journey of discovery.

Blake's house has long since been demolished and subsumed in
the Corporation of London's William Blake Housing Estate. Cycling along what is now a dusty short cut between Lambeth North
Underground station and Lambeth Bridge Road in heavy traffic,
I strain to see the blue plaque on the red-brick facade of the blocks
of flats marking where Blake's residence once stood ('William
Blake, Poet and Painter, lived in a house formerly on this site
1793') and wobble dangerously in the path of a bus as I pass Cen-
taur Street. A short stroll from his own front door, Blake would
have found himself at the gates of Lambeth Palace on the banks of
the Thames, the residence of the Archbishop of Canterbury and
thus the centre of power of the organized religion Blake so
detested. It is hard to think of a more powerful Blakean symbol of
the ills of society than a bishop sitting secure behind the walls of
a palace while destitute children patrol the streets outside.

There was one artist during Blake's lifetime widely associated
in the public mind with the moon. Abraham Pether was born a
year before Blake, in 1756, in Southampton. Initially he studied
music and was reputed to have been a skilled violinist; however,
at some point he must have made a decision that his best prospects

of gainful employment lay with painting rather than with music. From the first, he concentrated on landscape. Like many artists of the period, he was a man of what would today seem extraordinarily broad interests: he made musical instruments, telescopes, microscopes and air pumps; gave lectures on electricity that included demonstrations with equipment of his own devising; and invented a lead pencil. It was not until the 1780s that he began to focus on the genre that would earn him fame. Once he had set his artistic course he single-mindedly followed his vision, producing moonlit landscapes of such quality that he earned himself the nickname 'Moonlight Pether'. His *View of the Thames by Moonlight* returns the city to a mythic past, its neoclassical frontage on the river appearing as ancient as the Pyramids, its frenetic energy frozen into a glacial stillness. The full moon burns in the sky, gilding the river as far upstream as the silhouetted dome of St Paul's.

Pether had a model within his own family of an artistic career; his cousin William Pether, twenty-six years his senior, had moved from Carlisle to live in London, where he began as a landscape painter but enjoyed his greatest success as an engraver. One of his most fruitful collaborations had been with the leading British eighteenth-century painter of moonlight scenes, Joseph Wright of Derby. Some of Wright's greatest works, including *Lecture on the Orrery* and *The Alchemist*, were made known through William Pether's skills, their dramatic chiaroscuro effects transferred to the engraver's plate. The unholy radiance of the phosphorus in the alchemist's bottle and the gleam of the full moon through the window high above his head are as dramatic in Pether's version as in Wright's original. It seems fitting that these brooding nocturnal scenes should be rendered in mezzotint; the technique was nicknamed *manière noire*, as the image was extracted from darkness, the plate first inked totally black and then lightened by a process of burnishing.

The two artists became friends. On occasion when Wright came to London he stayed at William Pether's establishment at Great Russell Street, from where he organized the sale and exhibition of his works. Pether was part of a circle of young artists and radicals, including the painter John Hamilton Mortimer and the architect James Gandon, which would have been attractive to someone of Wright's wide interests in science and the arts. For his part Wright, with his connections to eminent thinkers in the Midlands such as Erasmus Darwin, would have been an object of fascination to the London circle. The importance of William Pether's contribution to Wright's career can be judged by the fact that John Leigh Phillips, Wright's obituarist in the *Monthly Magazine* in 1797, assumed that to his readers Wright's paintings of the 1760s would be 'well known by Pether's *mezzotintos*'.

For an eighteenth-century painter of the night sky, the secrets lay beneath the surface. To achieve the appearance of a source of light actually within the picture, to make a painted moon glow, there must be a layer beneath the topmost one that will reflect light back into the viewer's eye – acting, in fact, much as the moon itself does. Mastering such arcane science was part and parcel of the moonlight painter's art. A book entitled *A Practical Treatise on Painting in Oil Colour*, published in 1795, gave detailed advice:

To represent the sun or moon with amazing force, lay on the spot or place where it is intended the greatest light or glow shall be, some varnish, or body of fine white; upon this stick gold or silver leaf (whichever is to be painted, sun or moon) and glaze over with yellow-lake, brown-pink or Naples yellow, in proportion to the effect of sunshine or moonshine. This, well-managed in the glazings or re-touchings, will produce a wonderful effect.[*]

[*] Anon. (London, 1795), p. 210; quoted in Rica Jones, 'Wright of Derby's Techniques of Painting', in Judy Egerton (ed.), *Wright of Derby* (London: Tate Publishing, 1990), p. 268.

Microscopic analysis has revealed that Wright himself experimented with the use of such materials on one or two occasions; to intensify the incandescence of a white-hot iron bar or increase the heat in his depiction of a forge. Mainly, however, he relied on preparing his canvas with a highly reflective white ground, a double layer of gypsum bound in oil, deadened in most of the picture but allowed to show through in, for instance, a moonlit cloud or reflective sea to achieve a luminous effect. Abraham Pether had his own secrets, doubtlessly guarded carefully as they were the foundation of his reputation. They did not, however, go with him to the grave when he died at the comparatively young age of fifty-six.

Wright's untimely death forced Pether's widow to go into business (to support her nine children) as Pether and Company, selling 'Improved Black-Lead & Chalk Pencils (Invented by the late A. Pether, esq. F.S.A.)'. The artist had ensured that at least one of his children had a way of earning a living. By the time of his father's death, Pether's son Sebastian was a fully trained-up apprentice in the moonlight painter's trade. The young man took up his father's mantle as a painter specializing in night scenes. When he in turn had a son, Henry, born in 1828, he too was inducted into the family business, continuing the family tradition of painting 'moonlights' into the second half of the nineteenth century. At the beginning of his career, Sebastian followed the market, travelling as far as Naples to paint nocturnal eruptions of Vesuvius. Henry is best known for his depictions of the Thames at night, from Chelsea down to Greenwich, combining nocturnal effects every bit as skilful as his forebears' with astonishing accuracy in their depiction of architecture, making them a valuable record for historians of the river. And so a dynasty of moonlighters was established, unique perhaps in the history of art, active for almost a century.

Popular in their day and represented still in many public

collections, the Pethers are now largely forgotten (or, in some instances, mixed up with one another) by art historians. (Wright also languished in the art-historical shadows for many years, dismissed as an insignificant provincial, until undergoing a critical renaissance in the last twenty-five years.) Perhaps the key to the Pethers' fall from grace lies in the question, what does moonlight *mean* in their paintings? As we have seen, in his personal life Abraham Pether seems to have had just as much intellectual curiosity as Wright, yet his choice of subject matter means that none of his paintings captures the spirit of his age for a modern audience as Wright's do. In Pether's moonlight scenes he is instead reaching back to the old masters, to Adam Elsheimer's *Rest on the Flight into Egypt* (1609) (Pether painted a version of the same theme), or to the nightscapes of the seventeenth-century Dutch master Aert van der Neer.

In Pether's paintings, the moon comments on the action only by providing the contrast of its own glacial calm. In 1809 Drury Lane Theatre caught fire and was completely destroyed, an event that galvanized London. In *The Burning of Old Drury Lane Theatre*, Abraham Pether portrays the event from a mile or so downriver, near the opposite bank. A spout of flame from the burning building rises vertically into the air, like a volcanic eruption, and the clouds above it have been arranged into an arch, emphasizing its height. Though distant, the fire is so powerful that it paints the sky and river orange. A full moon, its light diminished, is partly hidden behind a cloud. In the foreground, three silhouetted figures observe the scene from a barge, with the detachment of the Romantic aesthete. Pether has chosen a viewpoint that allows him to demonstrate his skills, contrasting the heat of fire with the cold light of the moon, with special attention to the reflections in the glassily still waters of the Thames. He has created an elegant stage set, populated with the same contemplative types that appear at the rim of Volaire's volcanoes.

Twenty-five years later the city was once more visited by fire; this time captured in a very different manner by a very different artist. In 1834, J. M. W. Turner joined a watching crowd of thousands, some of them cheering and jeering, as the Houses of Parliament burned to the ground. In contrast to Pether, and like a modern Pliny the Elder, he got as close as he could to the blaze, hiring a boatman to row him out on the water, making rapid sketches from the south bank of the river near Westminster Bridge and also from further east at Waterloo Bridge. *The Burning of the Houses of Lords and Commons* depicts a maelstrom; we can almost feel the pull of the hot wind sucking us towards the conflagration, hear the roar, and catch the reek of history being eaten by the flames.

Abraham Pether has left one unlikely memorial that does connect him to the scientific advances of his day. Robert John Thornton was Lecturer in Medical Botany at Guy's and St Thomas's Hospitals in London, and keenly interested in the latest botanical research. Towards the end of the eighteenth century he became gripped with the idea of commissioning the finest artists of his day to produce a series of prints illustrating the reproductive functions of plants. What made his vision particular was that he wished each plant to be depicted in an appropriate setting rather than against a neutral background, so that the prints would combine the scientific and the artistic in a way that would appeal to a wide public. The work was to be known as *The New Illustration of the Sexual System of Carolus von Linnæus, comprehending an elucidation of the several parts of the fructification.* Among those artists enlisted for the project were Abraham Pether, Francesco Bartolozzi, John Landseer, James Opie, Henry Raeburn and Philip Reinagle. Pether, as London's leading purveyor of moonlights, was commissioned to provide the setting for the illustration of *The Night-blowing Cereus.* Several cacti share this name, but the species depicted in the illustration appears to be that known as the Queen of the Night, native of the southern Arizona desert, the very landscape through which I took my moonlit hike. With its waxy, perfumed, nocturnal flowers that blossom on just one night of the year, it must have seemed impossibly exotic to European botanists. In the illustration, the plant itself is painted by Reinagle. The luxuriant, overblown bloom, with its pronounced stamen reaching out to the viewer and framed by petals, is shown growing not in a desert but against a moonlit background of a lake; next to the lake stands a ruined tower, the hands of its clock pointing to midnight, the hour at which the Cereus reputedly opened. It is a striking image, Reinagle's acute scientific observation offset by Pether's gothic special effects. It is as if one artist has been commissioned to depict the scientific truth of the plant, the other its myth. Today, Thornton's collection is better known as *The Temple of Flora* and is revered by devotees of botanical illustration. Pether's contribution is still the most widely reproduced of its plates.

One place embodies the occasionally uneasy alliance between those who have made their living on the Thames and the artistic community that lived at its edge. In the nineteenth century there was a boatyard at Chelsea belonging to a boatman and skiff-builder named Charles Greaves. He and his family lived near by on Lindsey Row, in a section of houses now forming part of Cheyne Walk. Today their house is separated from the river by Chelsea Embankment, constructed in the mid-nineteenth century, but they grew up in more immediate proximity to the river. As Greaves's son Walter remembered, 'Our house was so close to the water that when lying in bed at night we could hear the river's wash beneath the walls.' Their business – the building and hiring out of boats, as well as the provision of ferry services to passengers who wanted to go out on the water – was of a kind that had continued along the river's reaches for centuries.

However, in their lifetimes the river itself was to be confined in a way it had never been before. Repeated outbreaks of cholera had made it clear that a new sewage system was vital to London's health. It was not until the long, hot summer of 1858, otherwise known as the Great Stink – when the combination of low water levels, raw sewage and effluent from industries resulted in such a stench coming off the river that Parliament was forced to hang limed sheets over its windows in order to continue sitting – that the funds were made available for work to begin.

So it was that the irregular, tidal foreshore of the Thames, which boatmen like the Greaveses had known all their lives, disappeared beneath the monumental embankments of the nineteenth-century city. However, it was not just the river that was changing. The newly landscaped neighbourhood had also begun to attract artists, drawn by its river views and bohemian reputation, and for the Greaves family these new residents would impact on their lives in unexpected ways. A valuable source of employment, they also brought with them new and unsettling ideas. The first and perhaps the most famous of all arrived somewhat surreptitiously. J. M. W. Turner had an 'official' residence in Queen Anne Street, with a studio near by and a gallery in Harley Street. He also maintained an establishment on Cremorne Road, at the western extremity of Cheyne Walk, a six-roomed house maintained by a woman variously believed to be his housekeeper and his wife. She was, in fact, his mistress, Sophia Booth; to many of his neighbours, Turner was known as Admiral Booth, a sharp-eyed, hawk-nosed old man of around sixty years of age. One afternoon in the late 1830s, he strolled with the painter John Martin and his son Leopold through the city to the house, which the fastidious Leopold described as 'a squalid place past Lindsey Row . . . very poorly furnished, all and everything looking as if it was the abode of a very poor man', although admitting it had 'a magnificent prospect of the river in both directions'. For Turner, the place was inspirational. He took his visitors upstairs to the room facing the river and showed them the view from its single window. 'Here you see my study,' he told them, 'sky and water. Are they not glorious? Here I have my lesson night and day.' His house, now demolished, is depicted in a drawing by Walter Greaves, dated 1860. Its front gate is just half a dozen paces from the river, where steps lead down to a floating pontoon at which boats are for hire. On the roof there is a wrought-iron balustrade, such as is found on harbour masters' houses, allowing a good view of shipping on the river. A minute's walk upstream, the trees of Cremorne Gardens give the scene a rural aspect that would have been tempered by the sight of the manufactories on the opposite shore.

Turner had been studying his river lessons for a considerable time already. His first painting to be exhibited at the Royal Academy in 1796 was a marine night scene, demonstrating a precocious ability to render waves made semi-transparent by moonlight. This was followed the next year by *Moonlight, a Study at Millbank*, a naturalistic rendering of the Thames under a full moon, from a viewpoint on the foreshore near the present site of Tate Britain, the museum that houses the works he left to the nation. In this early painting Turner is more likely to be competing with seventeenth-century Dutch masters, much admired and collected by his English contemporaries, than with any British painter. He was aware of Abraham Pether, and admired his moonlight scenes, but felt them too much the creation of the studio rather than of the direct study of nature, which for him remained the touchstone of true art. His first biographer, Walter Thornbury, tells us that 'Turner used to say he found moonlights very difficult.' It was typical of the man therefore that his first publicly exhibited paintings tackled the problem head on. Once installed at Chelsea, he regularly

employed Charles Greaves to row him across to the opposite
bank from where the luminosity of the river could best be captured. The boatman came to play a vital role; Turner depended
on his knowledge of the tides and his ability to read weather
conditions. Together they were out on the river at all hours.
St Mary's Church, Battersea, where William Blake had been
married in 1782, was a regular destination. Turner painted the
Thames from the churchyard and from the vestry window of
the elegant Georgian building, its spire dwarfed today by a zig-
gurat of condominiums designed by the architect Richard
Rogers. Greaves had no idea at first who his passenger was, but
described him as always wearing a faded old brown coat and a
top hat. The rather stout Mrs Booth was often sent ahead with
provisions. It was probably from a Chelsea pier that Turner
travelled by river to Wapping, where he had inherited another
property, the Ship and Bladebone public house. Here too he was
thought to be a retired naval man rather than an artist, and it
may well have been here that he took models to a discreet room
to paint the erotic watercolours discovered among his papers
after his death. At first taken to be sunsets, they were later recognized by Ruskin, Turner's champion and the self-appointed
guardian of his critical legacy, to be rather more intimate in
their subject matter; without hesitation, Ruskin sent them to
the flames. In the Victorian age the inquiring mind was permitted to investigate the heavens, but not to turn its attention to
uncharted territories nearer home.

In 1848, John Martin and his family moved to Lindsey House,
previously occupied by the Brunel family and just a short walk
from Turner's residence. Martin's interest in the river was not
purely aesthetic. For many years he had been campaigning for
the introduction of new sewage disposal systems and improvements to London's water supplies, publishing pamphlets at his
own expense that anticipated Bazalgette's proposals by quarter

of a century. Martin regularly accompanied Turner on to the river, rowed out by Greaves to see the sun go down. On stormy nights Greaves stayed up to watch over his boats and Martin had an arrangement that if the moon was particularly fine, Greaves would send one of his sons to knock at Martin's door. He would emerge on the two-storey, iron-pipe balcony, attached to the house by Sir Marc Isambard Brunel, to try to catch the wild night sky on paper.

Greaves's children were raised, therefore, in a society in which artists and the people of the river had shared business. His sons, Walter and Henry, as well as being taught all the skills of a waterman, were painters themselves, learning their skills decorating the prows of the ornate Thames skiffs at their father's mooring. There was money to be made selling genre river scenes also, depictions of the streets of Chelsea and the boat races and other festive events that regularly contributed to the gaiety of London life in the mid-nineteenth century. These they often worked on together, signing them 'H & W Greaves'. Gradually a small bohemian enclave developed, set slightly apart from the rigid rules of class and etiquette that governed British society. It was not Paris, but perhaps it was the nearest London could approach to a Parisian artists' quarter at the time.

Into this small world arrived one artist who had experienced the bohemian life in Paris first hand, and whose depiction of the River Thames at night was to take centre stage in the greatest art controversy of the age. James McNeill Whistler was an American who had spent part of his childhood in Russia and part in the United States, where he had trained as a draughtsman. Like so many artists before and since he travelled to Paris to study art, where he fell under the influence of Gustave Courbet, whose dominance he eventually found repressive. International in outlook, cosmopolitan and exceedingly ambitious, with family connections in London, Whistler moved to Chelsea, hoping to create art there that he could promote both in Britain and France. London itself would provide him with subject matter.

Whistler did not arrive at his mature style immediately on arriving on British shores; instead he put his art through a process of 'education' that lasted a decade at least. This involved exposing it to the latest theories, whether derived from other artists, literature or even science. As an artist, he was keenly interested in the nature of perception. By the 1830s, Newton's Particle Theory had largely been superseded by the wave theory of light. This proposed that light was made up of waves, travelling through an invisible substance called the luminiferous ether, which acted as the medium of their support in much the same way that water did for ripples, or air did for sound waves. To talk of light as akin to sound chimed with the contemporary fascination with synaesthesia, the overlapping or intermingling of the senses, allowing Whistler to argue for an aesthetic theory of his own: that just as complementary sound waves produce musical harmony, complementary light waves could produce visual harmony. Such visual compositions therefore could work directly on the senses, negating the need for the narrative element that was such a feature of much of the painting of his contemporaries. Whistler's theories were reflected in the titles he started to give his paintings in the 1860s: *Harmony in Blue and Silver: Trouville* (a seascape with beach); *Symphony in White* (two young women in white languishing on a sofa); *Arrangement in Grey and Black No. 1* (the famous portrait of his mother, this last from 1871). This approach echoed the synaesthetic imagery of Baudelaire's poem 'Correspondances':

> There are perfumes fresh as children's flesh,
> Soft as oboes, green as meadows,
> And others, corrupted, rich, triumphant,
>
> Possessing the diffusion of infinite things . . .

Whistler's half-sister Deborah was married to the surgeon, collector and amateur artist Francis Seymour Haden. Haden's home in Sloane Street was Whistler's first base in London when he moved to the city as an adult, determined to make his name as an artist. From it he could stroll to the river at Chelsea, which still ran up to the water gates at the Physic Garden, lapping against steps and old walls of brick. Whistler's first artistic engagement with the subject he was to make his own was through a series of exquisite etchings known as *The Thames Set*, made in the late 1850s. They show the river with its thickets of masts and its jumble of wharves and warehouses dwarfing the tiny figures hurrying about their business on its surface or along its banks. This was the Thames as a site of industry rather than a scene of contemplation. His knowledge of optics is also apparent; a rendering of East India Dock has the foreground and distance in focus, with the middle ground and peripheries slightly blurred, replicating the way that human vision works. Whistler took rooms in Wapping in east London to get close to his subject matter, spending long hours sketching in an area that would have been regarded at the time as dangerous to a gentleman artist of the upper classes, with its drinking dens frequented by longshoremen and criminals, prostitutes and their attendant pimps. Baudelaire, the supreme urban poet of his age, praised the etchings in an article in 1862 as representing the 'profound and intricate poetry of a vast capital'.

Haden and Whistler had planned to collaborate on the publication of a more extensive set of etchings of the Thames from London right down to the sea, but their relationship deteriorated, ending in a brawl in Paris in 1867 during which Whistler pushed his brother-in-law through a plate-glass window. They never spoke again. When *The Thames Set* was finally published in the 1870s, the astonishing skill and subtlety of Whistler's etching technique, which contemporaries compared to that of

Rembrandt, confounded critics set on attacking his paintings as the work of a charlatan. Whistler portrayed an alternate and infinitely engrossing aspect of the city. This was the London that fascinated French writers and artists and also, Whistler hoped, French collectors: vast, sprawling, ugly, at once excitingly modern and already in decay.

The etchings betrayed the influence of Courbet in their close observation of the lives of working men and of an earlier hero, Hogarth, in the detail of their portrayal of the city; Whistler had discovered Hogarth as a teenager and had long believed he was the greatest of all British artists. However, it was to the art of another culture entirely that Whistler was to turn for inspiration when moving to the next stage in his career. Japan had been opened up to Western trade in the 1850s and Whistler was galvanized when he first encountered Japanese prints and porcelain in Paris; he soon became an avid collector. For him, Japanese art was vital in a way that much European art had long since ceased to be; its emphasis on the decorative and the flat picture plane provided an escape route from the suffocating heritage of European civilization. Quite simply, it offered a new way of looking at the world.

To arrive at a satisfying synthesis of these influences, Whistler needed a subject that would inspire, but not dominate his pictures. He found it, once again, in the River Thames, but this time at night. One of his most enduring memories of his first visit to London, when he was nine years old and on his way to live with his father in Russia, was of being rowed out on the river 'by lamplight and starlight'. As a child in St Petersburg he visited the Hermitage Museum, where he would have seen Joseph Wright's *Vesuvius Erupting* (1778) and *An Iron Forge Viewed from Without* (1774), both moonlit scenes. (He himself was later to make two etchings of forges, attracted to the same effects of light and shadow that had intrigued Wright.) Through his brother-in-law, Francis Haden, Whistler was amused to discover, he was related by marriage to Joseph Wright; moonlight was, if not in the blood, at least in the family.

It was while working on his mother's portrait in 1870 that Whistler painted a view of the Thames at night which was, little did he know it, to launch an entirely new phase of his career and involve him in a level of public notoriety that even a man of his apparently limitless ambition might have baulked at. It was a view of the river that he initially called a 'moonlight' (taking the expression from Turner), painted in his studio in Lindsey Row, Chelsea. The elderly subject of his portrait had grown exhausted with lengthy sittings and so he had taken her out to get some air. Returning to Chelsea as evening drew in, they found the river, as his mother wrote to a friend, Kate Palmer, 'in a glow of rare transparency an hour before sunset'. Whistler had already experimented with such effects in the paintings he had made of shipping in Valparaiso Bay at dusk. Now he rushed to his studio, conscripting his mother as his assistant to hand him his paints. By the time he had finished his sunset picture, an August moon was hanging before his window and his mother urged him, 'Oh Jemie dear it is yet light enough for you to see to make this a moonlight picture of the Thames.' However accurate his mother's recollection of her part in the evening's creative activity, Whistler did produce a painting that night which pushed his treatments of water and light further than ever before towards the abstract. While the effects of moonlight on water in the resulting work may have been taken from life, the scene was rendered entirely from memory, as it depicts Chelsea seen from the opposite bank at Battersea. The Chelsea shore floats above its own reflection as indistinct as a cloud, identified only by the rectangular tower of the Old Church, its silhouette formed by scraping away the top layer of paint and revealing the grey ground beneath. Sky and water are rendered in almost the same tone. The river is free of

the paddle steamers that churn its waters to mud during the day
(Whistler never condescended to include them in his paintings)
and the disgusting outpourings of sewer and slaughterhouse are
invisible. A single figure, evoked in a few brush-strokes, stalks
the near shore, where a ghostly barge, painted out of scale, carries a single light. The moon itself is not visible, but the whole
scene is charged with a subtle luminosity. Whistler has discovered a world as minimalist and restricted in its colour palette
as any of the Japanese woodcuts he had studied. Soon he had a
name for this new genre of painting, contributed by his patron
of the time, Frederick Leyland, to whom he conveyed his appreciation in an undated letter from the 1870s.

I can't thank you enough for the name 'Nocturne' as a title for my moonlights! You have no idea what an irritation it proves to the critics and
consequent pleasure to me, – besides, it really is so charming and does so
poetically say all I want to say and *no more* than I wish.

Thus we now know his first painting of the London night as
Nocturne: Blue and Silver – Chelsea.

The word 'nocturne' was already well known as a description
of a musical study through its use by Chopin, who had appropriated it from the Irish composer John Field. That it was
thought the night could somehow be evoked through the language of music is clear from the well-known description by
Chopin's lover George Sand, in her *Impressions et Souvenirs*, of
the master composing at the keyboard in the company of the
French painter Delacroix.

Chopin is at the piano, quite oblivious of the fact that anyone is listening.
He embarks on a sort of casual improvisation, then stops.

'Go on, go on,' exclaims Delacroix, 'that's not the end!'

'It's not even a beginning. Nothing will come . . . nothing but reflections, shadows, shapes that won't stay fixed. I'm trying to find the right
colour, but I can't even get the form . . .'

'You won't find the one without the other,' says Delacroix, 'and both will come together.'

'What if I find nothing but moonlight?'

'Then you will have found the reflection of a reflection.' The idea seems to please the divine artist. He begins again, without seeming to, so uncertain is the shape. Gradually quiet colours begin to show, corresponding to the suave modulations sounding in our ears. Suddenly the note of blue sings out, and the night is all around us, azure and transparent. Light clouds take on fantastic shapes and fill the sky. They gather about the moon which casts upon them great opalescent discs, and wakes the sleeping colours. We dream of a summer night, and sit there waiting for the song of the nightingale . . .

Although Whistler was not as great an aficionado of music as Leyland, the appropriation of the language of music suited his purposes very well. He was still using it in his Ten O'Clock Lecture, delivered in 1885, to argue both the superior calling of the artist and to deny any obligation to merely copy nature.

Nature contains the elements, in colour and form, of all pictures, as the keyboard contains the notes of all music.

But the artist is born to pick, and choose, and group with science, these elements, that the result may be beautiful – as the musician gathers his notes, and forms his chords, until he brings forth from chaos glorious harmony.

To say to the painter, that Nature is to be taken as she is, is to say to the player, that he may sit on the piano.

When he came to live in Cheyne Walk, Whistler lost no time in connecting with its artistic heritage; he hired Charles Greaves's sons, Walter and Henry, as his assistants and oarsmen, and was entertained by their father's tales of rowing Turner out on the river. It also amused him to enrol the two young boatmen and amateur artists as his pupils. As Walter remembered it, 'he taught us painting, we taught him the waterman's jerk', the latter a short, sharp oar stroke passed down among Thames families, designed to propel a boat effectively through the river's silted, turbulent waters. The brothers learned to prepare Whistler's canvases or wood panels for the nocturnes with a red or grey ground, on to which he would wash what he called his 'sauce', a runny mixture of oil paint, linseed oil, turpentine and a mastic called copal. This medium was so liquid that canvases had to be placed on the floor to prevent the image slipping away entirely (Whistler's fingermarks are visible at the edges of *Nocturne: Blue and Silver – Chelsea* where he did so). As he explained to his pupil Otto Bacher in 1881, 'the paint should not be applied thick; it should be like the breath on the surface of a pane of glass'.

Whistler spent many evenings at the Greaves's house, eating supper, dancing with their teenage sister, Tinnie (who he also painted), enjoying his own electrifying effect on their home. Once old man Greaves died in 1871, there was nothing to prevent the brothers falling under Whistler's spell, abandoning the bright, primary colours of the boat limner for his subtle tone palette (they soon learned that he would not tolerate any return to their realist style★). They never entirely shook off the feeling that their relationship with the river was somehow different to their master's. As Walter was later to put it, 'to Mr Whistler, a boat was always a tone, to us it was always a boat'. Under his direction they made themselves useful decorating his frames, his living quarters and the rooms in galleries exhibiting his works.

They also accompanied him on his evening expeditions to Cremorne, the last of the great pleasure gardens on the Thames, to which paddle steamers and hansom cabs brought visitors from far and wide. Here Whistler discovered another great nocturnal

★ Whistler later and somewhat brutally dropped Walter Greaves when his marriage dictated he abandon his bohemian contacts, and also, perhaps, when his pupil's art threatened to distract attention from his own. The confused and heartbroken Greaves spent much of his subsequent life in poverty.

subject. By the time he moved to Chelsea, Cremorne was in its
final decade of existence, its noise and the clientele it attracted
increasingly at odds with the upwardly mobile neighbourhood.
During the day, families still enjoyed the extensive grounds,
well planted with trees. Entertainment included a show by
underwater acrobats in a vast aquarium; waltzing to an orchestra
in a Chinese pagoda on a circular dancing platform; a maze; a
gypsy's tent; and a theatre that featured ballet and vaudeville
performances. Ever-more spectacular events were put on to
attract the crowds. A tightrope artiste, billed as 'the female Blon-
din', crossed the Thames on an illuminated tightrope, her
progress captured in a drawing by Walter Greaves. Hot-air balloon ascents from the gardens were almost commonplace and
had to include an added element of danger or spectacle to attract
the crowds. On one occasion, the Belgian Flying Man, Mon-
sieur de Groof, was lifted in an ingenious machine made of cane
and waterproof silk by hot-air balloon to an altitude suitable for
flight. A sudden wind blew the balloon off course, towards the
steeple of St Luke's Church. The balloonist was forced to cut de
Groof loose, whereupon his machine, which featured bat's wings
thirty-seven feet long, simply spun downwards, landing with a
sickening thud near the kerb in Robert Street, from where he
was carried through the crowd to Chelsea Infirmary to die.

If members of the public were asked to name just two things
they associated with the gardens, however, they would probably
have mentioned fireworks and prostitution. Whistler painted both.
In *Cremorne Gardens No. 2*, he depicts the complicated ballet of
glances and gestures between a man and a group of women painted
in muted colours in the ambiguous twilight. The man is bowing
but stands with his feet well apart, not the body language of a Victorian gentleman in the presence of ladies. A woman holds her fan
open to signify her availability. In one corner of the painting
another man lounges indolently, legs crossed, in frock coat and top

hat, the archetypal Chelsea dandy. Many have taken this to be a self-portrait of Whistler; it could equally represent his doppelgänger and slavish imitator in the manner of dress, Walter Greaves, who appears in such an outfit in several photographs and self-portraits of the time. In Cremorne, Whistler found a British equivalent of Japan's Ukiyo-e woodcuts, which depicted a demi-monde where aristocrats mixed with courtesans and geishas and strolled between theatres, tea houses and brothels. Flanked by the two sturdy boat-building brothers, his bare-knuckle samurai bodyguards, he was a frequent visitor to Chelsea's version of the Floating World.

The gardens were particularly renowned for their fireworks, which could be seen far downriver and reverberated throughout the neighbourhood, as spectacular as those at the Castel Sant'Angelo in Rome in the previous century. The pyrotechnicians at the gardens created themed displays, including the re-staging of sea battles, for which paddle steamers were commandeered, and a cast of hundreds in full uniform, bearing weapons, brought a martial atmosphere to the otherwise sedate streets of Chelsea. A regular feature was a recreation of the eruption of Mount Etna (rival attraction the Royal Surrey Gardens featured a firework Vesuvius).

Nocturne in Black and Gold: The Falling Rocket was painted in 1875, two years before the gardens were closed, in the face of sustained pressure from residents of the increasingly gentrified district. (A petition against the renewal of the gardens' entertainment licence had over 400 signatories, including thirty-three curates.) The picture is a bravura performance, an opportunity to explore the different effects provided by smoke, sky, water and drifting sparks. On one level, Whistler is following in a long artistic tradition particularly of artists who had been on the Grand Tour of Europe. At the same time, to a London audience, the combination of fireworks and rockets very specifically meant Cremorne; the display marked the time when families generally left the gardens and gentlemen, disgorged by their

West End clubs, arrived in droves, their appearance coinciding with an influx of women of somewhat different social origins. This was the painting that launched the famous libel trial, in which a powerful art critic of the previous generation, albeit one who had defended Turner against charges of wilful obscurity, was pitted against a representative of the new. Ruskin's intemperate words, published initially in a pamphlet addressed to 'the workmen and labourers of Great Britain' but widely syndicated in the press, have lost none of their venom.

I have seen, and heard much of Cockney impudence before now: but never expected to hear a coxcomb ask for two hundred guineas for flinging a pot of paint in the public's face.*

Perhaps the decision to label the American-born, Russian-raised and Paris-educated Whistler a 'Cockney' was a signal of Ruskin's approaching mental breakdown. In any case, he was too ill to attend the ensuing libel trial. This is not the place to rehearse the arguments heard in court, a battle, as Whistler later characterized it, 'between brush and pen'. Although he won the case, he was awarded damages of only a farthing, so highly did the judge value an artist's reputation. The expense of bringing the case hastened Whistler's slide into bankruptcy and his departure from Chelsea, severing, for the time at least, his connection with the river that had been so central to his work.

II

A new obsession grips me; it seems that my journey won't be complete unless I go out in a boat on the Thames by moonlight. I decide to contact Andrew, a friend I have known since my

* John Ruskin, *Fors Clavigera* (London, 1877), Letter 79.

teens, who is the proud co-owner of a small cabin cruiser on the River Lea, a tributary that joins the Thames in east London. A few months previously we had spent an evening together, sitting on the deck of his boat drinking beer and catching up. He is the drummer in a rock band and has spent much of his life traversing the world at speed in aeroplanes and tour buses; his escape is to nose along London's waterways at something a little above walking pace and out into the countryside beyond, an anonymous traveller exchanging the noisy crowds of his working life for an audience of coots and swans. On the evening we spent together his backwater tour had ground to a halt, something to do with the air intake of the cruiser's diesel engine, but he was arranging for it to be repaired. For now, it is as immobile as the *Cutty Sark* at Greenwich. I told him I wanted to get out on the river in moonlight and we made a loose kind of determination to do so in the future, once his boat's broken heart was fixed and ready for new adventures.

So I think it worth a try to drop him an email and check on his whereabouts:

Hi

Don't suppose you would be free (and seaworthy) to go out on the river this Thursday night (full moon)? Just on the off-chance . . .

To which I receive the reply:

Hello James, what a happy coincidence! We are casting off on Thursday morning to go upriver for a week and a bit. You are of course most welcome to join us.

He goes on to say that his children and his partner would be away on Thursday evening, so we would be free to 'moonlight' wherever we wished. The chance seems too good to miss. The Lea is not the Thames, but it is one of its feeder tributaries; I can take a change of clothes to work with me and spend the night on board. On Wednesday night the moon is magnificent, rising huge above the allotments behind our house, the sky a constantly changing series of effects, as though someone off stage was turning a winch to demonstrate every possible combination of moon and cloud, as featured in the works of the great painters of the past.

At noon on the day of the expedition I take a break from work to go outside and check on the weather conditions. The sun is hot and the sky, though hazy, is relatively clear. By early evening I receive a text message from Andrew, telling me the boat has travelled twelve miles and is moored within walking distance of Cheshunt Station. The sky is darkening; I check the weather on the BBC website and see, with a sickening feeling of familiarity, that a band of heavy rain is expected to hit southern England within the next few hours. There is even a severe weather warning in place. I leave work around six o'clock and instead of heading home make my way to Liverpool Street Station. The rain has started in earnest, but I am hoping it will pass over quicker than the weather service predicts. I imagine getting up in the night, on a silent river, to find it bathed in moonlight. But my troubles are not limited to the weather. At the station, crowds of bewildered-looking people are scanning departure boards almost empty of trains. It seems that on the evening I have chosen to travel, workers belonging to two unions have walked out on strike and there is only a skeleton service still operational. One train is running to Cheshunt, but I will have to wait for over an hour for it to arrive – after that there is nothing. My phone rings and it is my wife, checking up on my progress. When I update her – it is pouring with rain and there is a train strike – she splutters with laughter and says, 'You must be . . .' but she fails to finish her sentence.

I must be what? I ask.

'You must be cursed!'

I hadn't thought of this possibility before, but as I wait, watching the queues build up for the few trains that arrive at the platforms, it begins to seem more and more likely. There is nowhere to sit; in any case, it is important to remain alert, and to position myself strategically so that I can make a dash when the platform for my train is announced, as otherwise I might not get on at all. This combination of boredom and enforced vigilance, a feature of modern travel, is particularly irksome. My train arrives and I somehow succeed in securing a seat, opposite two nuns in grey habits, who sit telling their rosaries, raising them to their lips as we leave the station. We trundle past Hackney Downs without stopping, cross the River Lea and run along beside the reservoir, where elegant pylons like Chinese pagodas usher us into Tottenham Hale. At Cheshunt I disembark beneath a sky that is uniformly grey, unleashing sheets of rain. The journey has only taken thirty minutes, but we have left the city behind.

As I get off the train I can dimly see a group of figures waving at me from the other side of the tracks. Andrew's partner and her daughter, along with a friend, need to get back to London as the girls are going off on holiday. Their dog, too, a large, friendly Alsatian-cross who has cruised up from London with the party, is leaving. News of the strike has not reached the boat. They have just found out that the last train running back to London that day has left. 'It's only a few miles,' Andrew says, 'why not get a cab? It can't cost that much.' We walk over to a minicab office next to the station, all of us, including the dog, thoroughly soaked by now. The fare, predictably, is astronomical. In addition, the controller says that none of the taxis will take a dog. Why not? 'Because it's raining and the dog will make the cab smell.' Behind this explanation is another: minicab drivers, vulnerable as they are to passengers running off at a red light without paying, are forced to make generalizations about their customers, and a fare to the East End with a large dog on board does not sound like an attractive proposition. But he's a clean dog, my friends insist. With a slight air of desperation, they attempt to dry him with a spare pair of socks they find in a rucksack, a process he submits to good-naturedly. Despite his size, it is hard to take a creature that allows itself to be dried with a pair of socks as a serious threat and I can see the controller wavering. Finally he takes pity on them and radios several drivers, but they all confirm that they have no intention of taking a wet dog home to Hackney. It's raining, there's a train strike, they can afford to pick and choose. So this is why Andrew and I return to the boat accompanied by a canine companion. He looks back at us and whines continually as we walk.

Why is he doing that? I ask.

'He just does it to annoy me,' Andrew says. 'Actually, he doesn't do it when I take him out on my own, but now you're here there's someone else to worry about – it's his herding instinct, it makes him anxious.'

He can't handle the responsibility?

'Exactly. Also he's epileptic. He's on medication, that might have something to do with it.'

The boat is moored on a quiet stretch of the Lea, near the evocatively named Thirsty Marsh, in the Lea Valley Country Park, a strip of greenery that runs twenty miles out from the city. Cheshunt is not far from the orbital motorway that rings London and the land to the west of the river is heavily built up. To the east is a string of meadows and flooded gravel pits, a clear space on the map criss-crossed with expanses of water. Andrew had hoped we could go upriver in the moonlight and maybe explore the meadows on foot. As it is, on the night of the August full moon, two men and a large, wet, epileptic dog, as well as several cans of beer, are confined to the cabin of a Dutch cruiser in driving rain. And so it remains all night. We laugh together at my wife's summary of my situation when she heard I was stranded at Liverpool Street. At times like these it is impossible not to feel a little ridiculous, my pursuit of the moon a fool's errand. Cursed or not, at least my quest has given me the chance to spend time with an old friend and to gain this insight into his hidden life afloat.

'So what is it you're doing exactly?' he asks. 'Travelling around to see moonlight?'

I do my best to explain, and tell him a little about my trip to Arizona and the hallucination I experienced at night in the desert, when I thought I saw a snake.

'I experienced something like that,' he says, 'the time I saw a ghost.'

He tells me the story. When he was a teenager he had spent a week or so in November camping up on the South Downs with a bunch of his mates from school. Every evening they would walk back from the pub across the hillside to the copse where they were sheltered and build a blazing fire to keep warm. One night as they were returning to their camp, a night on which there was enough light from the moon and stars to distinguish gorse bushes grey against the open landscape, they saw an object the size of a small person gliding to and fro across the smooth downland. It had no noticeable features and was transparent, not solid. It's a ghost, somebody said. They decided to approach a little nearer; the spook didn't fade away, as they expected, but continued making the same strange, unnatural movements as before. As one, they were seized with terror. Andrew said he felt his hair literally stand on end. They ran. The incident obviously remains vivid to Andrew, one of those things that happen in life for which we have no explanation. Later he learned that a bloody battle, the Battle of Lewes, had taken place on that spot, which concluded with one army being driven over a steep drop by the other. This was not the end of the location's historical significance. They had chosen to make their camp at the site where, during a period of Catholic supremacy, Protestants had been taken out of the town and burned at the stake. If you believe in such things, these overlapping histories would be perfect qualifications for rendering the place haunted. Alternatively, Andrew's experience is another demonstration of moonlight's ability to deceive the eyes and evoke the uncanny.

No small, transparent apparitions are seen on the towpath during the night. There is only one train running the next day that will get me to work on time and I sleep fitfully, anxious not to miss it. I am up early enough to hear the whistle of a swan's wings as it flies in low alongside the boat, aquaplaning to a stop 100 yards upriver. I join an unfamiliar gang of commuters on the small platform, most of whom, I am guessing, have spent the night on solid ground. A gentle rain persists, but clears during the morning. That evening, of course, the moon rises into a clear sky. Before retiring, I go to the end of the garden and raise a glass to it in ironic salute. The moonlight magnifies my gesture as shadow. OK, I have got the message, I feel like saying. I cannot confine the moon to any schedule of my own. It is not interested in my book, will not appear when it happens to be convenient for me. I think of Li Po, the Chinese poet, and his poem 'Drinking Alone under the Moon'.

> Among the flowers, a jug of wine.
> Drinking alone, without companion.
> I raise my cup, invite bright moon,
> and my shadow, that makes three.
> The moon knows nothing of drinking.
> My shadow merely follows me.

> But I'll play with moon and shadow,
> joyful, till spring ends.*

According to legend, Li Po drowned in the Yangtse River, drunkenly attempting to embrace the moon's reflection. Perhaps it is as well the moon didn't appear over the River Lea after all.

At the weekend, family commitments take us to the Kent coast and we spend an afternoon on the beach at Hythe. My son and I buy ice cream from a van, then enter the cloudy, pale green water between fishermen lined up at the tideline. This scruffy stretch of coast might not be as glamorous as some, but it is still the sea, vast and on this day welcoming, holding us up gently in its palm. That evening, as we come out of a restaurant, we see the moon, orange and smudged with purple cloud, rising from the water. I remark on it to my companions. A man, sitting on a wall with his pint of beer while his children play in the car park, overhears me and mutters something disparaging to his drinking partner, doubtless related to the idiocy of moon-gazing day trippers, because his son, who looks about twelve years old and has followed the direction of our gaze up at the sky, says, 'No, Dad, you shouldn't say that, because it *is* amazing,' and then scoots off across the tarmac on his bike, out of harm's way. I hope that the moon and our presence won't have brought him bad luck later.

After my abortive attempts to find the moon on the River Lea I am determined not to let a night like this escape, and announce my intention to go for a night walk. We are staying at the foot of the North Downs, that ridge of hills scored with pilgrim paths that conducted Chaucer's characters from London to Canterbury. Smaller and more complexly wooded than the smooth whale humps of the South Downs, skirted by motorways and urban conurbations, they still offer some fine open

---

* Trans. J. P. Seaton, from *The Shambala Anthology of Chinese Poetry*, ed. J. P. Seaton (Boston: Shambala, 2006), p. 92.

spaces from which to observe the sky at night. What is immediately apparent is that my son will be accompanying me; he is as dogged as a terrier and after the usual, tiresome adult remarks about the lateness of the hour I give in. I am glad to have his company as we park next to an ancient Norman church at the end of a deeply rutted track leading across the ridge of the downs; his excitement at being out so late, beyond the city in this unfamiliar place, matches and sustains my own. Even on this peaceful night, an urban paranoia infects these hills; the church has been fitted with a powerful security light that comes on as we get out of the car, temporarily blinding us, relenting only as we leave the car park. At first the track is confined between high banks overhung with hazel and alder trees, a pool of shadow as dark as ink to our spotlight-dazzled eyes, so that I take a wrong turn and we start descending into the valley and have to retrace our steps. Once we are out on the hilltops we are in bright moonlight. The heads of a field of corn glisten to our left; this is the same escarpment Samuel Palmer rambled over with his friends on August nights, drunk on the 'raving-mad splendour' of the moon, fifty miles or so to the west. Unexpected and unplanned for, shining moments like these more than make up for the grey skies I have encountered on my journey. Crickets sound in the long grasses of the bank beside the track and I stoop to pick up a glow-worm, the first I have seen in this part of the world. He sits apparently unconcerned on my palm, still emitting his green glow, until we replace him in the hedgerow. 'Imagine if the moon was made of glow-worms,' my son says jokingly, and as a theory on this particular night it doesn't sound implausible. We lie with our backs against the bank, looking up at the sky, and then watch as the valley below us fills with mist, silvered by moonlight, gradually climbing the hill towards us.

Moonset

Blue Moon on Stonewall Hill

November comes round again. It is now two years since I began my extended moon-watch. Getting off the train one evening when the sky is clear and the air has a touch of frost I notice the moon is capped with a partial halo, a rainbow fragment sitting askew on its crown like a yarmulke. Even as I watch, the corona begins to coalesce. I keep my eye on it as I cycle through the city, whenever the traffic and the elevation of the buildings permit. It triggers a distant memory of watching a photograph develop in a tray of chemicals in my father's toilet-darkroom when I was a child. (Has the sky become for me a darkroom for developing ideas?) Now the first halo completely encircles the moon and, something I have only seen previously in a woodblock print by Kuniyoshi, a second ring has formed around the first. Inside the inner circle all is pale, moonlight-inflected. Between the first and second ring a new colour begins to emerge, a turquoise blue, shot with green. It is the kind of light you might see through the wall of a crevasse in a glacier, or glinting on an iceberg. The moon, with its white and blue rings, looks like the iris of some exotic bird (it is only later that I stumble across the fact that the word *iris*, coined by the Greek physician and anatomist Galen, means 'rainbow'). I am cycling at walking pace. Around me people stroll and talk, heads down, unaware of what is happening in the sky above. I am tempted to shout to get their attention, to tell them to look up. Before I can, and before they decide to call an ambulance, the sky goes out of focus and the vision dissolves once more as the moon slips behind a cloud.

This experience, then, is available in the heart of a

twenty-first-century city, on an overcrowded European island, at a quarter past eight in the evening. No arduous journey is necessary. All that is required is a sense of expectation: I knew where we were in the moon's cycle, was aware that the weather was promising, and automatically checked the sky when I stepped out of the train. In return I had a glimpse of a spectacle that lent a lunar afterglow to the rest of the night.

December in the year 2009 has two full moons, making the second what is known as a Blue Moon. Even more unusual, this second full moon will fall on New Year's Eve. Others have noticed this coincidence and excitedly post about it on the internet, erroneously claiming it as the last night of the decade, advertising their intention to celebrate the event with all kinds of activities. We decide to spend New Year with family in Wales, as far from the big city as possible. Snow has fallen and remains three or four inches deep on the hills that encircle the small town in Powys we have come to visit. At night, temperatures fall to nine degrees below zero. The moon rises on New Year's Eve at three in the afternoon. As the sun is setting at five o'clock a small group of us climb Stonewall Hill, high above the Welsh Marches. Driving conditions are treacherous, with snow banked up on either side of the narrow lane and frequent patches of black ice where the thaw in the weak sunshine of afternoon has frozen once again. An Arctic wind is blowing as we leave the shelter of our cars; grey snow clouds are stacked up on the horizon. In the east, the moon's presence is announced by an ominous apricot light, cast downward as if from behind a veil, a pale answer to the sunset over the Black Mountains to the west. However, the cloud is moving, bringing the promise of a clear night. It is too cold to linger, the group agrees. Two of us resolve to return in an hour; we are expected for dinner and then at a party and I know that once the New Year celebrations begin, any opportunity to observe the moon may be over for the night.

By six o'clock we are back; all residual glow from the sun has left the sky in the west and it has grown colder. The occasional distant lights from farms folded into the surrounding hills merely serve to demonstrate how sparsely populated this place is. My companion is a photographer by trade and is carrying a camera and tripod. We crunch through crisp snow up on to the brow of the hill. The moon has emerged, softened only by a faint haze of ice particles that give it a rainbow aura. In the snowfields our tracks are text in the pages of a book – except they are not the colour of print. Moonlight is captured in the depression made by each footstep; they glow brighter than the grey-white of their surroundings, visually reversing like the dark marks in a photographic negative so that they appear to float above the surface of the snow. My friend is fiddling with his camera, battling with frozen fingers, the eye pressed to his viewfinder weeping from the cold. He tells me that he has set the focus of the camera to infinity, which seems appropriate, as a lunar drama is unfolding in the sky above us. The moon should be at its fullest shortly after seven o'clock, yet tonight there is a partial eclipse. For an hour or so the moon will move into the earth's umbral shadow and we are ideally positioned to see it. On cue, the thumbprint of the earth's presence appears like a smudge of grey mascara at the moon's lower edge; a mystery that would be inexplicable to anyone around the world unaware of what is happening.

Conscious of our families already sitting at table in the valley below we return to the car, parked at the edge of the road in a gateway. Predictably perhaps, given the falling temperature, its front wheels spin uselessly, and with every growl from the engine it digs its nose deeper into a drift. A five-mile walk home and social disgrace begin to appear likely. For the next few minutes we try different strategies to extricate ourselves. I am on my knees in front of the car pushing when I notice the full moon swimming in the metal bonnet in mocking reflection, an inch from my face. Eventually our combined effort frees us and we are able to slip and slide our way back down the hill. We are the last arrivals but we are swiftly forgiven. For the next few hours we celebrate between walls that cut us off from what is happening outside, eating, dancing and drinking together as humans will on these occasions.

Returning home at two in the morning, we are preceded by our marionette moon-shadows, cast by a now-perfect disc in the icy sky. Down here in the valley, there is no snow at all. In the darkened streets the frosted roofs of a housing estate have become glowing lunar panels. The local authorities have taken to turning off at least a percentage of their street lights at night in this town. Apparently the discussion process was difficult; it included posting a map in the local library on which each lamp could be identified so that residents could petition if they felt a pressing need to keep their road or house illuminated. After the predictable arguments a settlement has been reached, and up to 20 per cent of the town's streets have been reprieved from their usual tangerine pallor, the night sky restored. This experiment is running in several towns across the county, surely providing a model that could be rolled out across the nation; already the saving in terms of money and carbon emissions must be considerable.

Even as our over-loud conversation bounces off the buildings around us I am looking upwards, resolved to return to the hills the following night if the weather holds. In the end, my search for moonlight has mostly been a solitary one. I find it hard to be alert to anything but the presence of others when I am in a crowd. Even a naturally discreet and self-effacing photographer becomes a distraction as I wonder if the shutter of his camera will still function in the plunging temperatures or worry about how long I can reasonably ask him to linger outside when he would rather be with his friends and loved ones. To get the most from the moon I have to seek out what Coleridge called, in 'Frost at

Midnight', 'that solitude, which suits / Abstruser musings'. So it is that the next night I point my own even less reliable vehicle up into the hills. The radio waves are cluttered with warnings from the authorities against travelling on the roads unless it is absolutely necessary. Someone quietly suggests I take a phone with me; otherwise my departure is unremarked, which is as it should be. I decide to drive beyond the point we stopped at the night before; I don't know the road but hope to find another place where I can pull up and abandon my car. If I'd thought to ask I could have brought a map. As it is I am approaching the summit when my wheels start spinning and the car begins to slide backwards down the hill. Around here, locals know which roads to avoid at certain times of year; I am merely demonstrating my status as an ignorant visitor. Inching in reverse in the dark down an icy Welsh hillside is not an altogether pleasant experience; I rely largely on my flashing hazard lights to avoid going off the road into a snowdrift. There is no other traffic. Eventually I find a place to leave the car, facing downhill with two wheels on the road, and cross a gate into a field. The moon is partly obscured behind hazy clouds, but they are moving southward, so I resolve to wait. It is not silent up here. I can hear a dog barking across the valley and somewhere the distant grumble of a jet. A sound like an approaching train is the bitter wind in a stand of pines. The noise my boots make breaking through the brittle surface of the snow turns each solitary pace into a battalion's stride, marching in step on a parade ground. I stop walking and stand quietly as the edge of high cloud inches closer to the rim of the moon.

My back is turned at the moment it emerges and my shadow leaps across the field from my feet. The snow is dazzling; sprinkled across it are thousands of sparkling ice crystals, each one emitting its own lunar signal, a miniature beam of refracted moonlight. I squat down to appreciate them better, just as I did before the moonlit waves in Normandy. I feel drunk with moonlight, energized; I have forgotten the cold. It is bright enough to read the notes I am making on a scrap of paper retrieved from the depths of a pocket. I blow on my fingers to warm them enough to hold a pen, thinking of all those from around the world and throughout history who have made art, poetry and literature that incorporated this moment, this light. What is the source of our deep and enduring fascination with the moon, that has placed it at the centre of our consciousness since prehistoric times and that still works on the human mind today? Perhaps the answer is beyond words, something that must be lived.

I set off across the fields, convinced that if I choose I could walk all night. In the moonlight, distances are deceptive. What I take to be the lights of a far-away village as I crest a ridge turn out to be the decorations on a Christmas tree outside a solitary farm, dark among the trees. As I walk I think back over the cast of poets and painters, visionaries and eccentrics I have encountered on my journey; and of the moon's place in myth, mankind's unofficial history, repository of a certain kind of truth not recorded elsewhere. Finally I remember the alabaster reliquary in the museum in Florence containing Galileo's finger, still pointing upwards, urging us to tear our eyes from the virtual world we have created for ourselves and look to the skies. The euphoria I feel crossing the moonlit snowfields does not leave me, even when I return home.

I spend a restless night, the burning moon imprinted behind my eyelids. I rise twice to draw aside the curtain and see the shadows of trees striping the wall. To experience moonlight at this intensity in a semi-urban setting in the twenty-first century feels like a privilege. At the same time, it can only hint at what a moonlit night would have been like before the arrival of human-kind in the furthest corners of the earth. Such experiences are accessible today for most of us only through the words of a poet like Tu Fu, writing in China in the eighth century AD:

The circle without blemish.
The empty mountains without sound.
The moon hangs in the vacant, wide constellations.
Pine cones drop in the old garden.
The senna trees bloom.
The same clear glory extends for ten thousand miles.★

The moon connects us to a longer cycle than the artificially speeded-up one we have devised to regulate our time on earth. However, knowing the moon's timetable will not guarantee its presence. Clouds and rain, mist and fog are like the vagaries of our daily lives, frustrating our plans; the moon an instructor in primitive philosophy, teaching us to accept such setbacks with equanimity, yet to remain alert to the unexpected, seizing lunar opportunities whenever they occur. Each generation gets the sky it deserves, bequeathed to it by its parents. Distanced and diminished as it is by human brightness, today's moon demands of us greater attention, a little more effort.

My search for moonlight has taken me across the world and out into my own back garden. I have looked for it on mountainsides, beside rivers, in deserts, in the middle of some of the world's great cities and in the streets of my own neighbourhood. What have I found at the completion of my journey? Not an ending so much as an ongoing process. With the moon, after all, there are no such things as endings; this seems to have been the point of it, as far as humans were concerned, from the beginning of time. Each period of darkness is merely punctuation in the script; an opportunity to count the days until we can close the door behind us and venture out once more on to moonlight's unwritten page.

★ From *Songs of Love, Moon and Wind*, trans. Kenneth Rexroth (New York: New Directions, 2009). Italics my own.

Acknowledgements

I have received more help, forbearance and hospitality on this expedition than I had any right to expect. Special mention should go to early readers, critics, informants and hosts on my journey, including Lutz Becker, for his insights into German Romanticism and the life of Rudolf Hess; my agent, Catherine Clarke; Cressida Kocienski; Chris and Danielle McConnell; Fabrizio Nevola; Christiana Payne; Simon Prosser, Juliette Mitchell, Anna Kelly and Sarah Coward for navigation, advice and vital work under the bonnet; Anna Perring and Nick Jacobs; and Wes 'the Rock' Williams.

Thanks above all to Charlotte, co-pilot through all kinds of weather.

Permissions

The picture of Rudolf Hess on page 237 is taken from footage by Eugene Bird.

Lines from *Selected poems of Hugh MacDiarmid*, edited by R. Crombie Saunders, Glasgow 1944, reprinted by permission of Carcanet Press Ltd.

Lines from Johann Wolfgang von Goethe, *Italian Journey* (1786–8), translated by W. H. Auden and Elizabeth Mayer, Penguin Classics, 1970, reprinted by permission of Penguin Books Ltd, by permission of Curtis Brown Ltd for the estate of Elizabeth Mayer and by permission of The Wylie Agency for the estate of W. H. Auden.

Extract from *The Narrow Road to the Deep North Woods and Other Travel Sketches* by Matsuo Basho, translated with an introduction by Nobuyuki Yuasa (Penguin Classics, 1966). Copyright © Nobuyuki Yuasa, 1966. Reproduced by permission of Penguin Books Ltd (print rights) and by permission of The Agency (London) Ltd (e-rights).

Lines by Saikatu, translated by Nobuyuki Yuasa, taken from the introduction to *The Narrow Road to the Deep North Woods and Other Travel Sketches* by Matsuo Basho. Copyright © Nobuyuki Yuasa, 1966. Reproduced by permission of Penguin Books Ltd (print rights) and by permission of The Agency (London) Ltd (e-rights).

Lines by Ōe no Chisato, translated by Timothy Clark, from *Kuniyoshi*, Royal Academy of Arts, London, 2009. Reprinted by permission.

Lines by Abe no Nakamaro, translated by Matthi Forrer, from *Hokusai: Prints and Drawings*, Royal Academy of Arts, London, 1991. Reprinted by permission.